I Joke Too Much
The Theatre Director's Tale

Michael Rudman was born in Texas and educated at Oberlin College and Oxford University. His career began in the UK at the Nottingham Playhouse, where he was Assistant Director and Associate Producer to John Neville from 1964–1968. He was Director of the Traverse in Edinburgh from 1970–1973, after which he took up the post of Artistic Director at Hampstead Theatre until 1978 when he was invited to join the National Theatre by Sir Peter Hall and directed many successful plays there over the next ten years. He was the director of the Chichester Festival Theatre for the 1990 season then went on to become Artistic Director of the Sheffield Theatres. He has directed plays on Broadway and the West End to much critical acclaim. He lives and works in London.

Capercaillie Books

I Joke Too Much
The Theatre Director's Tale

Michael Rudman

Capercaillie Books

First published by Capercaillie Books Limited in 2014.

Registered Office 1 Rutland Court, Edinburgh

© Michael Rudman

The moral rights of the author have been asserted.

A catalogue record of this book is available from the British Library

ISBN 978-1-909305-82-3

Acknowledgements

I must thank a few people for their help and guidance. First, Helen Mumby and Dinah Wood and Victoria Gray who introduced me to both of these excellent women. And special thanks go to my diligent and intelligent assistant, Karen ('Billie') Curran.

Note on the Title

The title is taken from a speech by Willy Loman in Arthur Miller's play *Death of a Salesman:*

> **WILLY:** A man oughta come in with a few words. One thing about Charley. He's a man of few words, and they respect him.
>
> **LINDA:** (*smiling*) You don't talk too much, you're just lively.
>
> **WILLY:** (*smiling*) Well, I figure, what the hell. Life is short, a couple of jokes. (*to himself*) I joke too much. (*the smile goes*).

Another Note On The Title

When I was directing Dustin Hoffman and John Malkovich in *Death of a Salesman* for Broadway, we were on tour in Washington. I was walking with Arthur Miller near the Watergate Hotel when he told me that unfortunately Malkovich wasn't well and might have to withdraw that evening and Dustin was very upset about it.

I said, 'I hope it doesn't make him cry.' This was a reference to the fact that I was always trying to stop Dustin from crying in the play on the theory, attributed to Edith Evans, that 'the less you cry the more they will.'

Arthur didn't think that what I said was at all funny and he got extremely angry and said, very loudly, 'That's enough of your goddamn jokes.'

Chapters

PART 1

Starting Out

Some Years in Provincial Theatre

Interview For The Nottingham Playhouse

Time   Afternoon

Place   The Café Royale, London

Date   Autumn 1964

Post   ABC Television Trainee Director's Scheme

There is a large table, raised, at one end of a richly decorated room. Several judges sit there facing the interviewee who, along with eleven others, is questioned in turn. On either side are two representatives of each of the six regional theatres participating in the scheme. The two men from Nottingham, John Neville, in a blue suit, and Peter Stevens, stand out. They laugh out loud occasionally.

The candidate wears an ill-fitting suit. He is young and conscious of being American. He answers questions about Shakespeare. Frank Hauser asks, 'What is the thing you would most concentrate on in a production of *Macbeth*?' The answer, 'the plot'. Nods of agreement from John Neville and Peter Stevens.

The form is for the committee to choose six of the twelve and then for the representatives of the theatres to determine which one of the six they want. The candidate is not one of the favoured six, but Neville and Stevens break the rules and choose him.

A good result.

John Neville

My arrival in Nottingham was not auspicious. It was a Sunday evening and the M1 was only complete as far as Leicester. Driving quickly, the journey took three hours from London and we arrived in a small, drab Midland town to find that the first three people we asked had never heard of the Nottingham Playhouse.

When we did find it, it was beautiful. Set in a quiet square very near the city centre, it was white and new and modern. Part of the reason that the locals had never heard of it was that it was only a year old and news travels slowly in Nottingham.

But everyone in the town soon knew about it and the main reason for that was John Neville.

At Nottingham, John was the boss. With his blonde hair and aquiline nose, his springy walk, his talent, his vivacious wife, his six children and his unquenchable good humour, he seemed invincible. He had the perfect mixture of arrogance and fun. He was the best kind of actor-manager.

One night, John had played Richard II to the customary full house, and went into the Playhouse bar for the customary Guinness or three. To get to the bar, unless you wanted to walk in the cold Midland rain, you had to pass through the Playhouse restaurant, which was peopled by local toffs and their ladies.

Fine. He would get through quickly. Most of the tables were on a lower level and the aisle that led from the theatre to the foyer was one level above the tables. No problem. He would nip in one door of the restaurant, walk twenty paces or so very quickly, wearing a jean suit (he was 41) and out the other door into the bar. He didn't look down and he didn't look from side to side. He carried himself well. Perhaps a smile at the restaurant manager as he entered the sanctuary of the bar.

But, on this occasion, John forgot something. He got through the restaurant to the door to the bar, then he turned round. He went back through the restaurant, back into the foyer, up to his office, made a quick phone call, then came back. Through one door of the restaurant. Twenty quick steps. He was about to open the door to the bar, when came this deep voice:

'Oh, Mr Neville.'
John stopped.
'Oh, Mr Neville.' The deep, cheerful, toffee voice again.
The restaurant was now silent.
'Would you kindly shut the door, Mr Neville.'
Short pause.
'I'll sing the bloody *Desert Song* for you if you like.'
I served willingly as this man's assistant.

Casting was difficult at the Nottingham Playhouse. I remember offering the part of Volpone and being refused by literally eighty-four actors and this was in the heyday of regional theatre. The person would have played Volpone with John Neville as Mosca, so it was a good job.

Some of the shows were successful to the world in general, as well as the Nottingham audience. The Nottingham audience adored almost anything that John did, but the national press were more snooty. John's forced resignation was partly a result of the national press being over critical of his 'popular' programming. But one of the shows that everyone liked was *Measure for Measure*, which I directed with John.

Judi Dench was superb in this production, playing Isabella and bringing her experience of Peter Brook's work with it. In particular, the famous pause towards the end of the play before Isabella decides what Angelo's fate will be.

The success of this production meant that we extended the run into the second half of the year and Edward Woodward, who had been brilliant as Lucio, was off making his career elsewhere. The part of Lucio was taken over by Jimmy Thompson, a personable man, famous for his *Pinky and Perky* programme on television, but utterly new to Shakespeare.

Once, we were working hard on a scene between Judi and Jimmy. Jimmy was trying everything that he could to avoid simply saying the lines. He must have known, somehow, that he would never learn them, and that when he did he would never understand them, and that it would be better if he kept busy in as interesting a way as possible. He kept making suggestions like, 'Could I walk up and down here?', or 'Could I sit down there?' and each time Judi talked him out of it. She was practiced at this and very diplomatic.

One day Jimmy said 'Oh, err, could I smoke a cigarette here?'
Judi looked at me. I couldn't think of anything.
'He can't do that,' she finally blurted out.
We both looked at Judi.
'I'm all dressed in white.'
That seemed to satisfy everyone.

For two years, John and I picked the company for Nottingham in the office of Spotlight, the people who published the casting directory. The current artistic director of the Nottingham Playhouse will be green with envy if he or she reads that we were choosing about thirty-seven actors, including six acting ASMs (junior stage managers who were given small acting roles). Of course, it was the lowly ASMs who went on to glittering careers as television and film directors (Alan Dosser, Jim O'Brien, David Leland), but John and I concentrated on the actors, especially those who would play the middle-range of parts. The leading actors were usually already in the company and were chums of John from his years at the Old Vic or people whom John knew well. We were choosing a company for the entire season, so they had to be versatile and easy to get on with. Temperament was not allowed. John was loyal to those who did come and they might well stay for years.

One actor whom we met was neither versatile nor easy.

The room was tiny and this chap seemed to fill it. Also, he was Canadian and soft-spoken. He was what John would call 'worrying'. He had huge shoulders and a tiny head and spoke in a flat, western accent. His answers to questions like what he had done and what parts he liked playing and what he hoped to do were, to say the least, laconic.

'Yes', 'No', 'Some', were examples of his line of chat. He was heavy going. Most directors would have had him out of the room in three minutes. Not John Neville. John was an actor and very courteous to other actors, especially untalented ones. But finally, the conversation ground to a halt. I wasn't about to help and the combination of John's courtesy and this chap's monosyllables was leaving us with nothing but silence. Finally, I spoke:

'Well.' I was hoping that he would take his string bag filled with groceries and go.

He also said 'Well'.

The room seemed even smaller.

'Shall I do something for you?' he asked.

Oh, no. The longest sentence yet from the Canadian, and the one I feared the most. John was surprisingly negative, but pleasant.

'It's not necessary,' he said.

'I've got a speech prepared,' he said, with a quiet determined edge.

Oh, no, I thought again. It's like playing a bit part in some dreadful western.

'Usually we only meet with people and have a bit of a chat,' said John and that was true. John found any audition embarrassing and we almost never did them.

'That's right,' I joined in. 'We don't normally audition people.'

'I'll do something,' he said.

We were trapped.

He stood up. He was even taller than I had thought. He took off his pullover. He had rolling muscles under his t-shirt. He turned his back on us and raised his head. He moved his chair to a corner of the room. He had about three square feet in which to manouvre. We waited.

Then he began to make strange sounds. 'Huh, huh, huh.' And then, very quietly, 'Hah, hah, hah. Huh, huh, huh.' I recognised these as warm up noises. They were tiny, but shrill. He sounded like a dog experiencing pleasure. John, being strictly RADA and Old Vic, had no idea what they were. I looked at John. He was about to laugh. We realized that we must never look at each other again until this was over or we would be in hysterics. The huge young man turned to face us. Then the sounds became louder and were accompanied by movements of his heavily muscled arms. The room now seemed to have no more space in it. It was like being in the back seat of a car with an ape.

'Hit, hit, hah, hah, huh, huh, huh.'

I wasn't at all certain that this chap was sane.

I started biting the knuckle on my right forefinger to keep myself from giggling. Then the noises stopped. Silence. He turned his big back again.

I bit my finger harder. White teeth marks appeared on the knuckle.

Then the man wheeled around and in a voice loud enough to shake that little room and all of the adjoining rooms in that small old building, he began to scream:

Once more into the breach dear friends, once more!

We chortled. Both of us. A sharp, hacking sound, quickly choked back. Both of us pretended to have coughed. But this man was not deterred. On he went. Even louder.

Or close the wall up with our English dead!

He didn't pause. He didn't lower his considerable voice, when he touched on softer subjects. No. He yelled even louder.

In peace there's nothing so becomes a man as modest stillness and humility.

It really was too much to bear. I expected to hear banging on the walls from people in the adjoining rooms, but I don't suppose we could have heard much of anything. On he shouted, each word as loud as the next, with no change in emphasis, until he finished. Then he sat down and became monosyllabic again.

John thanked him. So did I. We said that we would let him know. He dressed himself and left. John and I were drained. We were numb. I showed John the first knuckle on the forefinger of my right hand. There was a little blood on the white bite mark.

After we had seen the next three actors, there was a gap. We were about to ask for a cup of tea when there was a knock on the door, very small, very delicate. It was the Canadian. He had come back for his string bag and his groceries. I thought that he was going to thrash us for laughing, but I don't think he was capable of violence, only silence and noise. He lived his life in one or the other, unlike a real actor who moves between the two, but never touches either.

Being the assistant director to an actor, especially one who is running a large building, is an unusual job. I was given a great deal of responsibility for the programming at Nottingham and for the direction of shows that John was directing. The billing would be 'directed by John Neville and

Michael Rudman' but I did a great deal of it, especially when John was playing a leading role. One day, he called me into his office.

'We're doing *Moll Flanders*,' he said with a look of 'Don't you think that's a bit startling and wonderful?'

'Great,' I said, trying to be unstartled and positive. That was what he liked. Jokes and optimism were at the basis of John's work.

'We're doing it as a musical.'

Now I was taken aback, but I disguised my reaction.

'Who's directing it?' I asked with a great deal of self-interest.

'Ronnie and I,' said John as if it was a good idea that he had only just thought of. Ronnie was Ronald Magill, the Associate Director.

'Whose version are you using?' I asked, to hide my disappointment.

'We'll write it ourselves,' he said. 'In rehearsal.'

Oh dear, I thought. He's heard about that somewhere. But so had I.

I thought about nothing else for a few days. I read the book. Twice. There was hardly any dialogue in it. How could this thing be 'written in rehearsals'? I thought I'd better have a go.

Every morning, before rehearsals, I went into my little office in the annex and I tried to make a theatrical scene out of one of the incidents or some of the characters of this novel, which was barely a novel at all in that it was so picaresque it had virtually no plot. It was more journalism than fiction. It was a documentary on the life of a woman in the eighteenth century.

Some of the scenes I made up entirely, some followed the book, but my plan was to have a sketch of every scene and a pattern for the show, which then some writer could use to produce a proper stage version. Then, of course, the songs would have to be written. We had someone good for that, Iwan Williams.

Also, I had an ulterior motive. Having shown such interest in the show and having had so many good ideas about it, I thought that John might change his mind and that I might be allowed to direct it as Ronnie would almost certainly be in it.

I finished the sketched version one lunchtime when we were not rehearsing. I took it to Vivien Hancock, John's secretary, and asked her to give it to him. For some reason, which I can neither remember nor understand, he came out of his office and said that he would read it straightaway. This made me unbearably nervous and I went for a walk, something I'm not very good at.

I saw that the local cinema was showing *The Sound of Music*. I thought that I would drop in and pass the anxious time watching a tedious family musical.

I think I cried five times.

First, when she makes clothes for the children out of the curtains. Also, when he proposes. And most gallingly, when she comes back. That was the worst of all because I thought to myself, 'She's coming back. I know she's coming back and I know I am going to cry'. And I did. I think that I was emotionally labile that afternoon, but I also think that *The Sound of Music* is a damn good movie.

I got back to Vivien at about five o'clock.

'Where's John?'

'Oh, he's gone home for tea.'

Vivien was firm and protective. You couldn't ring John at home because he was with Caroline and the kids. In the three and a half years that I worked for him, I don't think I ever rang him at home. Not even once.

'What did he think of the script?', I dared ask.

'Which one, Michael?'

'The *Moll Flanders* script. The one I gave you and that you gave him earlier today.'

'Oh, that's it there,' said Vivien, gesturing to the duplicating machine. My God.

'He told me to print it up,' said Vivien.

'Why?'

'He said that we're doing it.'

And that is what happened. I became a sort of writer. The outline version that I gave him as my audition to direct became the rehearsal script. Ronnie Magill directed it and it played to full houses and it wasn't at all bad.

It wasn't too good either, even though Harold Hobson quite liked it. But it happened and it was popular and that was what things were like at Nottingham under John Neville. Things happened and they were popular.

Glasgow Citizens Theatre

When I left Nottingham, I had nine months with the RSC and then I was a freelance director for a while before I got the job as Director of the Traverse. I worked in Coventry, Bath, Watford, Sheffield and Glasgow.

In Glasgow, as Willy Loman would say, I was liked but not well liked. I had once had a good experience working for Giles Havergal in Watford, where he modestly admitted to drawing a 'working-class audience'. This was amusing coming from an ex-Guards Officer, but it was true and it was what he wanted. I directed *Look Back in Anger* for him there and we got on well, so when he took over Glasgow Citizens Theatre, he invited me to do the second production. It was Albee's *Delicate Balance*.

I couldn't cast it. The four main parts were patrician Americans in their sixties and Giles was paying thirty pounds a week. No one of the right age or caliber was interested. I sat on a sofa in Dartmouth Park Hill and begged Giles over the telephone to let me cast it a different way.

'Why don't we get four actors in their early thirties? We could get Giles Block and Neil Stacy. Both of them age well and do wonderful American. The audience would accept it once it got going, and Giles and Neil would do it for the money. Please, Giles.'

Giles refused, but I modestly admit to believing that he used that conversation as the basis of his casting policy for the next twenty years.

In the end, we did get some good older actors including Terence De Marney and Euen Solon. Not long into rehearsals, there developed a rivalry between these two that was partly caused by Euen's huge dog barking whenever Terry (as his character) raised his voice at Euen or criticized him in any way. As it was a play by Edward Albee, the dog was kept fairly busy. Euen had demanded that his dog join him at rehearsals and I had agreed. No one much liked the dog being there, but Terry was patient. He had been around. He had once been refused a role in Hollywood because when they needed a Welsh actor, he had gone up for the role only to be told 'No, we want North Wales.' As he was Irish, Terry didn't argue, left the office, twisted his face up a bit and made a good living playing American gold prospectors and old codgers in Westerns.

One day the rivalry between Terry and Euen reached a peak. I wouldn't put it any higher than that. It was quiet, but intense. The gist of it was that Euen was demanding Terry be downstage of him at almost every point and as Euen had most, if not all, of the long speeches, this made a certain amount of sense. I let it go, knowing Terry would look after himself.

On the final run-through, the day before the dress rehearsal, Euen began his long crack-up speech, the one where a perfectly healthy looking rich American goes to pieces before your very eyes. Terry was dutifully standing downstage with his back more or less to the audience. Euen cracked up and cracked up. He ranted, he squealed, he spoke in broken sentences, many of which were written that way. Terry stood still. Then Euen reached the high point of his speech and, just as his nervous breakdown was about to reach a climax, Terry slowly turned his head, set on a slim old frame. He was facing the audience. Two great tears slid down his face.

Euen went quiet. The dog barked quietly. I applauded softly. Everyone in the room was spellbound. Terry was never instructed to move downstage again.

Sheffield Playhouse

Just before Christmas 1969 in my first year as a freelance, after I had left the RSC, I was sitting at home feeling dejected when Colin George rang me and asked if I would direct *Henry IV, Part One* at Sheffield. Yes, I said. I certainly would.

Colin wanted me to use his company of actors. In those days, the regional theatres had resident companies mostly consisting of young actors with a few middle-aged ones who didn't mind living there until something better came up. At Sheffield they were employed for the entire season and had to be cast in every play if at all possible.

I met all of these people, but found no one to play Falstaff or Prince Hal. Colin was loathe to let me cast two big parts outside the company. It meant at least another seventy-five pounds a week, but he gave in eventually.

I had seen Nigel Hawthorne, who was about forty at the time, a few weeks earlier in Bond's *Narrow Road to the Deep North* at the Royal Court and I enquired about him. Also, I cast Mike Gwilym as Hal. I had seen him working in Bath.

Then I got a strange phone call.

'Hello, is that Michael Rudman?'

'Yes. Who's that?'

'It's Nigel Hawthorne here. My agent, Jimmy Viccars, said that you had rung about Falstaff.'

'Oh, yes. I certainly did.'

'Are you sure that you've got the right actor?'

'Positive,' I said. 'I saw you being wonderful in *Narrow Road to the Deep North* at the Court.'

'Yes.'

'That was you, wasn't it? Nigel Hawthorne?'

'Oh, yes. That's me. I'm Nigel Hawthorne.'

'Well, do you want to do it? I'd be thrilled if you would. I don't think I can get them to go higher than forty pounds a week, but…'

'Michael.'

'Yes, Nigel.'

'I've got a very light voice, you know.'

I thought fast. 'That's the way I want Falstaff played,' I said. 'Like a gentleman. And your voice isn't all that light.'

I've done seven shows with Nigel and I don't ever remember thinking that his voice was light. I suppose that every actor has some secret criticism of himself that he wants corrected.

My production of *Henry IV, Part One* at the old Sheffield Playhouse was simple. Fifteen actors, one basic costume, one big bed, which was used by both Henry IV and Falstaff – Henry IV for his bedroom and Falstaff in the pub – and two cannons. It began with Henry IV having a nightmare about all the men killed in battle. The Bishop of Carlyle appeared and recited his curse from Shakespeare's *Richard II*.

I speak to subjects, and a subject speaks,
Stirr'd up by God thus boldly for his king,
My Lord of Hereford here, whom you call king,
Is a foul traitor to proud Hereford's king

And if you crown him, let me prophesy,
The blood of English shall manure the ground
And future ages groan for this foul act;
Peace shall go sleep with Turks and infidels,
And in this seat of peace tumultuous wars
Shall kin with kin and kind with kind confound;
Disorder, horror, fear and mutiny
Shall here inhabit, and this land be call'd
The field of Golgotha and dead men's skulls.
O! If you rear this house against this house,
It will the woe fullest division prove
That ever fell upon this cursed earth
Prevent it, resist it, let it not be so,
Lest child, child's children cry against you
'woe!'

This enabled the audience to understand the King's place in history and Shakespeare's view of him. Then we began the story of Hotspur's revolt and the education of Prince Hal. For the second Act, the already spare set was removed and only a bare stage remained with two cannons, one on either side of the stage pointing to the audience.

But, although the set was simple, the production was not. There were many 'trumpets and alarms'; much firing of canons, lots of fighting and almost more entrances and exits than this little band of actors could accomplish. David Howey, for example, would dash off as Bardolph and reappear immediately as Westmoreland.

In the final technical run-through, we were putting all these bits and pieces together on that tiny stage. It was working well, but it was taking a long time.

Then the stage was bare. Then all the lights went out. Nothing happened. Then one of the actors rushed on brandishing a sword. Then he saw no one to brandish at and so he went off. Then five soldiers rushed on looking warlike. Then one of the canons started to roll towards the audience. Then the lights went out. Then there was a roar of cannons and thunder and then, twenty seconds late, there sounded the music that was supposed to herald the entrance of the first soldier. His opposite number raced on, but found no opponent. Then the wrong lights came up. Then another canon roared. Then the lights went out. Everything was silent.

Then the electricians turned up the house lights, illuminating the stage and the auditorium with a harsh, bright light. Onto the empty stage came the production manager, alone, dressed in baggy corderoys, shielding his eyes from the light.

'It's all right, Mike' he said. 'It's technical.'

Two hours later, I took a call on the backstage payphone telling me that the Traverse Theatre was interviewing for the post of Artistic Director and a member of the Board wanted me to apply.

But before I tell you about my experiences north of the border, I should describe my experiences with the Royal Shakespeare Company, which was, to say the least, educational.

The Royal Shakespeare Company

Interview For The Royal Shakespeare Company

Time	3.00 p.m.
Place	Peter Hall's office at the Royal Shakespeare Theatre in Stratford.
Date	November 1967
Post	Assistant Director.

John Barton is wearing trousers and a green pullover. Peter Hall is absent. David Jones is wearing a tie. Terry Hands is wearing black. Trevor Nunn wears slacks and a pullover. The interviewee wears a jacket and tie.

'What have you done?' The young man is staggered by that question and stammers. Then Terry Hands asks, in a challenging manner, why the interviewee is interested in doing a West End production for Peter Bridge? (How did he know that?) How would he choose between that and the RSC? A quick self-defence. Many compliments are flung at the Royal Shakespeare Company, most of them sincere.

'Why would Trevor Nunn be interviewing me? He's only an Assistant,' thinks the utterly abashed young man.

Would he be interested in running Theatregoround? What on earth is Theatregoround? Why all this grilling? This job was a certainty. They had asked him to come there several times. He would be going from the post of full director at Nottingham, with several highly praised productions behind him, to a mere Assistant Director at the RSC. Why are they being so difficult?

That evening, after a long drive, a shattered interviewee sits in front of the television news. It is announced that Peter Hall is leaving the Royal Shakespeare Company and that his successor will be Trevor Nunn.

John Barton

My first job at the RSC was to assist John Barton on his production of *Julius Caesar*. John has a good method of teaching and directing verse speaking which, stated briefly, is this:

In a line of iambic pentameter, the actor should treat the last word of every line as the most important. That word should, with few exceptions: (i) get the most emphasis; (ii) be given an upward or rising inflexion, and (iii) cause the actor to pause slightly before continuing. Thus, it should be

To be or not to be, that is the *question*.

Certainly there is no more important word in this speech than question. The entire speech is a question. Also, an upward inflexion takes the audience and the actor springing onto the next line. Also, a brief pause after that word is most effective for clarity of speech and understanding.

This is an excellent rule and can be applied, with profit and pleasure, to most lines in most speeches of verse.

It can become a problem, however, when very little else is discussed in rehearsal. That is what happened with *Julius Caesar*. There are many corollaries to the rule, dealing, for example, with the middle of a line where one also often finds a natural and helpful break. But the extensive discussion of these guidelines, and their constant application, made the rehearsals long and dry. By the time we reached the technical rehearsals, we were hoping for some excitement.

We didn't get it.

What we got instead was many hours a day, for one week, of moving the actors about, lighting them, testing sound cues, moving the actors about some more, changing their costumes, trying different kinds of blood, putting the actors in the crowd and the soldiers into different positions, changing the costumes more, working on lighting effects and, yes, moving them about even more. In those days, the director was given an entire week in the theatre, from early morning until late at night to work on the technical aspects of a production with the actors. Present day union regulations do not allow anywhere near this number of hours.

Throughout this testing period, I was constantly at John's side, though he never spoke to me, except to say 'Coffee!', meaning that I should go to the Green Room and get him some coffee immediately. And, once in a while, he would give me a message to deliver.

Finally, we reached the dress rehearsal stage. Those of us on the production team sat three quarters of the way back in the auditorium, with a makeshift table in front of us which held the lighting charts, the text, two or three ashtrays, nearly full, and several half-finished cups of coffee. This 'table' was really a plywood board laid across the backs of five seats in the auditorium.

John Barton could be abrupt physically, disjointed, and seemingly unaware of his body. A story is told that once, while instructing a company of actors, he fell backwards off the stage, landed on the floor, stood up and continued to speak as if nothing had happened. It is also said that he chewed razor blades, but I didn't see that. When I worked for him, he was never without a filter tipped menthol cigarette in his mouth.

As we waited for the dress rehearsal to begin, all our nerves were jangling. The lighting designer had gone off for a moment and John and I were alone. John reached abruptly for a light for his next cigarette. He upset the tabletop. Eight half-filled coffee cups spilt onto my lap. My trousers were soaked. I looked at John.

'Coffee,' he said.

I got up, brushed the stuff off my trousers and started towards the canteen on the quickest route I knew. The dress rehearsal was about to begin and I didn't want to be late and I certainly didn't want John to be without his coffee. The quickest way was across the stage. I stepped onto it. After two steps, I heard Roger Howells, the stage manager.

'Michael Rudman.'

'Yes,' I said.

'The dress rehearsal is about to begin.'

'Sorry.'

'If you don't mind.'

I stepped back into the auditorium and found a different route to the canteen.

The director is one of the most powerful figures in any production, often the most powerful, and yet he (and increasingly she) is never in the limelight. The star comes out of the stage door surrounded by acolytes, is stopped by an even larger number of admirers pressing for an autograph. The director hangs on the fringe of these groups of people. Occasionally, in New York, an autograph hound will come up to him and ask, 'are you anybody?'.

This is a lesson in humility for the person who has been bossing everyone about a few hours or even minutes before. But these lessons are often learned much earlier. For the aspiring director, the early stages of his career are the years when he is treated like dirt and then asked to sweep more dirt off the stage, when he is sent for endless cups of coffee at all hours of the day and night, and when he is humiliated in front of the actors and designers by the abrupt dismissal of his suggestions.

These lessons in modesty and keeping ones mouth shut, valuable to be sure, were perhaps best learned at the Royal Shakespeare Company. At the Royal National Theatre, one is in London and help is available. In Stratford, cut off from loved ones, deprived by numbers (ten men to one woman was the ratio) from meeting new loved ones, the assistant director got booted about and seldom found comfort. If he was lucky, as I was, he might get invited for late night to early morning drinking sessions in the Dirty Duck by the likes of Michael Jayston, Norman Rodway and Alan Howard. Those hours provided the most valuable time I spent at the RSC partly because later Jayston recommended me for the job at the Traverse and Alan acted brilliantly in productions at three of the theatres where I have since been in charge.

But late night drinking with adorable actors was not the rule. The rule was to tag along behind John Barton and join him as a close-mouthed artistic and technical batman at every rehearsal and every meeting for a production of *Julius Caesar* that cannot, must not, be described. Another rule was to pretend to perfectly intelligent actors like Ian Richardson and Charlie Thomas that one understood what was going on, indeed, that there was something going on, apart from endless drilling of RSC Pentameter-Speak and soldiers marching and soldiers standing still.

Early one morning, around one o'clock, there was a session of notes for the technical staff in the make up room backstage. Three or four technical rehearsals had been held. The actors were either in their beds or in the pub. I was with all the designers who were being given minute criticisms by John Barton. I was tired from not doing anything all day for weeks. One of my small tasks was to host the Japanese observer who, as he staggered back to his hotel that night, had said to me prophetically, 'Wrong day.' He meant 'long day' of course but how right he was.

At one thirty in the morning, it was decided that Barrie Ingham, who was playing Brutus, was required for yet another costume fitting for the leather tunic or jacket that had already cost more than most of us. Where was Barrie to be found? He would be in the Dirty Duck. Who was to go and fetch him? The assistant director.

They let me into the pub, which was crowded. Barrie Ingham was nowhere to be seen. Probably he was hiding from me. But Elizabeth Spriggs found me. I looked over at her and smiled. I had never spoken to her. She was playing Portia beautifully, but John was changing most of her inflexions daily and I thought she was getting a bit peeved. But, she certainly didn't look cross. She managed the distance across the crowded pub very well. She had a large drink her in her left hand. With her right, she took me by the elbow and steered me expertly but slowly to a window seat.

'I have to find Barrie Ingham for a costume fitting,' I said.

'Never mind that,' she said.

Then she began. This woman that I hardly knew, had never spoken to, began to dress me down and tear me apart and analyze me psychologically and insult me. She never stopped smiling except to occasionally sip from her large drink. She said that I was a joke, that I was useless, that everyone considered me stupid and that I had no business being a director or an assistant director. This went on for about half an hour. I was trapped, like a frightened animal. For some reason I couldn't or didn't move away or even say anything. Much of what she said had some truth in it. At least it was based on accurate observation. I was as much amazed by her observations as by the fact that she was using them to attack me. Her main targets were my jolly demeanor, my lightness of tone and my tendency to make jokes. By now, we all know that this is a necessary concomitant of my work and indeed the title of a humorous and instructive book. But Liz Spriggs didn't like it one bit. She went on and on. I didn't say a word. I tried to smile. Then my memory started to click. I remembered that a year before Liz Spriggs had visited Nottingham and had seen the version of *Moll Flanders* I had written. I hadn't met her, but her enthusiasm had been widely reported, as is often the case in a provincial theatre when a well-known actor visits from out of town. She had, apparently, said that *Moll Flanders* was 'wonderful' and 'exciting' and that it should definitely be taken to the West End.

As she went on and on, now working over to the way I dressed and wore my hair, I quietly confirmed the accuracy of this report of her visit to Nottingham in my own memory. I decided that it was correct and if I ever got a chance, if she ever stopped this smiling catalogue of inadequacies, I would counter-attack with a defence based on her over praise of my version of *Moll Flanders*.

Finally, she stopped.

'Well, what have you to say for yourself, you jumped up little American joke smith?' she smiled.

I couldn't say anything.

'Well,' she repeated.

'Didn't you go up to Nottingham last June to see *Moll Flanders*?'

'Yes, I did,' she said.

'Didn't you tell everyone that it was wonderful and exciting and that it should transfer to the West End?'

'Yes, I did,' she said, still smiling.

I paused for effect.

'Well, I wrote that.'

There was no pause.

'Then why on earth don't you write instead of poncing about pretending to be a director?'

I was finished. I couldn't think of an answer to that. I went off into the night to find Barrie Ingham, which I did. I took him back to the costume fitting.

Being an assistant director is a little bit like being an understudy. One is treated with the same glass-eyed contempt. They simply look straight through you, unless they decide that they want to have a joke with you, a meal, or possibly go to bed with you. And even then you are second choice.

Until the moment when you are needed.

If you want to see a real transformation, watch the understudy immediately before and immediately after he is called upon. A minute before he was a corduroy clad dark shape in a nondescript group; now he is the cynosure. Now they are all around him – stage-management, wardrobe attendants, leading actors, producer, all vie for his attention.

I suddenly 'went on', as they say of understudies, when that production of *Julius Caesar* toured to Manchester and Charlie Thomas had a throat hemorrhage. He couldn't go on as Marc Antony. Ron Daniels was to move up from Trebonius. This meant that all the actors playing conspirators and even some soldiers would have to move up to bigger parts to fill the gap made by Ron moving up.

This was quite a task and it had to be done between two and five-thirty on Monday afternoon. I did it. I did it well and with good humour. Ron Daniels and I had gone to see *Star*, the movie about Noel Coward and Gertrude Lawrence, on Sunday night. We had worked out what he was going to do and working together (Ron later became a successful director), we guided the company through all the necessary changes.

Liz Spriggs was impressed. She came out to dinner with a group of us and we all drank lots of red wine and she was bloody nice to me. Very complimentary and all the business. She was terrific.

I started to think that she was right. Certainly I advise all young directors not to be assistant directors at all but to find or, indeed create, a situation where they can direct. The formation of the Freehold by Nancy Meckler and Headlong by Rupert Goold are good examples of this.

Trevor Nunn

Trevor Nunn took over the RSC between the time I was interviewed and the time I took up my appointment as assistant director. Trevor and I had been near contemporaries at Oxford and Cambridge and knew each other slightly.

After I assisted John Barton and Terry Hands, I became Trevor's assistant on a revival of *The Relapse*. After the first day, when Trevor gave a two-hour talk, mostly about the Vicar of Bray, I contrived to stay away from rehearsals by organizing something in The Studio. I didn't think he needed another director of his own generation under his feet.

Directors seldom talk to assistant directors and this relationship was no exception, but just before we opened Trevor invited me for a curry and a chat. I hated curry, but I looked forward to the chat. I knew exactly what I was going to say. I was going to stress the need for something to be done about Frances de la Tour who, all through rehearsals, had been astonishingly good. But at the dress rehearsal, she had been impossible to watch. She seemed to be walking through the role. She was distracted and without energy. I was anxious to find out if Trevor had noticed it and if he had, what he planned to do about it. I anticipated a long and interesting conversation about this puzzling actress wherein I could demonstrate what I considered to be one of my main strengths: dealing with actors. Even John Barton had admitted in an unguarded moment that I could do that.

But the conversation was brief.

'I'm very worried about Frances de la Tour,' I said. 'She seems out of it.'

'Oh, Frankie wore contact lenses for the first time today. She'll be fine.'

The meal proceeded in barely interrupted silence.

Three days later I was standing behind Trevor during the final rehearsal before the opening night. He half turned to me.

'Match me, JJ,' he said.

It was a pretty good joke if you know *Sweet Smell of Success*. I laughed and lit his cigarette.

Peter Hall and Peter Brooks

When Peter Hall was running the RSC, and I first worked there, long before I met Peter, they began The Studio. This was meant to be for exploratory work but, if the truth be told, it was instigated mainly to provide activity for large numbers of actors who had been in the Company for months with little to do besides carry spears, shields and bodies, and understudy. The Studio was, in 1965, under the directorship of Michael Saint-Denis, but *bien sur*, he was not there. John Barton was running it.

I was one of a group of young, very young, directors, brought in to rehearse two or three scenes, or perhaps an 'experimental' idea with these actors who were not doing very much and then to show these 'projects' to the assembled company, including the leading actors, directors and administrators and Peter Hall. The showings took place over a period of two days in the main rehearsal room.

John Barton was very demanding but, I learned, was quite far down in the chain of command. Once, I was in his office, and we were deciding which scenes I should direct with which actors, the morning after I had read or skimmed through fifteen examples of Greek Drama in translation (I don't exaggerate), looking for likely scenes. John disappeared after a quick phone call. 'Back in a mo.' He returned, two hours later, and mumbled through his menthol cigarette.

'Sorry. Peter gobbled me up.'

At the same time, you see, they were all working on the television version of Peter Hall's production *Wars of the Roses*. This meant even more spear and body carrying for the workforce, more unrest, and more anxiety for The Studio and 'The Showings' to undo. The Studio Showings were an opportunity for many to work, to act and perform for virtually the only time that season.

Finally it was agreed that I would direct (i) some sessions on improvisation with large numbers of actors; (ii) a duologue from *He Who Gets Slapped* by Andreyev, and (iii) *Purgatory* by William Butler Yeats. The last two would be 'shown'.

I rehearsed *Purgatory* hard, but the two actors simply could not act. There are people like that. They each learned their words quickly and never, hardly ever, varied the inflexions. Neither of them has progressed in the profession. They were in the Company, as far as I could tell, because they 'looked Roman'.

As actors, their defects and nerves became more evident as The Showings loomed nearer.

On a cold autumn morning, this small and difficult Yeats play was presented without décor to many of the most important people in British theatre. Peggy Ashcroft was there and Eric Porter and Ian Holm. And Roy Dotrice and Hugh Griffiths, and Michael Saint-Denis himself. He had flown over from Paris. They were all there and *Purgatory* was the first play shown. To say that the audience remained cool would be an understatement.

And it was dull.

There was polite applause for the two young actors. The scenery, such as it was, was being changed for the next presentation and I escaped to the gents. I walked up to the urinal and prepared to do my business. A short man came in and stood next to me. He also prepared himself. It was Peter Brook.

Oh, no, I thought. Not Peter Brook. Don't tell me that he saw that rubbish.

'Hello,' he smiled.

'Hello,' I said and, as one does, returned to my business. I didn't think it appropriate to say that it was nice to meet him. I was in some considerable awe of this tiny chap standing next to me with his thing in his hand and his rabbinical look. Also I was having trouble getting started.

'Are you in one of the plays?' he asked, very pleasantly. He didn't seem ill at ease at all. In fact, he was charming. Also, he kept looking at me. It was disconcerting.

'No, I'm not an actor,' I said, quite loudly. 'I'm a director.'

There was a pause while he continued to do what he was there for easily and without looking. I, on the other hand, struggled against increasing odds.

'Are you in any of the showings tomorrow?' he smiled again.

'No', I said. And then, rather less loudly, 'I'm a director. I directed the last one, that is, the first one. The Yeats play.'

Peter Brook smiled at me as he zipped himself up. I couldn't smile. 'Will you be in any of the plays after lunch?'

I was beginning to think that he was being obtuse on purpose.

'I'm not an actor,' I repeated and zipped myself up although I hadn't done a thing.

'It was very nice meeting you,' he said and washed his hands and left.

Was he winding me up? Did he not hear me? Was he sussing me out? I suspect that I was not the first person to ask these questions about Peter Brook.

Terry Hands

In my second stint at the RSC, I assisted Terry Hands on his production of *The Latent Heterosexual*. This was one of four plays that the RSC presented at the Aldwych in 1968 as part of their American season. In truth it was a season of New York Jewish comedies. But the RSC could not, would not, admit that. The plays had to be seen as important. Major academic claims had to be made for any play presented by the RSC. *The Latent Heterosexual* by Paddy Chayefsky, *God Bless* by Jules Feiffer and *Indians* by Arthur Kopit could not be seen for what they were, namely metropolitan spoof comedies more like Neil Simon than Ibsen.

Huge sets had to be built which reflected the claims made in rehearsals and in the programmes for these little plays. The men who wrote the plays were more or less ignored because even they could not understand some of the arguments being put forward: Kopit ate huge dinners with his wife Lesley, his director, Jack Gelber and me. Chayefsky played poker with me and some of the actors while the giant construction that was the set for his comedy came together and fell apart and was put back together over a three day period on the Aldwych stage. Kopit couldn't understand it when Gelber, his best friend, was fired as the director and Chayefsky simply gave up and took the kudos of an RSC production as he had taken the money from the film people. That was one of his stories.

Paddy told us how he refused to allow the play to be done in New York. He would only allow one production in Dallas, with Zero Mostel, before this. He gleefully related how he held out for months against the blandishments of the Hollywood moguls, until finally, with great reluctance, he had given in.

Then he told us the story of a lunch at the Russian Tea Room when a movie mogul handed him a cheque for half a million dollars. Paddy took the cheque.

Then the mogul said, 'I'm so glad you took that, Paddy.'

'Why are you so glad Irving?' asked Paddy.

'Because now I know that I was right. You can be bought.'

Whereupon Paddy tore up the cheque.

But Paddy wasn't about to tear up the cheque from the RSC. He was perfectly happy to sit in the tiny canteen at the Aldwych, for several hours a day, while the artists and technicians above tried to operate the scenic design for his play. The set was a triangular mechanical mouth that opened at the crucial moment by the floor rising to become a second ceiling. Then blood was to pour down the steep rake towards the audience. How this reflected the world of a homosexual novelist who is seduced by Jewish accountants into being a heterosexual businessman was never clear to me. But, whatever it was, we were going to persevere, or, in the case of Paddy and me and Roy Dotrice, we were going to play poker downstairs while the others made the damn thing work.

After quite a few days of waiting, we were summoned to the auditorium. The thing was ready. There was to be a run-through. The actors climbed onto the stage. They went to their dressing rooms and put on their costumes. The lights went down. The lights went up.

Then the same thing happened that had happened to *Indians*. All the wry metropolitan Jewish wit was gone. In *Indians*, after they had fired the director, Terry had actually painted the faces of the actors red and white to give a style to the production. Now he had put these actors on a steep, slippery slope. Lee Montague, whose perfect American accent and understated playing had made him a model of Broadway comedy in the rehearsal room, could not register against the white walls and white light of the vast expanse on which he acted. The same was true of Barry Stanton and Tim Wylton.

I had been angry and upset when this intellectualism and stylization had been inflicted on *Indians* because Jack Gelber and Arthur Kopit had become friends of mine. Now, I couldn't be angry anymore. I became puzzled.

After the run-through, when everything that had ever been funny in the play had washed away with the stage blood at the end, Terry gathered us in the stalls for notes. He gave quite a few, mostly about the aims and style of the production. Either he had given up on the actors or he simply didn't care.

Finally, I resolved to ask one question. No one except Paddy and Roy had spoken to me for days and I wasn't even certain that they knew who I was, but I was determined to say something, if only to register to myself that I was there. After all, I was the assistant director. Perhaps my point might be useful.

I waited until the notes were finished. There was a slight pause. At any moment we would be dismissed.

'Terry?' I ventured.

'What is it, Michael?'

'That little metal sculpture at the apex of the triangle, that little thing on a stand. You know the one I mean? It looks like an American Indian symbol made into a coat rack, or something?'

'Yes. What about it?'

'What's it for?'

There was no pause.

'If you don't understand that, Michael, then you don't understand the entire philosophy behind this production. Isn't that true, Tim?'

'Absolutely true,' said Tim O'Brien, the designer who was also dressed in black. 'He simply doesn't understand.'

Now I was embarrassed as well as puzzled. Also, I didn't think that I would be asking very many more questions.

A few weeks later, I left the RSC.

Traverse Theatre

Interview For Traverse Theatre

Time   12.30 p.m.

Place   The bar at the Traverse Theatre, the Grassmarket, Edinburgh. The bar smells of stale beer and is cluttered with debris from the previous night.

Date   February 1969

Post   Artistic Director

The interviewee is wearing a suit. One member of the Board, a playwright's wife, is wearing a Laura Ashley dress. One accountant is wearing a jacket and tie. The other two accountants are wearing suits. The schoolteacher (female) is wearing trousers and a pullover. The schoolteacher (male) is wearing a jacket and tie. And the lawyer, the chairman, is wearing slacks and a white pullover.

The scene has been dramatically set by previous interviewee flouncing out. His name is Robert Kidd. Something has upset him. The present interviewee isn't surprised, having watched him on the plane and in the lobby of the Caledonian hotel where they both waited, separately, and drank, separately, at least ten cups of coffee.

The still quite young man, the interviewee, is struck by the innocent lack of knowledge of the committee. The questions, not testing, seem to be, as they later prove, genuine quests for knowledge. In reply, the young man, high on caffeine and lack of sleep, outlines at top speed a programme of work, mostly new plays, from notes literally written on the back of an envelope. These plays are all projects he has been considering as a freelance director. The committee seems impressed. No one is surprised and certainly no one mentions it when later, at the end of the first year, those suggestions, written down during the one hour plane trip, prove to be the backbone of the first season. This lack of surprise is surprising when it is a fact that this young man had no experience at all of either running a theatre or directing new plays.

After the interview, a teatime meeting with Clive Perry, Artistic Director of the Lyceum Theatre who tells him life in Scotland is hard and after dinner, the Chairman, Nicholas Fairbairn, corners the young man and implores him to accept the offer.

The plane back to London is cancelled. The interviewee sleeps on the floor of a student flat. Olwen Wymark, whose play was being performed at the time, was also meant to take the plane and also sleeps there. They travel down together the next morning. She implores him to take the job.

Never having been implored, and after discussing it with his agent Peter Murphy ('You will have your own patch'), he accepts the job.

New Plays

The Traverse theatre was in Edinburgh's Grassmarket. Burke and Hare robbed bodies there and sold them for vivisection. Wealthy men used to keep their mistresses there. When I was in Edinburgh, their wives came down to watch Lindsay Kemp and Stephen Berkoff. I don't know where the mistresses were.

My job was to be in charge of the theatre. This meant choosing the plays, directors and actors. We didn't have designers or lighting designers. One man, Gerry Jenkinson, designed and operated all the lighting and sound.

Also, I was responsible for finances. When I arrived, I was told by Ronald Mavor, the Director of the Scottish Arts Council, that if by the end of my first year we could not demonstrate that we were on our way to wiping out the accumulated deficit of the theatre (£12,000), he would close it down. I thought that was a bit rough, coming, as it did, from the son of a playwright (James Bridie).

But we did make a good start financially with the help of a good year at the box office and a cool £1000 from Eddie Kulukundis, a Greek philanthropist and theatre producer. Eddie did ask that he be put on the Board and in return would donate the same amount for three years. I believe that Eddie has saved a lot of theatres. He was certainly on a lot of Boards.

In order to do well at the box office, we had to do some conventional plays but the Traverse exists to produce unsettling and unconventional plays so in the main, that was what I chose.

The man who hired me went on to fame and back as cabinet minister. He managed to reduce Alec Douglas-Home's majority to fifty, but he did get into Parliament and, indeed, into Margaret Thatcher's government. But not for long. He was Nicholas Fairbairn, lawyer, fancy-dresser, active heterosexual, maker of phrases and gifted painter. I keep one of his water colours to remind me of the time that he agreed to the pornographic photographs in our production of *Lay-by*.

Lay-by was the first genuinely daring play that I produced at the Traverse. It was the genuine article. Written by a committee of Howard Brenton, Brian Clark, Trevor Griffiths, David Hare, Stephen Poliakoff and Snoo Wilson. It's subject was, put simply, sex, drugs and pornography.

About three-quarters of the way into the play, long after the incident in which a man is turned into jam, came a scene that required the actor, James Warrior, to pass large colour pornographic photographs round the audience. The Traverse was a small, well lit theatre and it was not only possible for everyone in the audience to see each photo, but also possible for everyone in the audience to see each person seeing each photo. I had been offered the play by Snoo Wilson after a special reading at the Royal Court during which, it was reported, Lindsay Anderson and Anthony Page chatted throughout and then said 'no'. The Royal court wanted to encourage these writers, but not that much. They wouldn't do it. I must admit that I was a bit worried, but the Traverse put up half the money and we scheduled it late at night during the Festival.

I saw a run-through. I liked it, but I was anxious. The photos were big, and there were lots of them and they were graphic. I simply didn't know what to do about them. They couldn't be defended as art and the Edinburgh police were always pestering us, looking for some reason to come down on us and even close the theatre.

I called Fairbairn. Not only was he Chairman of the Board, he was also an eminent advocate (barrister). The pictures were put along the wall, on the floor, and they stretched quite a long way. Nicky arrived around 6 p.m. on the night the play was to open. He was dressed appropriately, flashy and at least three decades out of fashion. He walked up and down in front of the exhibition. The more I looked at these displays of sexual athleticism and imagination, the more I worried. The play could not be done without them and if we cancelled it then our credibility in the avant-garde marketplace would be blown. Besides, it was rather good. I couldn't very well ring David Hare and say 'I'm sorry David, we're cutting the dirty photos.'

Nicky paused before one of the more lurid ones. This one had three people doing as much as possible to each other simultaneously and in colour.

'These will be fine. Let's have a drink.'

Later that night, that is early the next morning at 1.45 a.m., (we were doing five shows a day), when the lights went up on a packed house, I had reason to be grateful to Nicholas Fairbairn. After all, Nicky had a lot to lose. He had married into one of the grandest and most respectable families in Scotland and he had real political ambitions. It was a difficult decision to make, but he made it look easy.

When the photos were finally passed around the small auditorium, crammed to overflowing with many people sitting on the floor, one of the actors in the audience burst into uncontrollable laugher. He had been a model for porno shots like these. To see him laugh, to hear him laugh at these pictures and to join in with the rest of the audience, was to have prudery banished. For the moment.

The show was a success, commanding all of the national reviews the next day. Irving Wardle gave it four fifths of his column in *The Times*, relegating the official Festival's production of *King Lear* to a paragraph.

Lay-By was invited to the Royal Court. Of course.

We did a lot of new plays at the Traverse and it was there that I discovered I could actually do something well. I was thirty so it was not too soon. I learned that I could form a working relationship with a living writer, suggest things that would help the play and, aided by my position as director of a theatre, get the play produced.

One day, I had scheduled lunch with C.P. Taylor. Cecil was working on at least four plays at once and a television script and probably something for the Northumbrian Tourist Board as well. Also, he was juggling two marriages and two sets of kids. He was, in other words, trying hard to remain a living writer.

I had made a good suggestion to him about his play *Black and White Minstrels,* which we were hoping to do in the spring. I had suggested that he bring another character into the play to begin the second act and Cecil had, presumably, retired to his shed in the garden, moved aside four or five other scripts, and set to work. Three months passed. We were having lunch in the Traverse restaurant during a break from my rehearsals. He had sent me the rewrites a month before, but this was our first opportunity to talk about my reactions to the rewriting.

'Well, Cecil,' I said cheerfully. 'I have to tell you that the second act is terrific. This new character really works. The play is much better. It is definitely worth doing and we are definitely going to do it. I can't tell you how pleased I am.'

Cecil looked puzzled.

'Just remind me, Mike. What happens in the second act?'

The new character that was introduced into the second act was Maxie, a middle-aged Jewish lawyer, very respectable, who finds himself involved in a quartet of wife-swapping socialist Glaswegians through his unexpected sexual attraction to one of the wives.

I offered the part to a man called Harry Hankin whom I had met on a plane. He owned a chain of dry cleaning establishments, but had always wanted to be an actor. We had a long conversation on the plane and in the airport. He had been for a long time an active member of the amateur group called the Avraham Greenbaum players. I am not making this up. He used to come to the Traverse as a patron and once I saw him there, when we were casting Cecil's play, and I said to him, 'Harry, this is going to amaze you, but I am going to offer you a wonderful part in a wonderful play.'

'I'll read it,' said Harry.

It turned out by strange coincidence that Harry was a friend of Tom Conti, who was going to be in the play. Not so strange, I suppose, as Tom knows almost everyone in Scotland especially everyone who is either Italian or Jewish.

Harry read the play and we fixed lunch. The part was ideal for him and, in one short scene, he had ten guaranteed laughs. It was a gift.

'I can't do it, Michael. I can't.'

'What on earth do you mean, Harry? It's perfect for you. You're exactly the right age. It's your own background. Alan Howard and Tom Conti are in it. Tom is your friend. You want to change your career and be an actor. This is ideal for you and for us.'

'I can't do it. Look at this.'

Harry pointed to the speech about fellatio and wine drinking in the second act. It was a tough speech, explicit but delicate. The husband was trying to embarrass and deflect the man who was threatening to become his wife's lover.

'What's wrong with that, Harry? It's a beautiful speech. It's brilliant.'

'I tell you, Mike, the next step is shitting in the street.'

I thought about that for a minute.

'Harry, that is the dirtiest thing that anyone has ever said to me.'

Eventually we, mainly Tom Conti, convinced Harry to do the part and it was, indeed, the beginning of a new career for him.

I'm not sure he ever forgave us.

The fact that Harry was, basically, an amateur was very right for the Traverse which always had a rough, unpolished side to it. The people who criticized me always did so because they thought I had made the Traverse too 'mainstream', too conventional. Maybe.

The first new play that we produced in my regime, *Curtains*, was written by a man called Tom Mallin. *Curtains* was well received. It got very good reviews during the Festival and on transferring to the Open Space theatre, and, it marked the London debut in a leading role for Nigel Hawthorne.

It is the accepted practice when a theatre and a playwright have a success together, as we did with Tom on *Curtains*, that the theatre should, whenever possible, put on his next play.

Unfortunately, Mallin's next play was called *The Novelist* and even more unfortunately, that is what it was about. There was this novelist. He lived on a Greek island. He had a wife. His best friend came to visit. The best friend was attracted to the wife. It was dreadful. But we did it. And we had a superb cast, Robin Bailey, Barbara Jefford and John Turner.

Whenever I could, I invited the playwright to stay at my house so that I could get closer to him. After three days of discussing the play, cutting it, finding ways to perfect the many long speeches that novelists seem to make, I sat across the dinner table from Tom Mallin, who was a gentle, self-effacing man, and I asked him what he thought.

'What do you mean?' asked Tom.

'I mean what do you think we should do? What should we concentrate on? Should you write something, perhaps? Something more? Is it working?'

'I'm sorry, Michael, I don't know.'

'That's a bit odd, isn't it Tom? I mean, you are the playwright and you have been sitting there for three days in absolute silence, watching us work, re-work, and even, occasionally, rewrite your script. Don't you have anything to say to me?' I really liked Tom Mallin, that's why I was able to talk to him in this way.

'Michael,' he said, 'I can't think of anything to say. I'm so in love with Barbara Jefford, so utterly in love with her, that I don't have a single other thought in my head.'

'Hadn't you better get out of love with her? She is very married to John Turner and we have to get your play on.'

'I will try, Michael.'

We never did make a success of his second play.

Experimental Theatre

I think the most significant single idea I ever came across was that of W.B. Yeats who advocated putting on the 'mask of the opposite'. If I am running a theatre and it is known for its experimental work, then I like to pull that rug away and give the audience something conventional but successful, something that might make some of the regular patrons cross. Similarly, if I am the director of a conventional theatre, then I will put on a fair amount of innovative work. I never think an audience, a regular audience, should know what to expect. At Hampstead Theatre, I gave them much more experimental and 'near the knuckle' theatre than they had been used to: *The People Show, Fanshen, The Elephant Man,* Mike Leigh's *Abigail's Party* and *Dusa, Fish, Stas & Vi.* The fact that some of those shows turned out to be commercially successful was not my fault. It was simply that at that time and place the public's taste for something good and something different coincided with my own. Hopefully this phenomenon will occur again.

But much of our work was unconventional at the Traverse, which was the preference of most of the patrons. Chief among the patrons was Tom Mitchell.

Tom Mitchell was the President of the Traverse. Few people had any idea what this title meant, but certainly he received a great deal of respect and attention. He was the owner of the Old Traverse, the building in the Lawnmarket from which the theatre had taken its name, and for many years he enthusiastically allowed that building to be used by the Traverse Workshop Company under the direction of Max Stafford-Clark. In fact, Max lived there, as did several of his company.

Also, there was an interest free loan of fifteen hundred pounds that Tom refused to allow us to pay off, which in turn insured his prominence in our thoughts and our budgets, not to mention our notepaper.

It is fair to say that Mitchell had a lively interest in young people. He was sixty odd, with white hair, a white beard, strong arms and legs and a prominent stomach. Normally he wore casual clothes. He claimed to drink one bottle of wine every evening. He was reputed to be very wealthy. No one knew what he did, although he certainly owned many properties in Edinburgh and a fair amount of land in Cumberland, where he was also President of the Workington Rugby League Football Club. Mitchell's interest in young people extended beyond providing rent free accommodation and rehearsal space. He would often have dinner in the theatre restaurant and he would give small or large parties at one of his properties.

One night, after a performance by the Freehold, an experimental company that visited the Traverse on a regular basis, we were all invited back to Tom's flat for plonk and cheese and serious flirtation.

I had only been artistic director of the Traverse for a few weeks and was new to the experimental scene. Although I was thirty and older than most of them, I knew I would have to join the late-night sessions in order to maintain good relations with these groups. Also, I hoped to enjoy it. Pip Simmons, of the Pip Simmons Theatre Group, Nancy Meckler of the Freehold, Snoo Wilson of the Portable Theatre were all people whom I had to get to know in order to keep up the valuable relationship between the Traverse and the active fringe theatre groups.

On this particular night, I was hoping to have a chat with Lindsay Kemp whose mime troupe had performed quite often at the Traverse and who was hoping, I knew, to use the Traverse as a base camp for touring and thereby get good Arts Council grants. Lindsay had been very loud at the press conference when my appointment was announced and he had a reputation for being obstreperous. I wanted to get on well with him.

I wandered from room to room at this party, refusing various drugs but being, I hoped, quite charming and easy to meet. The Freehold members were all there with lots of hangers on and Max Stafford-Clark's company in force. Tom Mitchell was being very friendly. I was new to Edinburgh, new to the fringe and I was married. I was doing my best, but I was shy.

The bedroom area was quiet. There was noise, but it was quiet. I stayed away from there. The sitting room and the study were packed with people talking with intensity over the music. They seemed to know each other well. I heard loud sounds of enjoyment from the kitchen. I went in. The sounds stopped. Everyone looked at me.

Lindsay Kemp was on the floor, on his back with one foot raised.

Tom Mitchell was holding that foot and using Lindsay, as far as I could tell, like a mop. Everyone, including Lindsay, had been laughing until I came in. Silence. Then Lindsay spoke.

'Oh, Michael Rudgeman. I want to fuck you.'

I think he was joking.

He never did get my name right, even after we had presented several of his shows including the premiere of *Salome*.

Jim Haynes, founder of the Traverse, a theatre with five founders, came into my life there twice. Once he turned up for the theatre's twenty-first birthday party fundraising event with two young French women and helped us to erase the accumulated deficit. Another time, he pressed me to invite the Women's Theatre Group, under the leadership of Jane Arden, to create a show at the Traverse.

We turned the theatre over to these zealots and I turned my home over to them for two weeks while I went on holiday with my family. This was after they had opened to an indifferent Scottish press. Perhaps people who do political theatre can cope with anything but co-operation and indifference. If I had yelled and screamed at them and tried to manipulate their work, they might have been happier. Possibly they would have done better work. Instead, I employed Jim Haynes' method and left them to do what they wanted with very little fuss. They met indifference, they got angry, then they got bored and then they left. The only remnant of their stay was a bikini, belonging to my wife, which was cut up in pieces and left in a wastepaper basket in our home.

Actors

I was determined to get fine actors to the Traverse. Many of them were quite well known and others were to become extremely well known. They included Robin Bailey, Tom Conti, Fenella Fielding, Mike Gwilym, Nigel Hawthorne, Ian Holm, Alan Howard, Russell Hunter, Barbara Jefford, Nigel Planer and Jack Shepherd.

Of course, the committee, my bosses, were not that interested. Many of them were accountants and lawyers and they were concerned with the nuts and bolts.

I remember the evening that I told them the cast for the new play,

The Novelist by Tom Mallin, I said they would be delighted to know that it would consist of Robin Bailey, Barbara Jefford and John Turner. They did a sort of collective nod and went back to arguing about the stolen bar takings and how to find the culprit. It turned out to be one of our favourite people.

Stanley Eveling and Ian Holm

One memorable performance was Ian Holm's in Stanely Eveling's play, *Carravagio, Buddy*. Stanley was one of the many pieces of luck I had in my time at Edinburgh.

Stanley's work had been a mainstay at the Traverse for years. Legend has it that one day he marched up to the box office and demanded the return of the long-held manuscript of his first play. He was a successful philosophy don and was used to having his work read immediately. After this intervention, Max Stafford-Clark read the play and put it on and many more with great success. Stanley's plays were witty, elegant, profound, sexy, unusual, philosophical and, above all, fun. Our audience was more than fond of his work and the plays often sold out before they opened.

Carravagio, Buddy was a complex work in which a modern man embodies the persona of Carravagio, the painter. Like many of Stanley's plays, it demanded a charismatic, sexy actor with wit and skill.

Ian Holm was an actor I had relentlessly pursued. I had offered him five plays. He always read them quickly and turned them down politely. His agent was a charming man called Julian Bellfrage who never made us feel like poor cousins offering paltry wages.

But something about *Carravagio, Buddy* struck a chord with Ian and he agreed to do the play for a short season during the festival. Also, I had offered him so many plays he must have thought that I had good taste and that it would be okay to work with me.

The rehearsals were a delight. There was no set. The whole thing was played on one of the modules – small banks of seats that comprised the auditorium. The cast loved the play and relished the language and the comedy.

Stanley was an extremely accomplished squash player. He had been an Oxford Blue and also played some tennis. I loved tennis and we played all the time. I would say to my secretary that I was off for a couple of hours script conference with Stanley Eveling. We were pretty well evenly matched, but he usually won.

We found out that Ian Holm loved tennis and we both arranged to play with him. He wasn't very good so Stanley and I agreed that when we played him we would let the set go to five all or more before we won. This, we rightly thought, would keep Ian interested and fairly happy during the rehearsals and maybe he would do more than two weeks of performances. He didn't do more performances but he was pretty happy. One of my best memories is Ian coming into a rehearsal a few minutes late one day saying, 'I took that bastard playwright to six all, but he beat me. It was a great match. I'll get him next time.'

But, of course, he didn't.

Traverse Trials

But, we didn't only do plays. Malcolm Rifkind, Nicholas Fairbairn, John Smith and Robin Cook, all starred in something we called 'Traverse Trials'.

The format was simple. It was stolen from a television show presented, and possibly invented, by Ludovic Kennedy. Each side would have a barrister, usually someone like Rifkind or Cook, one from the right and one from the left, and they would have three expert witnesses each. They would debate an issue like 'Student Power Now' or 'Legalise Drugs Now' and then the audience, numbering about one hundred, would have a general debate and then vote.

Once I asked Malcolm Rifkind why a clever young Tory councilor with a beautiful wife would give up his Sunday evening to debate in a small theatre in the Grassmarket?

'Don't you realise,' he asked in his penetrating way, 'that this is a much larger audience than I will get at any political meeting?'

Malcolm got his audience regularly and improved his standing in the city. Also, he and Robin made sure that the Corporation quadrupled its grant to the Traverse. A fair exchange.

Usually the debates were within the realm of reasoned argument. The most heated one was about the Ring Road, although 'Education' did draw some blood and in 'Gay Power Now' there was a contingent who were bussed up from London and who attacked Professor Carstairs for being too moderate. One rather beautiful young man in tight jeans kept screaming at him, 'Have you ever fucked a boy?'.

Professor Carstair's reply was polite, firm, and negative, but he lost the vote.

The Traverse auditorium was simply a black rectangle with seven grey seating units. Once the doors were closed, you felt that you could not get out and certainly no sound came in. It was the perfect laboratory for theatre.

Sometimes, as I said, we experimented with conventional theatre, or theatre that seemed conventional compared to the drug culture non-linear work that was fashionable on the fringe in the seventies. Once we did a version of *The Relapse* by Vanburgh. Fenella Fielding agreed to play Berinthia. All went smoothly until the opening night, and even until the interval of the opening night. We had all been to the bar for a drink and a chat and now we were settled into our cushioned seats for the second act. So far the play, which we had edited severely but fairly, was working. We had cut all the Lord Foppington scenes, normally the most successful, and kept all that was to do with Loveless, Amanda, Berinthia and Worthy. We had dressed it á la 1930's and played it as a contemporary comedy of manners, rather like a Noel Coward play.

After the interval, as I sat in the dark auditorium, I was feeling pleased. I was wrong.

We waited two minutes. Then three. Three minutes is a long time to be in the dark with one hundred strangers, some of them critics. Then we waited four minutes. And five. Everyone was restless. No one could see his watch. I rely for my timings on the stage management reports.

The thing was, Fenella hadn't finished her costume change. With a twenty minute interval and another five minutes of us being in the pitch dark, you imagined it was long enough, but apparently not. I knew that she was nervous, although she was excellent in the play that night and every night, but I realised after a little while that she was the reason for the delay. The doors were shut. The lights were out. It was hot. You could smell panic. Then it was eight minutes. I was breathing heavily. I didn't know what to do. I was desperate. Then I felt a sharp pain in my scalp. Then another. What the hell could that be? Then I realized what I was doing. I was tearing at my hair. Eventually, the second act began and the play was a success.

Max Stafford-Clark

Although I was appointed Artistic Director of the Traverse, it was an appointment complicated by one proviso: the previous artistic director, Max Stafford-Clark, was to stay on, housed in the old Traverse (the original building) in the Lawnmarket. There he was to evolve two shows per year and he was to finance himself with a portion of the budgeted salary for one artistic director. He received fifteen pounds a week, which was five pounds less than me.

Many members of the Board let me know privately that they considered this arrangement temporary, that Max really should be going immediately and that I could insist on him going at any time, take the full thirty-five pounds a week, and they would back me.

In fact, I found the relationship with Max more than satisfactory and, although we never became close friends, or even friends, several good shows came out of the Traverse Workshop Company and we got on well, or at least easily. Their work was always new, often innovative and played to a strong constituency in Edinburgh. Also, it freed me to do some conventional new plays, which gave the Traverse a more balanced programme and a larger audience than it had had before. Max would evolve his shows from improvisation and work with the author in the old Traverse building.

His rehearsals and devisings sometimes took several weeks, or even months, and the Company lived and stayed together. Twice a year, Max would come in to my office and we would stare silently at a wall chart together. Max was canny and he would try to get the best playing time during the Festival that he could. As we were usually doing five shows a day, the amount of juggling was considerable.

In the end, there would be in the Traverse programme for the Festival, for example, a devised play by Max and his Company and a little known playwright alongside, say, a new play by Stanley Eveling and a new play by Cecil Taylor both directed by me.

Max is the sort of person who appears single minded, even selfish, but actually has based his life on co-operation.

As artistic director of the Traverse during the Edinburgh Festival I was, in effect, the Director of a small festival. We presented four or five shows a day: a lunchtime show, three evening performances, the last one beginning a little after and sometimes long after midnight and sometimes we would do something in the afternoons as well. By the end of four weeks, we all felt the need to unwind. One year, the restaurant was franchised out to an Italian. He and Tom Conti became friends because Tom loved food and fellow Italians. On the Sunday after the official Festival finished and Edinburgh became a beautiful ghost town again, Tom gave a dinner in the restaurant. We all paid for our own food and drink, but Tom was the genial host.

There were speeches and toasts and more speeches and there was a great deal of red wine. Then, about eleven o'clock, I took my wife home. But as we walked through the door of a flat in Oxford Terrace, I began to worry. All those merry people alone in the building. Romance might blossom, or worse, destructive tendencies. The police might come; always looking for an excuse to either embarrass us or threaten closure. I felt tipsy, but I went back.

As I was parking my car, very carefully, in the empty Grassmarket, I bumped the car behind, bumper to bumper, no harder than you might bang a table to emphasize a point. There couldn't have been any damage, but I was in that state of cautious inebriation. I got out to look at the car behind. It was an invalid vehicle, with only three wheels. I became even more careful and quite socially concerned. I could see no damage but, just in case, I tore of the top of my cigarette packet and wrote my name, my address, my office phone and my home phone number. Just as I was about to add my height, weight and NI number, two Scottish policemen appeared. They had been hiding in the small wooden hut in the Grassmarket across from the entrance to the Traverse. They had seen how careful I was being.

They asked me to blow up a little balloon. Fascinating. It changed colour. They took me to the police station in the Lawnmarket. Not so fascinating. They were quite rude.

'May I please go home? No one knows where I am.'

'You'll have to wait for an hour, then take a blood test.'

'Why?'

'We're very busy, sir.'

I sat in silence, wondering if my wife would worry, wondering what Conti and the others were up to, and wondering if I would ever be allowed to drive my car again.

After an hour of this, I felt sober. Then they took a blood test from my arm, which sobered me up even more. I thought of asking them for another balloon to blow up. Then they said that I could go.

'Could I please have my car keys?', I asked.

'No, sir.'

'Oh.'

'We can't possibly let you drive your car, sir.'

The word 'sir' was becoming a tiny whip.

'How can I get home then,' I was polite.

'Well, sir, you will have to phone one of your friends. We can't hand over the keys to you, sir.'

Phone one of my friends? I didn't have any friends. My wife would be fast asleep. Who would be awake at two o'clock in the morning on a Sunday night in Edinburgh? I thought of Max. He might very well be awake, talking with his colleagues and making interesting plans and he was nearby in the Lawnmarket. I rang him.

Max answered the phone immediately.

'Max, I don't suppose I could ask you a huge favour?'

'Of course, Michael. What can I do?'

I explained the situation, said where I was, and asked for his help. He said that he would be there in five minutes and he was. He walked into that station like any sober uncle come to help his naughty nephew. They gave him the keys and told me that I would know within a month whether or not I had been over the limit, and thus disqualified. I think they were slightly surprised that I could get a friend there at such short notice. I know that I was.

Max and I went into the cold air. We headed up the hill.

'Thanks a lot Max. I don't live far from here.'

'Oh, I mustn't drive you home.'

'Oh?'

'Sorry, Michael, but I am completely looped. I'm afraid I couldn't possibly drive a car.'

Actually, I don't think that Max is afraid of anything.

Do It

Not long after I got the job at the Traverse, I came across a book called *Do It* by Jerry Rubin. It was an account of his activities in the Yippie movement of the sixties and an incitement to more of the same. I had known Jerry at Oberlin College, in Ohio. I read *Do It* with great interest, but not much pleasure.

It is impossible for a theatre director to read anything without seeing a play in it. *Wisden* has possibilities. So does the *Rules of Golf*. Almost anything can become a play or a show, given the right treatment and the right place to grow.

I had seen the Pip Simmons Groups do one of their shows and I knew their work to be ballsy, brash and talented. I sent the book to Pip who read a few pages and decided that he would like to do a show. The Traverse gave him commissioning money and with a promise of a production, he set to work writing songs and improvising the text or, to be more accurate, adding rude words.

The show went on to be performed all over Europe at many theatre festivals and to big audiences in some pretty big places. But I think that its opening night in Edinburgh on that tiny stage with eighty astonished onlookers must have been one of its most interesting performances.

As eight singers, actors or musicians performed the history of the Yippie movement, complete with demonstrations in front of the White House, Bacchanalia, and obscenities of word and deed, we looked on with a willing suspension of taste.

Finally, we arrived at the compulsory full frontal nudity and sex scene, which I sometimes think was a *sine qua non* for grants from the

Arts Council for small touring. And Pip did nothing by halves. All eight of the cast, six men and two women, took off their brightly coloured hippy clothes. Flared jeans and t-shirts flew in all directions. A gang bang was forming before our eyes. The lights went up bright, bright, bright. Then the bodies plastered themselves against each other in a multi-sexual daisy chain. There was writhing and humping and pumping and pushing and there were noises too.

Then I remembered something. The chap in the dark brown suit, sitting in the front row, two feet away from the nearest performer, was a Bishop. He was the Bishop of the Church of England in Scotland. He didn't move.

My eyes were drawn back to the action. It was far too late to be worried about what the Bishop thought. What on earth did I think? That was my problem.

Then I saw smoke. Not the obligatory stage smoke of the sixties, but cigarette smoke. This is an astounding thing to see in a theatre, even on stage. The stage light catches it and heightens it. No, this smoke was coming from the auditorium from the first row. It was coming from the Bishop. With his eyes glued to the bodies glued together, the Bishop had unconsciously done something far more shocking that the writhing bodies. He had lit up. Right there in the auditorium. And the stage light was bright and spilling on to his face. But he smoked on. He was unaware of what he had done.

After the show, he collared me in the bar.

'Are you Michael Rudman?'

'Yes, I am. And you are the Bishop. Yes?'

'Yes, indeed.'

'Welcome to the Traverse, Bishop.' I suppose that is what you call them.

'I enjoyed it very much,' said the Bishop.

'Oh, great. I'm glad,' I said.

'A very good show. Jolly good.'

I was surprised, I must admit. He didn't mention the orgy and I didn't mention the cigarette.

Traverse Tattoo

In my first year as director, in addition to the plays we were doing, I initiated something called the Traverse Tattoo. This was, of course, half a joke. The main festival has a Military Tattoo that parades armed might and music. We, by way of contrast, offered the best and worst of the fringe in selected segments, every evening between six and seven. Because the Traverse was the acknowledged leader of the fringe and its social centre, it was ideal for many groups to show their wares. Many of them had no audience at all, but here they could perform a bit for their fellow competitors, the Traverse audience and some festival audience on their way to the shows. It became quite an event. Most of the fringe people wanted to be in it. I remember seeing Mel Smith and Billy Connolly and, on one memorable occasion, Jack Shepherd, Richard Eyre and John McGrath.

It was decided that on the last night of the Traverse Tattoo, a grand conglomerate show would be organized by three groups: The Traverse as host, 7/84, which had begun that year at Cranston Street Hall, and the Lyceum Company headed by Richard. It was a fraternal idea and fun, and we decided to rehearse it.

There was no director, but Jack Shepherd quickly began to call the shots both for the script and the production. It was to be an Aquashow telling the history of water, based loosely on the story of Moses crossing the Red Sea. All of us made contributions to the text. Jack played the villain/narrator and I played the Egyptian Pharaoh with a heavy Mexican accent. Richard and John also had good parts.

Jack's introduction was lengthy and included a credit for the fictional producing company, which he called the '7/84 Traverse, Royal Lyceum, Scoto-Yid Theatre Company'. The courtyard was packed. Everyone had heard about this and it was going to be some kind of valediction for all the work that all of us had put in for the past several weeks.

The only décor was a large metal tub of water left of the centre of the tiny stage. We had to step over it and around it whenever we had any movement and it seemed to be funny to the audience that we had to do this. In fact, almost everything we did got a laugh. We were all known figures to those watching and we were willing to play the fool for them in these informal surroundings with this makeshift jape of a show. In fact, they got quite giggly.

In the rehearsal, Jack, who has a strong anarchic streak, had said that at the end of the Water Show (he insisted on using the English version,) we would all shout 'Armageddon', pick up the tub and tip it over and soak the audience. This seemed like a good idea and we all agreed, but I thought 'Surely not'.

Towards the end of the sketch, I noticed that not only was the courtyard full but all the windows of the theatre, from the first floor up, were filled with people watching. It looked like the first truly modern, truly Scottish opera with a giant chorus leaning out of the windows. I also noticed a growing hysteria.

At those windows were mostly Traverse actors and technicians who had been working with little or no sleep for weeks to provide round the clock entertainment for the burghers of Edinburgh and their visitors. On the stage were the people who had been planning, writing, performing and directing these plays for months. Now, we were all laughing together. Now the show was coming to an end.

When we had all run down the backstairs of the Traverse and onto the stage like a football team going onto the pitch, I had said to each of the cast, at least twice, 'Forget the business of dousing the audience. Don't do it.' They had all nodded and accepted my right as host to exercise caution.

But now, as the hysteria mounted, so did my perception of the genius of Jack's idea and the need to touch or slap or smack or *frapper* this audience in a palpable way. This is what happened:

After about ten minutes on the history of water, including Moses crossing the Red Sea and many other much less significant events, finally, breathing heavily, Jack screamed the final line of the text.

'Armageddon!'

I moved to the tub. The others moved with me. I shouted.

'Armageddon!'

And we threw the entire contents of a large metal tub of water onto one hundred faces, twenty mink coats, fifteen nice dresses and quite a few duffel coats. And from above came more water. The technicians were flinging plastic buckets of water out of the windows, sometimes letting the bucket go as well.

The audience laughed more. Then, as they got drenched, they stopped laughing. Then they screamed. It was laughter and screaming, screaming and laughter, all at a high pitch.

It was a great release.

A Fringe orgasm.

Amazingly we had no serious complaints. The audience seemed to recognize our right to reply. One person objected seriously to being hit by a plastic bucket and bleeding a little as a result, but I think that she was proud to have been there

So were we.

Stephen Poliakoff

My office at the Traverse was small. A desk, two shelves on the wall, a year planner, a couple of telephones, and one small tennis shoe that my daughter Amanda had worn. Outside of festival time, not much happened there. During the festival, there were constant visits from the powerful and interesting.

One powerful and interesting person came to see me on one of the quiet months. Stephen Poliakoff. He was seventeen and he was blunt. He said that he was a playwright.

'I am only here because Richard Eyre can't see me today. I'm seeing him tomorrow at the Lyceum. I understand that you do new plays, but I doubt it. I am a very good playwright indeed. Margaret Ramsay represents me.'

His attitude seemed to be 'What are you going to do about it?' I had an idea. He was very young, but there was no reason to suppose that he couldn't write. He was arrogant, which was a good start. Margaret Ramsay was, in fact, his agent. I asked him to give me something he had written and to come back the next day.

I read some of his stuff. It was handwritten, I knew that Christopher Hampton submitted his plays untyped, without any corrections and that this was probably a borrowed conceit. Stephen's work had lots of corrections. It was smudged, but talented. He wrote the way some people speak. But these were middle-class people, not the working class characters fashionable in Royal Court plays of the time. Stephen lived with his parents in Holland Park and presented his plays in the sitting room with his friends and family acting the roles.

I couldn't make up my mind whether he was an identikit young playwright, a perfect poseur or the genuine article. Usually one can tell whether a person can write simply by being in a small room with him. With Stephen I couldn't tell. He might be a highly cultivated child prodigy playwright or he might have learned enough to play out the role perfectly. He was rumpled and long haired. He spoke in staccato sentences, calculated to throw me off balance. He chewed pencil tops. He stared at me. I decided to try to surprise him, perhaps even throw him off balance. The next day I met him again.

'I've read your stuff and it is very talented.'

'It's not very talented. It's very good.'

'Okay, Stephen. Very good.'

'Thank you.'

'What I'd like to do is to ring Peggy and commission you to write a one-act play. For this, we will pay you twenty-five pounds...'

'That's not very much.'

'No, it's very little. But I will tell you and I will tell Peggy, who will believe me when I say it that we fully intend to present the play as a late-night production here. Fully rehearsed and produced. So I am offering you a commission, which could mean nothing...'

'Quite. You could be just fobbing me off.'

'Yes, but also offering you a production. We've just done a one-act play late night. Martin Sherman wrote it. It worked very well. It was the first play of his to be produced. It was called *The Night Before Paris*. He was pleased.'

'But,' I said, 'I will also promise to get you an established playwright to direct the play so that you can be in contact with and learn from someone who actually writes plays for a living.'

'Who do you have in mind?'

'David Halliwell.'

'That sounds very interesting,' said Stephen. 'I'll think about it.'

Stephen thought about it and Margaret Ramsay thought about it (for about five seconds) and we presented *A Day With My Sister* by Stephen Poliakoff, directed by David Halliwell. Carole Hayman was in it and so was Nigel Planer. I think that David Halliwell learned more than Stephen Poliakoff.

Shakespeare revisited

At the Sheffield Playhouse, now the Sheffield Crucible Theatre, I had directed *Henry IV Part One* with Nigel Hawthorne and Mike Gwilym. When I went to the Traverse, we tried to give further life to that show by concocting (Nigel and Mike devised it) a show taken from both parts of the two *Henry IV* plays. We called it *Stand For My Father* and Nigel doubled pointedly the parts of Falstaff and Henry IV.

We did it with eight actors, all male. Job Stewart, in addition to giving a memorable version of Justice Shallow, played Mistress Quickly with relish, and all the actors doubled and trebled their roles. I handed out the parts as we went along.

We had in the company an actor called Roland Oliver who I knew from Oxford and who was one of those actors that they call a 'younger character actor'. He was a short, solid looking man with a round face and a receding hairline. He had worked for many theatre companies and had done a lot of Shakespeare, going back as far as the National Youth Theatre even before going to Oxford.

When we came to the scene in the pub in *Part II* where Falstaff and Hal learn that they must leave the stews and go into battle, I was, as usual, parceling out the roles. We came to the entrance of Peto.

'Roland,' I said. You had better play this.'

Roland took up his Penguin Shakespeare and rushed over to the entrance. When his cue came, he ran on with great urgency and much too much volume. He began acting and shouting as he ran. He hared up to Mike Gwilym and blasted him:

The King your father is at Westminster;
And there are twenty weak and wearied posts
Come from the North.

Then Roland stopped. He stared at the page in front of him. 'Oh, fuck,' he said.

'What's the matter, Roly?', I asked.

'I've played this part before.'

Then Roland straightened himself and very quietly, with considerable menace, entered again and read the rest of the speech to Nigel.

and as I came along,
I met and overtook a dozen captains,
Bare-headed, sweating, knocking at the taverns,
And asking every one for Sir John Falstaff.

The Traverse is the only theatre I have ever worked in where the writer was the most important person. The principal reason for that was that we had no set designers. We rehearsed the play on the stage where it was to be played and whatever doors or windows or ocean waves that were required were built or imagined or mimed as we went along. Part of the reason for this was the budget for scenery, which didn't exist. Also, the audience sat on a steeply raked seating modules so that they saw the actors against a background of the stage floor. Also, and perhaps most importantly, we tended to put on four or five shows a day during the Festival and these had to be changed over in fifteen minutes or, at most, half an hour.

If there is no set then there can be no design concept. Interpretation is more important than creativity in the production. Then the playwright maintains the same authority that he had when the script was read. Of course, I am not advocating a ban on the director and designer's role in the creative process. I am merely pointing out that fifty years ago, in the Grassmarket, some very good plays were produced and acted beautifully with the bare minimum of design.

Sometimes these plays would be taken up by commercial or semi-commercial managements and transferred to London. The production of one, a little sex comedy by Sid Cheatle called *Straight Up*, was instructive. As the play moved towards London, with each successive production, first at Leicester then on tour and in the West End, the physical production grew so that by he time the play had arrived at the Piccadilly Theatre, almost an entire house in South London was put upon the stage. Before there had only been two walls, one pink, one blue, made of board and quilting.

I am not saying that the designer and the director and the producers were not clever men. They were. But the play suffered. It was a funny play, but too slight to take on the weight of other imaginations.

It was a better play when the audience could enjoy the language of South London suburbia and imagine the wallpaper. The playwright had created the people and the way they talked; to themselves and to each other. These people created the correct environment for the play.

When a new play carries the baggage of design it can succeed, of course, but I think with greater difficulty. Many new plays have sunk under the weight of a large design concept and the ballast that has been heaved onto it and, more importantly, writers who had not done well in the commercial or major subsidized theatre have thrived in the smaller houses when forced by lack of success to take their work there and enjoy an absence of timber and painted things.

My time at the Traverse ended as abruptly as it had begun. I was asked to direct David Storey's *The Changing Room* at the Long Wharf Theatre in Connecticut, USA. It was a success. It transferred to Broadway. I went from earning twenty pounds a week to earning three hundred. Hampstead Theatre needed an artistic director. I had given the Traverse financial viability while maintaining its position in the profession as an important starting point for new plays. I had a success on Broadway, something that always intrigued the *Evening Standard*. I was invited to Hampstead. I left Edinburgh.

Hampstead Theatre

Interview For The Hampstead Theatre

Time   1.00 p.m.

Place   Scotts Restaurant, near Leicester Square

Date   April 1973

Post   Artistic Director

Three men are wearing suits: Michael Codron, Bob Swash and the interviewee.

This is a forgone conclusion. The important discussions have already taken place on the telephone. This is an invitation to take the job. This is also one member of the Board, the most important member, Michael Codron, showing another member, who is not convinced, that the right choice has been made. One year later, Bob Swash, still unconvinced, resigns from the Board because the work of Hampstead Theatre had not been directed enough to 'the community'. The grant from Camden Council, however, greatly increased.

In 1973, after eleven years in the provinces where one is fairly well protected, London is a tough place to work. For one thing, the critics are so near. When I was invited to be Director of the Hampstead Theatre, I was advised by many friends not to do it. But I wanted to get to London. I was in the middle of the road of my life and I had spent all my working days north of the Trent. It was time. I had directed a hit on Broadway. I had made the Traverse a success in its new home. I was ready for London.

Actually, I wasn't.

My first warning came when Ed Berman, then a big noise in North London running Inter-Action, told me bluntly not to come, 'I'll be getting all of Hampstead's grant from Camden Council. It's finished. You'll hate it.' I took that warning seriously. Ed was the flamboyant head of a successful and fashionable theatre trust. David Aukin also warned against. That was more worrying. I was standing in a phone box on a beach in California when I heard David's calm, but worried voice, telling me that with the Young Vic booming under Frank Dunlop, the Royal Court on a high and the National opening a studio theatre, there wouldn't be room in the marketplace for Hampstead, which had languished, and there certainly wouldn't be funding for it. For once, David was wrong. He reckoned without David Aukin, who played a major role in whatever success I had at Hampstead.

The hope at the Hampstead Theatre Club was to transfer plays into the West End. That was what most of the Board wanted. Michael Codron is reported to have said, about my appointment, 'Don't worry. Everything he does will transfer.' He was suggesting that the financial troubles would be over. They were over, but not because of the West End.

Expecting the tiny Hampstead Theatre to provide a steady flow of West End shows is like wanting your nine-stone weakling of a son to row for Oxford. He might, but it will be difficult. Better he should be the cox. Small theatres seldom produce plays that work in large theatres. Only three or four shows from Hampstead had ever transferred to the West End and made any money, or even gone into profit.

Why?

Hampstead took the potentially or possibly commercial plays that no commercial management was willing to take the chance on, and the leading roles were usually played by actors who were not quite stars or who might-be-about-to-become stars or both. This situation was good for the actors, good for the plays and good for the audiences, but not so good for the West End managers who would bung a few thousand into the coffers, have a flutter, read the reviews, and forget about the play. And the reviews are almost bound to be 'mixed' for a good new play, especially one by a new writer.

But, if Hampstead was not the place to catch an early (and cheap) look at a West End hit, it has always been the place to catch a star just before it rose, whether it was a writer, actor, designer or director. And the actors tended to be especially good because they were doing the play because they liked it and sometimes even because they believed in it.

Glyn Owen was a perfect example. He became quite a name because of *Howard's Way*, but he did several plays at Hampstead in the seventies before he was well known. He was what they call 'a good character actor'.

In the rehearsals for his third play there, I took him aside.

'Glyn,' I said. 'A minute ago you were talking about divorce. Are you divorced?'

He said that he was.

'But when I took the script round to your house, in Dartmouth Park Hill...?'

'Yeh,' Glyn said.

'I gave it to an attractive blonde woman who seemed to be your wife.'

'She was.'

'But you are divorced from her?'

'Yeh.'

'You are divorced from her, but you live in the same house? I don't understand.'

'I'm a cunt.'

But, of course, he wasn't. Like many others, like me, he was trying to explain himself with a joke.

The actors who work at Hampstead are the finest examples of what the British Theatre can produce and they were particularly fine in low cost circumstances. My theory, which I expound elsewhere in this book, is that all artists behave differently under different circumstances and that the chief variable is...guess what? Money.

If the writer or actor or designer or director thinks that someone is making money, lots of money, out of his hard work and discomfiture, then he can behave worse than a spoiled child. But, put this same artist in a place like Hampstead, where there is precious little going on, no lunches or cigars, no star dressing rooms and no splash ad's and you will usually find good behaviour.

Whenever you do transfer a play from, say The Bush or the Almeida or the Royal Court, it is amazing how quickly arguments develop about billing and wages, and advertising and most particularly dressing rooms. Where money drives, the ego rises. That is why so much good art was found in the comparatively co-operative, low-budget, non-profit atmosphere of a theatre such as Hampstead.

Although actors like Glyn Owen were the backbone of Hampstead, occasionally we would have a star. Usually, it was in a play that was doomed to obscurity. One of these was *The Day of the Triffids*, a lesbian-leaning psychodrama based on a little bit of the life of August Strindberg. Susan Hampshire was the star. Strindberg, as if he needs help, is one of those writers that other people constantly write plays about. I know that I have read, and avoided, at least five plays about F. Scott Fitzgerald.

Why do you think they send them to me?

Anyway, for the rehearsals of this Strindberg piece, we would gather at St James' Church hall, a modern building attached to an old church in West Hampstead. The hall had an overhanging bit of roof, which makes an appearance in this story.

The rehearsals were highly charged. Some of the actors were distressed from early on.

Georgina Hale: 'Bull shit, Michael, I want to play it for real.'

Peter Woodthorpe: 'I don't like the set. It will never work. I hate it.' and

Richard Moore: 'I don't want to be difficult, but....'

Susan was serene. She had learned the lines beforehand. She was mildly dyslexic and thought that she would never be able to learn them otherwise. It was a charming thing to do, but it did constrain her, until one day when something extraordinary happened.

In the second week of rehearsal, on a rainy Tuesday morning, between eleven o'clock and one, four actors did their nuts. Each one of them burst into tears and choked out an emotional speech about the obstacles that they were facing and the impossibility of overcoming them.

The set, the rehearsal room, the other actors, the director, all came under heavy fire. After each of these psychological cadenzas, the actor rushed from the room and into the rain.

But the actor did not stay for long in the rain. No, the actor managed to get under the little bit of roof that was protruding from St James' Church hall. It was the director who stood in the rain begging the actor to reconsider, to return to the rehearsal, and to understand that it was all going to get much better and that the performances, once integrated, would be terrific.

I suppose that when you are crying, you don't notice the rain especially if you are under a bit of roof. But, if you are directing and not crying, you do and I did. I noticed that I was getting very wet.

Often a play will engender in the men and women who perform it, the very emotions that the characters live through. Any good actor takes on the thoughts, the language and the behaviour of his character in the game, just as children do. It is natural. Not that actors are children. Far from it. They are gifted adults capable of understanding and imitating other adults. That is why, contrary to popular belief, they are on the whole an intelligent and mentally healthy set of people.

If the play touches many nerves, as this one did, and if the actors are highly strung, as these were, then you can get these outbursts, especially at that time of rehearsals, the second week, when it is the moment to start giving a performance and to feel what help or hindrance you are going to get from the other actors, the director and the designer. On this rainy day, the actors could see and feel only the hindrances.

And so the speeches went on. First Peter, then Richard, then Susan, then Georgina. And each one ran from the room in tears after the speech. And each time the director went out to find his place in the wet, and then he would coax the actor back into the room. Then we had lunch and after lunch, a good afternoon's rehearsal and after that everything was fine. I can't remember another cross word being spoken.

That evening, Susan gave me a lift back to the theatre where I had left my car. We had been friends for a long time. There was a friendly pause as we drove down Abbey Road. Then I spoke.

'Wasn't that remarkable?'

'Yes,' said Susan.

'I don't think I've ever seen anything like it. It must be the play. Or the rain.'

'I rehearsed mine,' said Susan.

'What?'

'My speech. I worked on it last night.'

'You knew that it was going to happen?'

'Oh, yes. Sooner or later. So I prepared a speech.'

'Well, Susan. It was a very good speech.'

'I know. I prepared it.'

'I hope you won't have to do another one.'

'I won't.'

And she didn't.

Being director of the theatre meant being a kind of impresario. It meant not only directing and finding plays, but also presenting a production that had begun elsewhere. Sometimes I had never seen the show, but knew that it would be good. How did I know? When you are very busy, you have to listen to other people, even critics.

Once Sam Shepherd rang me. He had a new play. Good. It isn't full length. Too bad. Could we put it on late night? We do that sometimes.

'It's called *Little Ocean* and it's about having a baby. Dinah (Staab) is very pregnant and wants to do it. Also my wife. Also Caroline Hutchinson. Stephen (Rea) wants to direct.'

'Okay, Sam. We'll do it.'

'It has to be in March. Just before Dinah has the baby. The play requires her to be eight months pregnant.'

'Okay.'

'Okay, what?'

'Okay, we'll do it.'

'Don't you want to read it?'

'Sam, I've got enough trouble reading the plays we're not going to do.'

True. Too true.

Late one night, or early one morning, I returned to England from one of my tennis, golf and smoking holidays in the Canary Islands. As always, I was fit when I left Gran Canarias and destroyed by the time I arrived home. The plane from Spain had been late. There were hours of delay; a return to the hotel, half a night's sleep and then back to the airport again. Finally, the train from Gatwick to London arrived. I managed to get my golf clubs and everything else into a taxi from Victoria at five in the morning.

This time I was greatly cheered by a message to ring David Aukin as soon as possible. I knew that it was good news because if it had been bad, it would have waited like his note the following year in which he informed me that Tom Courtenay was very displeased with the situation at the Duke of York's theatre and didn't want any jokes from me.

This time the news was that we had won an *Evening Standard Award* for Special Achievement. The award had only been given a few times before: once to Laurence Olivier for his work at the National and once, I think, to Peggy Ashcroft. Anyway, it was pretty hot stuff.

Immediately, I started to prepare my speech. I knew that I had about six minutes (we were limited to four) to let people know who I was and why we had won the Award. It was an opportunity to gain prominence and with it more people willing to work for the small wages that Hampstead offered. Naturally I chose jokes. Also, I wanted to thank everyone even though we had been instructed not to do that.

I said that I was accepting the Award personally because no one else was free. They were all back at the theatre making personal phone calls. I managed to thank David Aukin (I called him an 'Artistic Administrator', a rather prophetic remark) and everyone in my immediate family under the guise of not thanking anyone. I said of the little shack that we worked in that 'There is no reason why a temporary building can't last forever' and that got the biggest laugh of all, showing the British love for paradox and language jokes. I wish I knew more of them.

But the real joke was the effect of this speech and this Award. Trevor Nunn hugged me, he who had never answered my letters. Peter Hall laughed extremely hard at all the jokes, although we had never met. Famous playwrights blew me kisses. And all because of one little Award.

I never wondered again why we spend so much time and effort giving these things to one another.

The Award was for success, mainly with conventional work or unusual work that became successful. So we had to change or we would stagnate, and we had to turn to more unconventional work.

Like Mike Leigh.

Mike Leigh

Inviting Mike Leigh to devise and direct one of his plays for Hampstead wasn't easy. First I had to convince David Aukin, which wasn't that difficult. I reminded him that we were far too far ahead on money for the year and if we didn't lose a little or spend a little, or both, we would have to give it back to the Arts Council at the end of the year. That was not attractive. Also, I then pointed out, we had been far too conventional of late and Hampstead was beginning to look respectable. We were losing our Fringe status and we needed to take a gamble on something more experimental.

Having convinced David, he and I then had to convince Mike Leigh. I don't think that having a success with *Abigail's Party* ever seemed like a good idea to Mike.

Mike Leigh was known for his improvisational work. He would spend weeks evolving characters and a plot, and eventually a play or a movie would be made. He was very much on the Fringe. He was considered difficult and a perfectionist and expensive. He was a slight, bearded, questioning sort of man with a tendency to make you say everything that was on your mind. He had great ambitions, but no pretence. He knew that he was a considerable artist and he was always interested in whether or not you could see it. In time, we did.

Our plan was to give in to all of Mike's outlandish requests; eleven weeks rehearsal, set and costumes designed in rehearsal, whatever he asked, and simply soak up all the surplus money that we had made in that financial year. It would open at the beginning of the next financial year and we could then absorb the inevitable loss all through the year that followed.

Then the damn thing turned out to be a hit.

The rehearsals for *Abigail's Party* were fairly uneventful. The costume designer cried a couple of times. The actors looked agonized. Everyone wondered how a play could be made in rehearsal and most of us sneaked in under some pretence or other only to see Mike talking quietly to one of the actors and not at all worried by us seeing or hearing anything because, apparently, there was nothing to see or hear.

David and I had met Mike at the Wellcome Chinese restaurant in Belsize Village months before he began. He wondered what we wanted. We said that we wanted him to work as he always did, that we would give him whatever he wanted, within reason, and he must turn out the best work he could.

Did we want to know what the play was about? No, we said, we would leave that to him. Did we want a West End play? Not necessarily, I said, but that would be nice. David agreed. Mike said that he would give us one. It was fairly comical, we all thought, that Mike Leigh, a leading light of the Fringe, the experimental theatre director, should produce a West End play. To be honest, we doubted that he would produce anything at all.

We were wrong.

After two previews, it was clear that we had an extremely good and funny play on our hands, but there was something working against it becoming a well-wrought comedy. That something was Mike. He seemed to be opposed to it going smoothly. That is, I think, an important part of his talent. Mike Leigh is whatever it is in an oyster that makes the pearl. He irritates, he creates obstacles; he delays and, yet, he constructs entire plays and films in a relatively short period of time.

By the time we reached the third preview, Mike had more or less run out of things that he wanted to do. He had invited Jonathan Miller into rehearsals to help him with a heart attack at the end. Miller had seemed to want to direct the play so he had been asked to go. There was a terrific fuss over the stereo, but we bought him a new one and that was settled. He was ready for the opening night.

But David Aukin and I were convinced that it was not ready yet. It needed running in. We argued. Mike disagreed. We insisted the opening night was moved from Tuesday to the following Friday.

Abigail's Party had quite the most uproarious reception that a play at Hampstead had ever had. Bernard Levin, writing in *The Sunday Times*, actually objected to the audience, saying that they had laughed so much that it had prevented him from responding properly to the play. Everything was set fair for a West End transfer.

But Mike had fixed that. The leading lady was his wife and she was pregnant. So, in the end it was and it wasn't, after all, a West End play.

As always, Mike Leigh got what he wanted. And he didn't get what he didn't want.

The Elephant Man

If *Abigail's Party* was an unlikely success then *The Elephant Man* was an impossible one. Bernard Pomerance's play almost didn't get done, or even read. My colleagues at Hampstead were wary of showing it to me because I had been too sniffy about his previous one, a painful account of his mother dying of cancer. But I heard about *The Elephant Man* from Neil Johnston, and asked to read it.

The text was short and seemed not much more than interesting. Then I read the introduction. There, Bernard strictly forbids the use of make-up for John Merrick, a man utterly disfigured. When I read that I knew that the play had to be produced. I can't tell you why, but I knew that it would be good theatre.

The emergence of *The Elephant Man* as a hit can be attributed to several men and their tendency to be stubborn. Neil Johnston, who was pushing it, refused to be fobbed off with excuses and delays. Roland Rees insisted upon casting it the way he wanted to cast it. (Roland's company, Foco Novo, co-produced the play). David Aukin and I badgered Roland for changes in the production and style. Roland agreed to some, but adamantly refused others. He would not, for example, cut the cellist despite endless persuasive arguments of art and commerce. He was right. Bernard adamantly refused to rewrite. We absolutely demanded some changes, mainly to avoid dogma. Bernard agreed. And so on. And on. It was a battle, but a battle that all of us won.

One cold Saturday night, we watched *The Elephant Man* play to an audience of very few on tour in a draughty hall at Manchester Polytechnic.

David Aukin and Nancy Meckler were there. The designer, Tanya McCallin, and the lighting designer, Gerry Jenkinson, were in and myself and my two children. I didn't know the other eight people.

Also, the projector broke down. This was bad because the play relied upon a lecture with slides.

We said that we would meet the cast afterwards for a hamburger in Piccadilly Square.

When we got to Piccadilly Square, five of the cast were waiting outside the hamburger joint. It was very cold. I asked them why they weren't inside?

'We didn't think you'd come,' said Jennie Stoller.

'Why not?'

'It was so awful,' said David Schofield.

'It wasn't awful,' said David Aukin.

'It was terrific,' said Nancy Meckler.

'It's very nice of you to be nice,' said Jennie. 'But we know that it was terrible. We can do it so much better than that. That bloody projector. And there was nobody in. Only about twenty people.'

'I think there were about fifty,' said David Aukin without even pausing.

They did look pathetic. Five actors in duffel coats and old furs on a Saturday night in November, in an empty city centre in the northwest of England. It was hard to know what to say.

'Look,' I said. 'I've never said this before and I don't imagine that I will ever say it again, but this is going to be the biggest success of any new play that you have ever been in. It is not only good, and good in every way – the play, the acting, production, set, costumes – everything, but more than that, amazingly enough, everyone is going to like it. It's very good and very new. It is going to be a big success. Possibly the biggest success you will ever have.'

I don't think that I've ever seen five people more surprised. David Schofield didn't say anything. Neither did David Allister. David Aukin looked pleased. Jenny Stoller believed me and suggested that we go for a Chinese instead of this hamburger. We all agreed.

It was a terrible meal and the place is now closed, but the play is being done all over the world.

A couple of years later I was in New York on another Saturday night with my daughter, Amanda. We went to the Shubert Theatre, in the middle of Manhattan, we blagged our way into standing room at the back. The house was full. It was *The Elephant Man* and *Variety* reported that it was playing to 104% houses.

Rowan Atkinson

It was, and still is, I think, the custom for the Artistic Director of Hampstead to go to the Edinburgh Festival, especially the fringe, to see if there was something that might work well in Swiss Cottage.

At Oxford, I had done two plays for the Oxford Theatre Group. The group always took a play and a revue to the fringe in the summer, so naturally, I looked first at what they were doing. I went to the hall they were using.

I had been queuing for quite a while at the box office, when a brash young man with dark hair commanded the attention of the box office lady to book some seats. This took quite a while. When he finally left I asked who he was. 'Rowan Atkinson,' she said. 'He's in the revue.' I found out later that he *was* the revue.

I asked for a single for that night. 'Which performance?' she asked. 'Are there two performances of the revue every night?' I asked. 'Yes,' she replied. 'It's very popular.' That really surprised me.

I booked for the early evening show. The house was packed. Rowan was on almost every minute. The audience laughed all the way through, especially at Rowan. I didn't laugh once.

But I booked him for a show at Hampstead the following spring. It was called *Beyond a Joke*. There were major problems with the rehearsals mainly because the director, a chum from Oxford, dropped out and David Aukin summoned me back from a precious holiday in Texas with my two daughters to take over the production.

Partly because of jet lag and partly because I'm hopeless with revue, the show wasn't great. But the audience loved Rowan. John Cleese and others saw him and his career benefited, even though Bernard Levin, the then drama critic of the *Sunday Times* left at the interval on the press night.

John Cleese

Around that time, possibly because of *Beyond a Joke*, Cleese came into my life.

He decided that I was a funny man and, because I was American, he wanted me to write a play with him set in Hollywood. I was taken aback to say the least but I listened. He had in mind an evening of short, comic plays beginning with one that was well formed in his mind. He told me to be at his home in Holland Park at ten a.m. the following Tuesday.

He tends to get what he wants.

Unfortunately, I was ten minutes late. I couldn't find a parking space. He was very put out. I said I was never late. He didn't believe me. He offered me coffee. I took out a cigarette. He said not to smoke. I could smoke after our writing session. I wondered how long it would be.

'Two hours,' he said. 'No more. No less.'

And that's what it was. Exactly two hours. Then I was allowed a cigarette. It was the most intense two hours, outside of technical rehearsals, that I had ever had. He, of course, was the main writer but I did the writing, which is to say that I was the one with the pen and paper and I put down everything he suggested. He agreed with about half of what I suggested so I put that down too.

In the evenings, I would type everything up and do some adding and subtracting. I would show him the stuff in the morning and he always approved it.

He also took me into his social life. He invited me to dinner parties. He took me to a Chelsea football match with his girlfriend. The Marketing Director of Chelsea had run into Cleese's Bentley and, by way of apology, invited him and guests to sit in a box, which we did. I didn't like it. It was a lot of small men in blue uniforms running around defending.

People ask me what Cleese is like and I always say that he is generous in every way, especially intellectually, and he is a bit like Basil Fawlty.

One evening, there was a dinner at his home. There was fine food, some attractive women, a lot of red wine and we were getting into some serious flirting and having a great time when he suddenly stood and announced that the evening was over and we must all go home. He had work to do in the morning.

I hardly ever see him anymore, but I have followed, more or less, his regime for writing. Like Cleese, I treat it as a rehearsal. You have to start at a particular time and do the allotted hours.

Michael Frayn

My collaboration with Michael Frayn on two of his best plays was a hallmark of my work at Hampstead. But it began with a negative. Michael Codron urged me to do *Alphabetical Order*, and I refused. I thought the play was too conventional and too well focused. I thought that for a 'work play', a play about men and women set in their workplace, its lines were cut too clean.

Michael Codron rang me several times about the play. That was unusual for him. Apparently the author considered me the right director and Hampstead the ideal venue. Finally, I was swayed when Codron agreed to pay any losses on the production, thus guaranteeing us a balanced budget for my second year at Hampstead.

I had a minor medical procedure on the Saturday before rehearsals began, so I was dizzy during the talk that directors give to the actors and staff on the first day, in which we used the model of the set as a reference point, showing how various features of the play will be stressed in the production. At one point I felt so faint that I had to hand over to Alan Tagg, the designer, to present and discuss the second Act.

But from that day on, it was plain sailing. The actors were delightful and worked together well. The set was perfect. Michael Frayn and I got on very well. He did a few rewrites to make several things happen at once. I muddled up the clean lines of the play a bit and he kept me on the straight and narrow when I strayed too far. It was a good combination. No trouble. Then we had the first preview.

Michael Codron called Frayn and me to his office in Regent Street the next day. He was in a forbidding mode. He was not pleased. All of the acting was too extreme, he said, except for Billie Whitelaw (the only one we had been worried about); and Barbara Ferris was too strict and too tough as the lady who takes over the office.

What could we do?

'Tone everything down,' said Michael Codron. 'Stop the loud comedy acting. Make it more real. But above all, much less loud.'

What about Barbara Ferris?

'Think pink,' said Michael Codron.

'What?'

'Get her out of that deadly beige blouse and into something pink. She is a very attractive, appealing girl. For goodness sake, let's see it.'

We did both. We toned down the acting and we put Barbara into a powder blue blouse and asked her to be more appealing. She liked the blouse and found it easy to be appealing. The play worked much better that very evening. There were twice as many laughs.

Claire Tomalin had invited most of the clever and successful NW1 crowd to the opening night. Although the performance had gone well, there was a terrible mix-up in the second act when the newspaper library is torn to pieces by the staff. The lines went wrong and we lost at least ten good laughs.

Later that night, a large number of London's intelligentsia were gathered at Claire's house along with the cast. I couldn't face them. I went into a larder with James Cossins and we drank three-quarters of a bottle of whisky in half an hour. Then I went upstairs and sat on a sofa opposite Jonathan Miller and Clive James and listened to them talk about George Steiner.

I knew that they knew who I was and that a great deal of their conversation was directed at me as the most available and interesting audience. But I was nearly comatose. I couldn't respond. The odd name would float through my miasma and occasionally I would smile, just to show that the camera was, as it were, on them, but I wasn't capable of much more nor did I want to do much more.

Finally they mentioned the name Lindsay Anderson. They talked about him for a few minutes. Then with no preparation, I blurted something out: 'He's mischievous,' I said.

They both stopped talking and looked at me. I had only said it very softly, but they were aware of me. I didn't say any more and the George Steiner show continued.

The reason Jimmy and I got so drunk was that the key scene in the play had gone wrong. We knew, he from his actor's instinct and I from sitting in the auditorium, that the play should have taken off there but instead it remained still, nothing like what it could have been. We were disappointed that the critics from the national newspapers should have seen this performance.

But many months later, I learned a lesson. *Alphabetical Order* had good reviews and had transferred to the Mayfair Theatre. I happened to be there one night when Irving Wardle, *The Times* critic, decided to go on a busman's holiday to see it. He had liked it and wanted his wife, who hadn't seen it, to enjoy it with him. Now this pleased me greatly. All of us admire Irving and care what he thinks. Of course, we can dismiss his opinions when they differ from ours, but we always pay attention to what he writes. Indeed, the wife of a young theatre director once said, 'Thank God for Irving Wardle.'

I was very glad that Irving would be seeing *Alphabetical Order* the way it was meant to be played. I told him afterwards.

'It's really sweet of you to come again,' I said.

'I wanted Liz to see it,' said Irving, with as much diffidence as he could muster, which was a lot.

'I hope you liked it.'

'I liked it very much,' said Irving.

'I'm really glad that you were able to see it with the library being messed up properly and all the laughs there. On the first night at Hampstead, it all went wrong. June Ellis didn't say 'Over my shoulder goes Vietnam' at the right time and all the lines after that got out of sync and we lost an awful lot.'

'Oh, I didn't notice any difference,' said Irving. 'I enjoyed it very much both times.'

Critics. They see something different from what we see, feel something different, hear something different. Sometimes I think they sit there watching the words of the text jump off the page. They are writers, after all.

Clouds

Michael Frayn's second play to be produced at Hampstead was *Clouds,* which was a very easy ride. We began rehearsals on a Monday. We had opened his West End play *Donkey's Years* on the previous Thursday. We were confident. The cast was good. We blocked the moves quickly and hardly changed any of them. The actors were sharp, co-operative and ideal for their roles. It opened to good reviews and played, as they say, to packed houses.

The problem came when we tried to get it into the West End. By the time a theatre was available, Nigel Hawthorne and Barbara Ferris were not at all certain that they wanted to go. Then the theatre slipped away. Then the actors slipped away. It looked as though the play would never get a wider audience. I was frustrated because I was sure that it could be popular.

Michael Codron toyed with the idea of transferring the play for a while and one day he rang me. He thought he had a good idea. Vanessa Redgrave was interested and if she would do it, then it could open in the West End at almost any time, almost anywhere we liked. We arranged to have lunch with Vanessa at Chez Victor.

I was nervous. I knew that it was a good part for her and a good play, but I didn't quite know how to pitch it to her. How much, for example, should I play up the fact that it was a fairly sympathetic view of a communist regime? We all knew Vanessa to be left wing, and a staunch member of the Workers Revolutionary Party, but we also knew that she never mixed her politics with her work beyond politicizing a few stagehands.

Chez Victor is a small, narrow restaurant, about forty yards from Shaftesbury Avenue. When Vanessa arrived, her stature and her blue eyes seemed to fill it. Michael and I rose and sat deferentially on either side of her. Aperitifs were accepted and refused. Entrecote steaks were ordered, for this was in the land before fish, and we started to inch our way around to Michael Frayn's simple but complicated play.

Just as we were about to get round to the point of the lunch, six actors came through the door. They had been to see a screening of one of Tony Richardson's films. Vanessa greeted them. Then she turned to them. They were seated at the back of the restaurant. It became clear that this was a conversation she preferred to being inveigled into doing a play set in Cuba. Peter Jeffrey was there. He and Vanessa traded comments on the film and life in general. They talked fully for ten minutes. Finally, I said something very quietly to Michael.

'How do you think it's going?'

He didn't laugh, but he wanted to.

Finally Vanessa turned back to us. The conversation was halting. Compared to the animated chat she had been having with her fellow actors, the flattery and conniving of a producer and a director must have been very boring. We talked about the play. I looked into her blue eyes and tried to think what to say. Michael was charming. I tried to seem intelligent. Finally the lunch ground to a halt. I had a funny feeling that I would never see this lady again.

I took the tube back to Hampstead and rang Michael. I repeated my joke.

'How do you think it went?'

This time he laughed. Then he said, 'If you had mentioned 'revolution' one more time, I would have left.'

'Sorry,' I said. 'I was probably trying too hard.'

When an actor doesn't want to do a part, it doesn't seem to matter what you do, you can't talk them into it unless you are Peter Hall.

After five years at Hampstead, Peter Hall invited me to join the National Theatre.

I was delighted.

I went from Hampstead to the National thinking I would never return but, in fact, I did. Three times. Once for play I wrote (see the chapter entitled 'The Collected Play' of Michael Rudman). Once to direct a very good play by James Saunders and, finally, to direct *Berlin Hannover Express* by Ian Kennedy Martin.

When I had finished that one, I thought I had better not return but I did make one more contribution. I sent an anonymous letter offering advice to Edward Hall when he took over as Artistic Director.

Advice to Edward Hall when he took over Hampstead Theatre

1. Take one day a week completely off. Do not work at all on that day. Sundays are good. So are Wednesdays.
2. Take brief but frequent holidays.
3. Change everything at the theatre eventually, gradually, but change very little immediately.
4. Never read a play more than twice if you are seriously considering it.
5. Get up early. Get to work early. Try to take a twenty-minute nap every day.
6. Do not decide that reviews are bad until two weeks after you have read them.
7. Exploit any success with lots of publicity paid and unpaid.
8. Find an administrative partner who will be just under you, but definitely under you. Give him/her a lot of authority and a lot of credit.
9. Read books and articles that have nothing to do with theatre.
10. Have as much social contact as possible with people outside of show business.
11. Keep staff to a minimum.
12. Pay staff the maximum.
13. Be generous but let everyone think that you are stingy or better yet that your aforementioned administrative partner is stingy.
14. Limit any non-artistic meeting to forty-five minutes.
15. Delegate as little as possible. Do your own research when possible.
16. Swim as much as possible. Avoid breaststroke. Do crawl and/or backstroke.
17. Go to the theatre twice a week.
18. Avoid red meat and dairy products.
19. Limit conversations about critics to three minutes unless you are picking quotes.
20. Never tell anyone how hard you are working.
21. Never tell anyone how little you are sleeping.

22. Flatter all actors as much as possible, but always based on your genuine admiration for them.
23. Remember this quote from John Lennon: 'So I showed it to eight people who weren't me.'
24. Be positive about other people's work.
25. Never raise your voice to a subordinate.
26. Avoid plays that involve townspeople.
27. Avoid plays about therapy.
28. Don't do one person shows.
29. Never do a show mainly because somebody gave you the money to do it.
30. Keep your letters short, especially when turning down a play.
31. Be polite and welcoming to critics, especially after they have given you a bad review.
32. Cultivate relationships with other directors even if their work is not to your taste.
33. Encourage imaginative actors to write plays.
34. Encourage imaginative journalists to write plays (not critics).
35. Have a quiet secluded place where you can read plays without interruption.
36. Never leave a show before the end unless it is your own.
37. Always sleep on a play before deciding to do it. If you wake up in the morning wanting to tell people about it, then do it.
38. Never do a play because one famous actor wants to do it.
39. Avoid musicals.
40. Keep staff as long as you can.
41. Make sure that every play that is sent in is read and returned within a month if you don't want to do it.
42. Treat your benefactors, patrons and Board of Directors as your employers. But make it clear, in a very polite way, very early on, that you choose the programme and the staff.
43. If you are working on a play with an inexperienced writer and it is full of good writing, good ideas and humour but lacks shape, seriously consider beginning it with its second act.

44. Ideally the writer should come to the first four days of rehearsal and then go away, returning mainly to see sections of the play run. Most questions from the actors to the writer and notes from the writer to the actor should go through you. But be flexible on this.

45. Towards the end, but before the end of the fourth week of rehearsal, invite trusted colleagues (not friends of the actors) to a full run through which should be your second or third. Ask for their opinions. Don't get cross.

46. Stay at this theatre as long as you can and certainly until you have made it successful and don't leave until you receive an irresistible offer elsewhere. Even then think hard about leaving. If you are right for a theatre, then the theatre is right for you.

47. As you become more successful, you will be asked more and more to direct for other managements. Do this but do it seldom and try to get as much control over the production as you can. You will sorely miss being producer as well as director. Also, while you are doing this, try to ring and/or email your own theatre every morning and every evening.

48. It is not necessary for the show to go on. Some flops are never forgotten. If it looks as though it's going to be a flop, say for example a leading actor drops out, or none of your friends like it, or you wake up in the middle of the night knowing it won't work then you really don't have to open it. If it never opens, it will be forgotten.

49. Every show works once, usually at a run through. Make sure it works twice before you open it.

50. Avoid but don't abjure conflict.

51. Try not to do too many plays with leading characters who resemble you.

52. Remember that even a mediocre director can deliver a terrific production if you give him or her complete control.

53. Aim any conventional play towards the *avant garde* and any *avant garde* work towards the mainstream.

54. Fund raising is best accomplished subsequent to, or in inconjunction with, a success.

55. Treat every Board meeting as if it might be your last.

I don't know if Ed Hall followed any of my advice but he is certainly having great success in Swiss Cottage.

The West End

The West End of London is a very important place to me. I think that every show I have directed in Britain was aimed either consciously or unconsciously, either openly or covertly, at Shaftesbury Avenue.

Having a West End hit means not only that you are making money, but also that you are in a sympathetic relationship with what you might call the world at large. This is a great deal better than the world at small, which is the world inside one's own intimate circle or, worse, inside one's immediate family or one's own head.

Few people have any idea how important it is to distinguish between a success and a failure in the West End of London, and to determine who has been involved with which.

While we were doing the last minute technical work on *Donkey's Years* by Michael Frayn, not long before the first preview, I was sitting in the stalls telling the stage manager which lighting cues came where and where one or two of them might be improved. Her name was Roberta Graham and she was excellent. She was polite but firm with me; polite but firm with the actors and even more remarkable, polite but firm with the electricians taking into account that it was after lunch.

Bobby, as we called her, and we called her that so often it sounded like a Sondheim song or an Ionesco play, kept darting out from the prompt corner.

'Yes, Michael. I will when I can.' 'Penny, have you got your cue light? Is it working, darling, or should we move it? Good.' 'In a minute, Michael. Brian's cans aren't working.' A lot of that was going on.

An idle director can be mischievous. In one of the pauses while we waited for Brian to come back from coming back from lunch, I turned to Jo Scott-Parkinson, one of Michael Codron's right hand men, and I whispered loudly;

'She's good, isn't she?'

'Who?'

'Roberta. The stage manager.'

'Very, very good.'

'You know she's never worked on a hit.'

'Really? Is that really true?'

And he looked worried. He was very worried. I could tell. The track record of the stage manager was of some concern to Michael Codron's production manager.

After *Donkey's Years*, Bobby could say that she had worked on a hit. Indeed, she was one of the reasons for its success because the timing of the entrances got laughs when they were most needed, and these entrances never varied.

Perhaps she was particularly sharp because she knew that she had never worked on a hit before.

Robin Phillips

Robin Phillips is a man who has had many hits. At one time, the time that I was finally managing to start out, Robin Phillips epitomized the West End of London. I had very little contact with him, except for one Christmas party where I learned to my chagrin that he was tall, good looking, charming and better than me at charades. I didn't mind so much that he could play the game better, but I did mind that he seemed able to organize his team better than I could. Here, I thought, is a real director.

When Robin was in the midst of his first peak period, in the early seventies, he was walking down Shaftesbury Avenue with scripts under his arm. He met Charles Kay, a charming and chatty actor. The dialogue went like this:

'Robin, you look wonderful.'

'Thank you, Chas.'

'Have I seen you since I saw *Love's Labour's*?'

'I don't think so.'

'It was super. A really super production.'

'Thank you.

'I hear that *Abelard and Eloise* is a big hit.'

'Yes, it is.'

'Diana is wonderful in it.'

'We think so.'

'What are those scripts under your arm?'

'One is something I'm doing at Chichester next season.'

'Lovely.'

'And one is a play that I've written.'

'Gosh, Robin. You've written a play?'

'Yes.'

'What's it like?'

'Magic.'

Rex Harrison

Directing in the West End often means directing Rex Harrison, or someone very like him. Rex and I didn't get on terribly well. Here are some of the things that he didn't like about me:

That I wanted him to be on time for rehearsals.

That I wanted him to learn his lines.

That I wouldn't let him be rude to the actresses.

My clothes.

That I wanted to direct the play.

But Rex and I had an uneasy truce. I think that something in the back of his tired but combative brain told him that I was going to stick it out until the last possible moment, which I did. He didn't fire me until after the show opened successfully in Wales.

Rex preferred arguments in front of the large cast. In his hotel room, he would agree to anything. He was charming at the Ritz. Most stars are, but in front of the Company, he would throw his weight around, query every suggestion for a long time and criticize other actors.

One day I was trying to get him to stand up at a particular point.

Now, I knew that standing up for Rex was not easy. I knew that he was eighty-two, that he was tired and forgetful and hard of hearing. I also knew that if I suggested that he sit, he would want to stand and that if I suggested he stand … well, you get the idea. But I was pretty sure that at this particular point, it would get a laugh (which it did) and that it would be a laugh for him (which it was) and it would help make everyone in the audience like him (which they did). But it was hell's own job getting him to stand up on cue.

Each time we tried it, he questioned it. Then he started making fun of me.

'I don't understand these Canadian directors. So much bloody movement …'

I mentioned that I wasn't Canadian.

'All this bloody movement. What good does it do? I suppose that in Canada they do plays this way.'

I reminded him, gently I think, that it had been difficult to get him to sit down at all, but that now he was happy with it. Perhaps he would come to like standing up as well, especially if he got a laugh.

'Bloody Canadians. All this movement.'

That did get a laugh from the other actors, around thirty of them. It was getting out of hand.

'Rex, I'm not even slightly Canadian and I've directed seventy-five plays and some of them have movement in them.'

'I saw one of them.'

There was quite a hush.

'Oh?'

More hush.

'*Six Characters in Search of an Author.*'

Pause.

'At the National.'

Pause.

'It was bloody good.'

And there it was. The charm and wit and ability to think on his feet, once you got him there, and everyone really laughed, especially me, and the truce was renegotiated.

He paid me two more compliments: on the first night in Wales, he played the first Act exactly as we had rehearsed it and secondly, when he fired me, he said that John Dexter and I were the only two directors that he didn't get on with.

A.J. Brown

Not all actors in the West end are stars, but there are many who are rather wonderful. One of them was A.J. Brown.

AJ was a tall, slim man who was pretty old but full of beans. I first saw him at the Royal Court in *Savages* by Christopher Hampton and noted him down as someone who could still cut the mustard.

The first play I did with him was *Alphabetical Order* at Hampstead. He played the man who showed the newcomer the ropes. The play and the production were, at times, complex and difficult but AJ, who was well over seventy, had no trouble with the lines. In fact, if anyone else dropped a line he was right there to fill it in. Extraordinary. In rehearsal he was energetic, positive and very cooperative. We all made a mental note to be like him if we ever got old.

At one rehearsal, conversation turned, as it sometimes did in the Seventies, to therapy. One actor described his. Another told a funny story about hers. Then AJ said, to everyone's surprise, that he had tried therapy. We couldn't imagine how such a cheerful, clear headed, bubbly man could need therapy especially long before it was fashionable.

ME: When was that, AJ?

AJ: After the war.

(*He meant the First World War*)

ME: Was it shell shock?

AJ: No. I just felt that the world was against me.

ME: And what happened?

AJ: I found out that a lot of it was my fault.

When we did *Donkey's Years*, he played a similar part. An older man who was half character, half narrator. He was the College Porter, setting the scene and participating a little bit in the plot.

When we were on tour in Brighton, I was backstage and an announcement came over the tannoy. 'Ladies and gentlemen, there is a problem with audibility in the balcony.' AJ replied, 'I'm not having any difficulty hearing the balcony.'

Also in Brighton, there was a constant stream of ladies of a certain age asking to see AJ. They all had silver hair and a gleam in their eye. They wanted to see 'Jack' and they all said how fond they were of him.

Donkey's Years had been on for well over a year when AJ's eightieth birthday came up. I took him to dinner at Odins. I asked him a question I had always wanted to ask.

ME: AJ, tell me why your shoelaces are undone at curtain call?

AJ: Because, dear boy, it helps me to get home quicker.

When we opened, the advance was only £500. Somehow Peter Barkworth knew that. We were all worried. AJ said, 'Don't worry, chaps, this play will run longer than I will.'

And it did. But only by one month. One Saturday, AJ did the matinee. He did the first act and then passed on, quietly, with his shoelaces still done up.

Michael Codron

Many of the successful plays that appeared in the West End in the seventies and eighties came from the subsidized theatre.

Michael Codron was one of the first to bring plays quickly and easily from small theatres and make hits of them. He is known mostly for his parsimony and his charm. Also, of course, he is very brave. And, with the aforesaid parsimony and charm, he has also transferred plays that have very little prospect of earning him money.

Only a few plays that anyone took into the West End from Hampstead have made a profit. One of the few was *Dusa, Fish, Stas and Vi* by Pam Gems. It went into the black by the margin of a couple of hundred pounds in the last week of its nine month run at the Mayfair by virtue of a fee extracted by Codron from a television company employing Diane Fletcher for two days of that week. Nine months to make two hundred pounds. Not exactly a gravy train.

On the first night of *Dusa* in the West End, we were all in the foyer in our suits and smart clothes. We were dressed, as Lindy Hemming would say, like 'slightly successful young men'. We were all very pleased and smooth and smug, but there was one who was not dressed well at all. That was the designer,

Tanya McCallin, who was still in jeans dabbed with paint and a baggy pullover and she looked a bit desperate. For days, weeks maybe, she had been trying to dress the set and the actors for the very little money provided by the production budget. She had a battered list in her hand of those things she had been denied and, when Michael Codron was pointed out to her, she went straight to him.

'I am Tanya McCallin, Mr Codron, and I am the designer of this show and these are the things that I am told I cannot have.'

Now bear in mind that this was the first night and that Codron is a shy man anyway. He looked at the list. He read it carefully. It said things like 'mending sofa…£35.50' and 'costume jewellery…£15.00' and 'wastepaper basket…£7.56'. Michael looked at the list for a long time then he looked at Tanya. Finally, he spoke.

'But Tanya, I am a poet and a dreamer.'

Gloo Joo by Michael Hastings

Gloo Joo by Michael Hastings was the most unlikely West End success that I have ever had or, indeed, ever heard about.

It was about a West Indian man with no papers, no passport, no NHS documents, and no record of his entering England or even his existence. When I tell you that he ends up marrying a beautiful, young African girl at Gatwick airport in a Jewish wedding ceremony, you might guess at how funny it was. Also, it had a happy ending because he was allowed to stay in England.

Michael Codron sent me the play when I was at Hampstead. I read it the next day for all kinds of reasons, not the least of which was that he always did the same.

I really liked it. I thought it was funny and more than interesting. I rang him immediately. As usual, he was in his office and he wasn't in a meeting.

MICHAEL: I'm very glad you like it, but there is a problem.

ME: I don't see a problem. Oscar James is perfect for it and I know we can find a super African girl.

MICHAEL: The problem is that the Royal Court have it.

ME: How long have they had it?

MICHAEL: Ages. Let me see if I can get it away from them.

After a couple of days, we were offered the play. I rang Oscar and told him all about it. More or less as a formality, he read it and was keen. We found an amazing Ghanaian girl, Akosua Busia for the female lead. Everything was set fair.

Then came the rehearsals which were, to say the least, strange.

The play needed work. The playwright's knowledge of immigration law was a little sketchy and the crucial final scene, the wedding night, was, to put it kindly, underwritten.

Antony Brown and Dave Hill, who played the two awful immigration officers, were, it turned out, very good at writing and researching. Akosua was double clever and dogged. She was determined to get the final scene right.

What was Michael Hastings doing you may well ask? Michael came to every rehearsal. He always wore the same pullover. He sat next to me and smiled a lot. He hardly said a word. All around him people were acting, reacting, writing, rewriting, puzzling, worrying, arguing, agreeing, achieving and he never spoke except to ask for a cup of tea.

On reflection, I think he was right.

After three and a half weeks of this, we went before an audience. At the first preview, there were very few laughs in the first act. I have since learned that this is not unusual for a successful comedy. The audience is being led into the world of the play, the plot and the people involved. They are watching and learning. They are enjoying it but not prone to laugh much.

When we got to the wedding ceremony at the beginning of the second act, the little darlings laughed their heads off. They found it hilarious. It didn't hurt that many of them were Jewish. We could hardly wait for the opening night. We absolutely knew that it was going to work.

Then, the first of two big problems arose.

Problem 1 – Akosua's father died. Did I mention that he was the Prime Minister of Ghana? I asked her when the funeral was and, fortunately, we thought, it was after our opening night. I told her that we would certainly give her a few days off to go to Ghana and immediately started looking for an actress to play her part while she was away. There were a lot of gifted black actresses in London who, unfortunately, seldom worked.

But the problem was bigger than that. Because he was the Prime Minister, the funeral would go on for a long time. At least a couple of weeks. When? After the run at Hampstead. Good. What if it goes to the West End? Don't be ridiculous.

Problem 2 – Oscar is a big man. Athletic and strong. On the final preview, in his zeal, he yanked a drawer much too hard and wrenched his back. He was in agony. I took him to Dr. Sturridge who told us that Oscar had slipped a disc and must have complete rest. Oscar said he couldn't do that. The next day was the opening night and he was determined to do it.

On the Press night, Oscar was wonderful and the play went even better that we thought it could.

When I told Dr. Sturridge he was amazed. He couldn't believe that anyone could perform the leading role in a play in what must have been paralyzing pain. How could he do it?

'Well,' I said. 'It is probably something to do with the fact that he is black and has, for ten years been carrying spears for the Royal Shakespeare Company and driving a cab at the same time and he knows that this is his big chance and he knows how good he is.' Which he was and, bless them, the London critics agreed. The play went to the Criterion where it had a respectable run and won *The Evening Standard Award* for Best Comedy of the Year.

As for Akosua's problem, it did mean that as soon as the audience left on the opening night at Hampstead, we had to rehearse another actress, Mardelle Jardine, into her role so she could open the following night. She was excellent.

Akosua did go to Ghana for the funeral during the West End run.

This involved a procession all over the country. Unfortunately, she insisted on coming back to the show before she was ready having had very little sleep.

At her first performance back, I was in the audience.

After Akosua had done one scene, the stage manager told her understudy that she could go to a concert. This meant that when Akosua fainted halfway through her next scene, a white lady, an ASM who didn't know the lines, had to go onstage pretending to be black.

Surprisingly, the play still worked.

Akosua went to Hollywood where she played many parts including a main role in Spielberg's *The Color Purple*.

Oscar went on to have a successful career which included, I'm glad to say, coming to the National when I was there to play Pompey Bum in a Caribbean production of *Measure For Measure* and Aston in *The Caretaker*.

I still see him from time to time. He still calls me 'Whitey'.

To Be Continued

I will leave the West End now but return to it in a chapter called *Freelance*, which deals with much of my work after twenty-five years of being an Artistic Director.

PART 2

Back Story

Texas

And now, diligent reader, it is time to give you some of what movie people call 'The back story' beginning in Texas. I have always, like my idol, Arthur Miller, been partial to 'Flashbacks'.

Later in the book, I will digress to fill you in on my education which, although not wonderful, was thorough and intense: I more or less became what my father would have called, and sometimes did, 'An overeducated son of a bitch.'

I had two grandfathers. Both of them arrived penniless from Russia in the first decade of the twentieth century. Both of them began by selling household goods off the back of a donkey. Ike Rudman, whom I called Zadie, ended up as an oil millionaire. E.H Davis, whom I called Grandpa, managed to open an ironmongery shop but retired when he was in his forties in order to do next to nothing and play pool at the Dallas Athletic club. He took me to some baseball games. At one of them, he lost me.

Not long after I was born both of them were ushered into the maternity ward. Zadie looked down at me and said, after a long time, 'Tell me Davis. Is he smart?'

Seventy-five years later, we are still seeking the answer to that question.

Zadie's son, my dad, called himself 'The Duke', but that's another story. Anyway, my dad, The Duke, found himself in front of a Broadway theatre on the second night of my first success in New York. The play was called *The Changing Room* and it was about Rugby League football and England and many other things.

Because it was a wonderful play, I had a lot of good reviews for the direction. Anyway, my dad was standing there in front of the theatre, on the second night, in front of a more than life-size photo portrait of me and he was being congratulated in a way that I don't think he ever imagined possible when he first saw my skinny calves. I should say that The Duke was what they call a 'character' and as such had not been invited to the opening night for fear that he might do something like shout out for the director in the middle of the second act. Anyway he was being congratulated by all sorts of people and, as it was the second night, reviews were out and the congratulators were able to quote from Clive Barnes and to say things like 'Beautifully choreographed, Mr. Rudman'. 'Your son has done a wonderful job in this magnificently choreographed production.'

After about ten minutes of this highly sincere stuff, my dad, sought me out and, for perhaps the first time in his life, asked my instruction. 'This word, Mike, 'choreographed'. What the hell does it mean?' I said it was what they did with dancers to organize their movements.

The next time someone said 'Beautifully choreographed' to The Duke, he answered quickly, in a thick, possibly exaggerated Texan accent, 'Well, with twenty-two guys on the stage, somebody had better be dancin'.'

I think it's fair to say that I, like my father, have always been eccentric. I am, after all, the same person who, in 1953, stood in front of the assembled WASPS of Dallas, at the commencement of St. Mark's School of Texas and told them that by the year 1972, Cleveland would have a black mayor. I told them that Detroit would have a black mayor too. I had read these facts in a speculative article on demographics in the *Saturday Evening Post* and had worked them into my entry for that year's oratory contest. Lord, were they cross! Many of them stopped speaking to me.

So, we are talking about an eccentric. Someone who, encouraged by his dad, egged on even, could at fourteen, speak with the view that racial equality was inevitable so we might as well embrace it. Embrace it? In 1953? In Dallas, Texas? Are you serious?

Well, I was.

And I am.

I joke too much, but I am also very serious.

My dad never believed I had a job let alone a career until he saw my production of *Long Day's Journey Into Night* at the Nottingham Playhouse with Robert Ryan playing James Tyrone. After that he was willing to believe I was 'gainfully employed' as my mother would say, but he always thought, even when he was ninety and I was sixty, I would return to Texas and go into his business at his office.

The fact that I never did and pursued a career in the theatre should not have surprised him. After all, for a time he was in show business. He had severe asthma during World War Two and was declared unfit to serve in the armed forces. So, he produced, directed and starred in OAS shows for wounded soldiers.

The rehearsals were often held in our living room. One of my first memories from when I was four, was a chorus line of babes making rocking motions with their arms and singing

Put your arms around me honey
Hold me tight,
Cuddle up and cuddle up with all your might.

I think I have always tried to be different from my father. Where he was loud and braggadocious, I have tried to be quiet and laid back. Probably I haven't succeeded. When I gave John Barber, *The Telegraph* critic, a lift on my motor scooter, wearing a flowing leather poncho, he described me as 'flamboyant' which came as quite a shock.

My dad would exaggerate any accomplishment of his own or mine. He always pushed me to get more publicity, whereas I have avoided interviews and photographs as best I could. At least I think I have.

But, lately, I have become more and more aware of the truth of something Arthur Miller said to me when we were on tour with *Death Of A Salesman*: 'One of these days, Mike, you look in the mirror and you're shaving your father's face.'

I think I am more like my mother. I would hope that I have her dry wit. When she came to visit me at the Nottingham Playhouse, she made a lot of the actors laugh. There was one remark they found particularly funny coming as it did from a clearly provincial Texas woman in 1966.

I introduced her to Harold Innocent, a lovely bubbly man who was pretty obviously gay. They chatted at length over a couple of drinks. The next day I said to her, 'Harold Innocent liked you a lot, Mother. He said you could come to tea any time.' Her answer was, 'Yeah, but I bet he wouldn't want me to stay for breakfast.'

When I think about my time in Texas, I am mainly struck by how brief it was. I have been in England much longer and all of that time as an adult. So, how did Texas form me? As a theatre director, for that is what I am, my two principal tools are intellect and energy. For energy you could read health. Texas, and my father, literally trained me to be keen on sport and to be aware of my physical fitness. This kind of talk doesn't sound nearly so weird now, in 2014, but forty-years ago running in Central Park was considered odd.

In the mid-seventies, jogging up to an actor in Central Park whom I had met the day before at an audition, I said 'Hi', and he literally recoiled.

'Get away,' he shouted.

This story has two points. (1) Joggers, especially very slow joggers, were still rare in New York City in the mid-seventies. (2) For most actors, most auditions are a blur and the man who terrifies them and whom they loathe for judging them, is unrecognizable the next day.

Israel Horowitz said to me once about slimming for Jews, 'The gentiles celebrate Christmas; we celebrate weight loss.'

For most of my life, particularly the American bit, people have found it comical, or at least strange, that someone could be a 'Texas Jew'. The two characteristics don't seem to go together well. Probably not, but for health and fitness and enthusiasm for sport, it would be hard to find two kinds of people more similar than Texans and Jews. And certainly both heritages combine enthusiastically in my father who made me carry watermelons around when I was two years old to build my muscles (he failed); who stood on the steps of the Cotton Bowl Stadium in Dallas introducing me to his friends, trying to convince me that they were world class football players (he failed); and who founded, in the late forties, when nobody listened to him, the 'Texas Anti-Smoking League' and spent a great deal of time talking to people, including his sons, into becoming non-smokers (he succeeded).

Dallas is an interesting place.

Quite a few years ago, my mother took me to dinner with one of her friends, recently bereaved, but still young and attractive. She was the widow of a wealthy oil baron who had been married five times before, but she was his widow. He had been infirm and blind when they wed, but she had loved him. So she said. She still loved him. His eldest son, let's call him Jimmy Jnr. didn't like her at all and especially didn't like the fact that she was legally his only widow and getting all the privileges, not to mention funding, that the position guaranteed. Jimmy Jnr. was making her life a misery. Getting her kicked out of the Country Club for instance, when her widowhood guaranteed her associate membership for life.

When she finished her recital of all the evil things that Jimmy Jnr. was doing, I told her that in England where I was living, a television programme had recently become very popular. It was called *Dallas* and had she ever seen it?

'Yes,' she said.

'What do you think of it?'

'It's accurate.'

Well, it is, or was, and those are the people I went to school with, though of course many of us escaped. Like Steve Miller, Tommy Lee Jones and, of course, Adams.

Adams or John Quincy Adams III was a big part of my life and for many years, at Oberlin College, we shared a room and even a sense of humour.

His best moment was undoubtedly in Religion. That is, second year Religion class when the teacher, Burl-Sahl by name, strode into the classroom impressively. Partly he was impressive because he was big and had a limp. Also, he had thick spectacles. Anyway, he strode in as the bell rang and without any warning, went to the blackboard and started writing questions there. It was a 'spot quiz' to test if we had done our reading. No one ever did the reading for that class.

There was an awful pause.

'Jesus Christ,' said Adams, very loud, in Religion class, in Texas in 1954.

'What did you say?' said Burl-Sahl, wheeling round.

'Short prayer, sir,' said Adams.

Anyway, Adams got out of Texas and so did I.

But, I can't leave Texas, or at least the Texas that is in me, without telling the story of my dad and Pablo Picasso.

Pablo Picasso

The Duke met Picasso in the early fifties in Cannes where the painter was living in the hills above, and my dad was taking the waters, etc..

In Europe, Dad used to interview and sometimes employ secretaries and many of them were attractive. On one occasion he was sitting at a restaurant called Felix with one of those secretaries when Picasso happened by. Now you have to understand that to my dad, Picasso was not Pablo Picasso at all but more like a small out-of-work Mexican.

Anyway, this small Mexican, whom we will call Pablo, came up to the Duke's table and asked if he could buy him and his petite, blonde Dutch secretary a drink. My dad didn't drink so he had a vodka martini and the lady, who had a small child and no discernible husband, had a glass of white wine.

Whether it was the modesty of her drink order or something in herself that attracted Pablo, we shall never know but mightily attracted to her he was and he put it to my dad in his Mexican English that this young lady might be better off working for him than for my dad. The Duke could see nothing wrong with this and graciously offered to release her forthwith. Pablo was thrilled and offered another Martini, but Dad left thinking 'good riddance' and never thought to see the Dutch girl or the Mexican again.

He did see them, however, all the time. They were often swimming from the beach at the Carlton Hotel and swimming very well. In fact, my dad found himself thinking things like 'How can that little Mexican bastard, or Spaniard, or whatever he is, swim like that? He swims like a son of a bitch.' These thoughts, though aggressive, were complimentary to Picasso. The Spaniard beamed when my Dad voiced them. The Duke was always fulsome with his compliments. Soon Dad was invited to swim with the Spanish painter, as he was actually, and he always beamed when the compliments were repeated.

It was only by accident in the changing room that Dad found out that Picasso was wearing a small air balloon round his waist, under his bathing costume, which was a considerable help to his swimming speed and style.

For once, Dad kept his mouth shut and was invited to lunch. After lunch, Picasso was in an expansive mood. The post-prandial speech went something like this:

'I know that I have too much *vin rose* and that you, Mr. Texas, have complimented my swimming too much and been so gracious as to release this beautiful young lady to work as my secretary. I know all these things and I know that I shouldn't do this but I am going to have to act on this impulse. Look, *Monsieur du* Texas, look around you. What do you see?'

'Paintings,' said the Duke.

'Exactly,' said Picasso.

'Paintings of women with their tits hanging out and their faces all messed up.'

'You could say that,' said Picasso. 'Do you like nudes?'

'I love nude pictures,' said my dad. 'I got 'em all over my office at home.'

'Do you like these pictures?' asked the Spaniard.

'Not a whole hell of a lot,' said The Duke.

Picasso was not at all taken aback. He had heard this before. 'Even so,' said the painter, 'in return for your charm of manner, except in not liking my paintings, but I forgive that, and especially in return for introducing me to this charming lady....'

The Dutch girl said nothing.

'...and for releasing her. In return for all that, I am offering you any one of these paintings on any one of these walls in my villa. Take your pick.'

There was, I always think, an awful silence.

'They are quite valuable, or will be, one day,' said the Spaniard with evident modesty.

'No thanks,' said my Dad.

On his behalf, I apologise to all his heirs.

'Quite understandable,' said Picasso, and they all drink some more *vin rose*.

Texas led me in some ways to Europe. That might sound strange, but not too strange, I hope, considering what you have read so far.

Aristotle Onassis

My father went to Europe every year and Europe seemed a natural place for me to go.

Cannes, where my father met Picasso, was also a natural place to go, especially as my father was there, so, at the end of my first year out of college, before I went to Oxford, I met my father at the Cannes Film Festival and landed my first job, my first proper job, working as a stagehand for the Living Theatre on their tour of Europe.

Cannes was a good place for my dad because they understood eccentrics there and welcomed them, as long as they could pay their bills. And whatever else you may say about a Texan Jew who wears feathers in his hat, calls himself 'Duke', founded an anti-smoking organization in 1948, cuts everyone's hair, answers the telephone 'Henry's Mule Barn' and drives a yellow Cadillac convertible when he has no money at all, he is an eccentric.

Once dad did an unusual thing in Cannes that led to a good piece of advice. When he didn't have much money, but wanted to have a lot, he noticed Aristotle Onassis sitting in one of the cafes on the Croisette. Probably Felix. Not being shy, he went to Onassis' table.

'Aren't you Aristotle Onassis?' asked young Duke.

'I am,' Onassis answered with great charm.

'Do you mind if I join you for a minute?'

'Not at all,' said Onassis, 'please do.'

Then the young man asked Onassis for some advice. He was anxious to make a lot of money. How could he do that? How could he succeed like this Greek had done?

'I'll give you one little bit of advice,' said Onassis.

'Please do,' said my Dad.

'No matter how good your business is, no matter how bad...No matter how good your sex life it, no matter how bad…No matter how good your health is, no matter how bad…'

'What?' asked Dad.

'Always have a little bit of a suntan.'

St. Mark's and Aleph Zadek Aleph

Until I was thirteen, I went to state schools in Highland Park, a fairly leafy suburb, and Preston Hollow, a mostly concrete area. I did okay. I was even quarterback on the eighth grade football team. I was barely competent, but I did it and I didn't get seriously injured.

Then my mother decided that I should go to a private school, St. Mark's School of Texas. I had four unremarkable years there, except for one speech about racial equality which I have mentioned. There were some excellent teachers and some who were not so good. I did the minimum amount of work and was the founder, and later, editor, of the school newspaper.

We wore khaki uniforms and had to wear a tie. Considering that I was a smart-alec, it is a remarkable fact that I only had one fight. A boy called Tommy Gay persisted in challenging me until finally I had to agree to fight him. We went out front of the main building. There was quite a crowd.

Although small, Tommy was terrific at fighting. He kept knocking me down and pummeling me. Then he would stand up, thinking it was over, but I would stand up and we would go on fighting. This went on for a long time until both the crowd and Tommy got bored and the fight stopped. I was still standing.

It is possible to see that incident as a metaphor for my entire life.

St. Mark's was probably a good education, but there was very little laughter. In the classroom I made a few jokes but, according to some masters, I always went too far. (See title.)

But I found laughter and fellowship and a different kind of education in an organization called *AZA, Aleph Zadak Aleph*. This was the boy's section of BBYO, the Bnai Brith Youth Organization, which was Jewish and probably Zionist. Also, and this was important, there was a sister branch called BBG or Bnai Brith Girls. We didn't have girls at St. Mark's.

Henry Zapruder was tall, charismatic and handsome. I knew him from Temple Emmanuel, the reform Jewish temple in Dallas. He was the year above me but in breaks we all played touch football using a shoe as the ball and we had fun. And some laughs.

He asked me if I had ever heard of *AZA* and I said that I had, dimly. He invited me to the next meeting of the Henry Monsky Branch. It was way across town in Lakewood so he gave me a lift.

I don't think I have laughed so much and for so long in my entire life.

Jay Ungerman, a handsome, dark, young man with a prominent nose, was the President or *Aleph Godol* of the Chapter. At one point during the meeting, he addressed himself to the problem of one of the former officers; I think he had been secretary, or *Aleph Mazkir*, of the Chapter. I don't remember his name. Let's call him Meyer Nathan in honour of a boy from Houston who became a friend.

Meyer's father had decided to relocate. The whole family were moving to San Antonio. A collection was made to pay for a present for him. It was a book, but it was nicely wrapped.

Jay narrated this in detail for the benefit of all, but especially prospective members like myself. Throughout, his eyes were sparkling and a wry smile played on his lips. He was always just on the point of chuckling, but he never did.

The present had been gift-wrapped and the card was full of glowing tributes to Meyer's accomplishments. And it was arranged that Meyer would come to the next meeting to receive it. But there was a hitch.

Meyer's father had decided to stay in Dallas.

Jay described how the governing committee had found this to be a knotty problem. How the discussions had gone late into the night.

Should the gift be returned to the shop? They refused to reimburse the money. They would only exchange it for another book. Was anyone else leaving? Should we give the Meyer the book anyway? Should we keep the book in case anyone else decided to leave? Did anybody know anyone who might be leaving soon?

Jay went on and on. Everyone knew that he was spinning it out but he was so hilarious that we wanted it to go on forever. I resolved there and then to join *AZA* and I am very glad I did.

Twenty years later I was sitting in the auditorium of the Morosco

Theatre on Broadway after the successful, if not triumphant, opening night of *The Changing Room*. Remember that *The Changing Room* is a dour play, virtually a documentary, about a grim and gritty game played in the north of England by men who are, for the most part, laconic and tough and who are, quite often, nude.

Also, remember that in 1973, the theatergoing audience of Dallas, Texas was mainly fun-loving, wealthy, churchgoing, hard working men and their wives who went to the theatre for an evening of colour, movement and entertainment.

So, I am sitting there alone on the opening night, as I often do, remembering and savouring what has just passed.

Onto the stage came three or four men and their wives from the Dallas Jewish community led by Jay Ungerman. With a half smile on his face, he looks around at the drab set and the empty auditorium, sees me and says, 'Mike, this play would go very well in Dallas.'

Eventually, after a year and a bit, I became *Aleph Godol* and learned to control a room full of people. I could never make people laugh as much as Jay, but I did pretty well. I'm sure that the experience of chairing meetings and organizing activities was good preparation for life as a theatre director.

Also, Henry Zapruder and I became lifelong friends.

Henry progressed far in *AZA* which was a national organization. He became *Aleph Godol* of the entire district, which stretched from Texas to Georgia and had thousands of members. At the district convention, he appointed me to the non-existent job of recording secretary. My main task was to help him govern and in particular to whisper to him the name of the member who had his hand up for recognition at one of the many large meetings.

Henry went on to excel at Harvard Law School and to become successful representing, among others, the Hitachi Corporation, and the Getty family. We never lost touch.

Henry, as I have said, was tall, attractive and smart. But, most of all, he was confident in everything he did and said. As you can imagine, he was a favourite with the girls. Even though he was a terrible dancer, he did it with such élan that he was very effective.

Sometimes, at night, girls would go with Henry in his car to a parking area near White Rock Lane. They would, as the expression was in the fifties, 'make out'. According to Henry, he was pretty good at this but, whether he was or not, he was certainly confident.

One night, quite late, some boys who had been drinking came up to his parked car. First, they threw pebbles at it. This upset the girl. Then they started singing and hitting the car with their hands. She got even more frightened. Henry tried to remain confident but he was apprehensive.

Then he remembered he had a toy gun in the glove compartment belonging to one of his nephews. When the taunting and singing got louder and more scary, he opened the glove compartment and took out the gun.

'I'll take care of this,' he said to the girl. Holding the pistol, he got out of the car and locked it. The boys came towards him singing louder. When they saw the gun, they stopped. There was silence.

And then, I'm sorry to report, Henry shouted, 'Get the hell out of here or I'll fuck your shootin' guts out.'

Everyone collapsed with laughter and the boys went away. The girl, of course, only liked Henry all the more.

It's worth mentioning that Henry's father, Abraham Zapruder, was the man lucky enough or, unlucky enough, to be in Dealey Plaza with his super 8 camera when Kennedy was assassinated. He took the crucial footage that has been seen millions of times all around the word.

Abe had been a very quiet man who hardly spoke. He was a Russian Jewish immigrant who owned a small dress shop near downtown Dallas. I don't remember him ever saying a word. But after the incident, he became garrulous. He once talked to me through an entire game of pool.

I suppose *AZA* was to me what boarding schools are to English boys. It gave me hopes, aspirations and confidence and introduced me to boys who became lifelong friends. I was a lucky boy in many ways, but *AZA* was my biggest piece of luck.

Rose Rudman

My Bobo was my father's mother. She died when she was one hundred and one. I was on the golf course. I had managed to get on the first green in three and was about to putt when a man in a golf cart drew up, looking at me, and stopped. I knew it wasn't slow play because it was the first hole. I asked him what it was because he was looking at me. He said, 'Go ahead and putt and then I'll tell you.' I said 'Tell me now,'. He said, 'It's about your grandmother.'

I knew it wasn't flu.

Bubba was the sort of person that you could rely on. I used to ring from time to time, and I knew her number by heart. Once I rang her from the rehearsal room in New York when we were rehearsing *Death of a Salesman*. Kate Reid and I were early. I asked if she'd like to talk to the woman upon whom I based my ideas for Linda Loman. Kate said she would. So I rang Bubba from the rehearsal room. The number was 430-592-6445.

The conversation went like this:
'Hello Bubba'.
'Who's that?'
'It's Michael.'
'Hello Michael. Where are you?'
'I'm in New York.'
'Are you working?'
'Yes Bubba.'
'Who's that?'
'It's Michael, Bubba.'
'Where are you?'
'I'm in New York, Bubba.'
'Are you working?'
It was a kind of a loop.

Her husband, my Zadie, was, as they say in England, a weird cove. He used to work from very early in the morning until the afternoon when he would come home, have a nap, wake up and work some more.

He would send letters to me when I was at summer camp, addressed to himself. They would be quite long, typed out usually a full page, describing all the activities that I was having, and he would ask me to sign it and send it back to him. This was his way of saying that I wasn't writing to him enough.

Rose Davis

My mother's mother was a Communist. I can't put it more plainly than that.

I was twenty, a keen student of political science, and curious about most things. I was also Chairman of the Ohio-Indiana region of the National Student Association. I was respectable and I was on a duty visit to Grandma Davis' small bungalow on the outskirts of Dallas. After the taking of cookies and iced tea, my mother was talking to her mother and I was leafing through a magazine that I had found on the coffee table. It had an intriguing title: *New World*. The first article was a defence of the Imry Nage trial in Hungary. Imry Nage was a student who had committed some minor offence of dissent, largely unproven, but his trial had been made a showcase and he had been imprisoned. All of us in the NSA had managed to become enraged at this traducing of free speech and I was appalled to find an article defending it on the coffee table of my little grandma in North Dallas, not far from two Methodist churches and three country clubs.

Until that time, I had thought of my grandmother as a kind woman with a strange Russian accent, who was married to a man who had retired at age forty-five with no visible means of support. She was mother to four children: a doctor, a shopkeeper, a company executive and my mother. There were strong rumours that the doctor was an official in the ultra right wing John Birch Society.

But there was this article. And worse, when questioned, my grandmother turned out to have great sympathy for the regime in Hungary and indeed the regime in Russia and indeed all of the former regimes in Soviet Russia. It became clear that all grandma Davis wanted, now that her children had grown up and produced comfortable and acceptable grandchildren, was to get enough money and time to visit Mother Russia and see all the miracles that Lenin and Stalin and their successors had worked.

I was amazed. She sat there in her Doris Day bungalow surrounded by labour-saving appliances, defending the worst excesses of the Soviets, including the murder of millions of people during the purges. Her hair was soft grey. Her eyes were clear and sweet. But she was a communist. My grandmother.

Apparently, in her village in Russia, most of the Jewish children had been taught opposition to the Czar from the cradle. They had tied signs around the necks of pigs with 'Capitalist' written on them. She told me that she had been in a big demonstration in Moscow as a young girl in 1905. I calculated that to be the March on the Winter Palace.

I was just getting ferociously interested in all this when my mother pulled me away. Literally. And I was told never to discuss this conversation. My mother, the peacemaker in the family, was almost always right about these things so I did go away and I did keep quiet. I don't think I ever mentioned it again until years later, at the National Theatre, during the strike when I got a reasonable laugh with the line 'Does it seem right to you for someone whose grandmother marched on the Winter Palace to drive through a picket line in a BMW?'

Josephine Davis Rudman

But we were not communists. Certainly not. We were Jews and we were liberal, especially about being Jewish.

Once, when I was Director of the Hampstead Theatre, I teased my mother about her next trip to England to see her grandchildren. She had chosen, with extreme care, and months ahead, a particular day in September.

'But you can't travel on that day, mother.'

'Why not?'

'It's the second day of Rosh Hashanah.'

'Le'me tell you something, Mike,' she said in a thick Texas accent. What, mother?'

'I don't give a shit about the second day of Rosh Hashanah.'

My mother was called Josephine Davis Rudman. She was a mother, card player (Bridge and Canasta), golfer (best round – 63 for nine holes) and *bon vivante*. She said, many times, 'When I die I don't want them to say I haven't lived.' This former schoolteacher was perhaps best known for her remarks about her marriage to my father. 'I've been married to your father for fifty years, but he's only been married to me for twenty-five.' Also, 'When I married him he looked like a Greek God. Now looks like a goddamn Greek.'

Josephine Davis Rudman was a devoted grandmother. Once, long ago, when my two daughters were young and I somehow got them to Texas on their own, we were all sitting around watching television and a film appeared called *Midnight Express*. Good looking young men in appalling circumstances enthralled my daughters, aged twelve and nine at the time, and I was quite taken with the excellence of the direction and the acting. But my mother wanted to talk to her grandchildren.

The movie went on. My mother knitted. More attractive men came on the screen, hitting each other, craving drugs, suffering, making speeches. Many of them were covered with dirt. My daughters became transfixed. My mother began to find it impossible to get answers to her questions. Finally she gave up.

Then, after about half an hour of us watching, very hard, and her managing as well as she could to remain silent, she suddenly blurted out a question.

'How could all this happen on a train?'

Shirley Maclaine

I was about to direct Richard Harris in *Camelot* at the Apollo Victoria theatre (don't ask) and my mother was staying in London. The Apollo Victoria was presenting Shirley MacLaine in her one-woman show.

'Would you like to see Shirley MacLaine? I can get free tickets, and good tickets, because I'm directing the next show there.'

My mother was delighted at this prospect and I picked her up from her hotel in plenty of time because she, like Somerset Maugham, was the sort of person who arrived at the station so early that she caught the train before, if you see what I mean.

A young golf pro Mitchell Spearman who, at that time nobody had ever heard of, indeed not many people would speak to, begged me, when he heard I was going to see and meet Shirley MacLaine, to take him along. I don't know if I would have agreed had I known he was going to wear a pink sports jacket, and bring a large box of chocolates, and his fiancé, but he had been nice to me and we had played golf on many occasions when he would probably rather have been doing something else, so I said I would.

After the show, we went backstage and said to one of the minders that the director of the next show, Michael Rudman and his mother, and a young man and his fiancé, would like to meet Miss MacLaine. We were told to stand in the queue, which we did. The queue was long, stretching down several floors and past the lift on the ground floor of the theatre. My mother was not at all aware of the fact that we were being treated shabbily and in fact seemed quite happy to stand there, in her rain-hat. It was pouring and we'd had to walk round the theatre to the stage door. Eventually, we got to the top of the stairs and a tall man, who was called something like Michael Flowers, asked who we were. I said who we were. He went inside the dressing room and came out with Shirley MacLaine.

Shirley is very tall, which surprised me. The other thing that surprised me was that she wasn't at all interested in me, even though I was a director of some repute, and she wasn't at all interested in Mitchell Spearman, even though he was a good looking young man in a pink jacket and destined to become David Leadbetter's chief assistant.

No, Shirley was interested in my mother.

My mother said 'Oh my God, Shirley, you were so wonderful. So wonderful. Ethel Merman had better be glad that she is retired because you are the tops. Shirley you are just so wonderful.'

Without a pause of one second, Shirley grabbed my mother's arm and said to Flowers, who was her assistant, or husband, or both, 'I must have this woman. This woman will get me my Academy Award.'

Mother went fairly quiet at this point. She stared at Shirley MacLaine as though something wonderful was happening.

'This woman is going to be my technical advisor. When I go to Texas, I want this woman with me all the time. I want her accent. I want to be like her. She is going to win me my Oscar.'

Shirley was referring to the Academy Award, that she did indeed later win for *Terms of Endearment*. She knew she was going to win it long before the movie was made. I don't know how. Perhaps she had been reading some of her own books. And at that moment she convinced herself that my mother was going to be instrumental.

My mother completely believed this. I may say that I didn't but I did give Michael Flowers all my mother's phone numbers – that is one – and her address, and my father's business address and telephone number.

My mother didn't speak much after that. As we were driving down the Strand, I finally said something.

'Mother, what are going to say to Daddy? Daddy is the one who knows all the film stars. Daddy is the one who travels round the world. Daddy even got Van Heflin to invest in an oil deal once. You're not supposed to know all these people, or be involved in all this. What are you going to say?'

'I'll just say Shirley is a friend of mine.'

The sequel to this story is a little depressing so I won't relate it, but it did involve my mother writing about twenty letters to Shirley, none of which was answered. I promised myself that if I ever met Shirley again, I would mention this to her and indeed I did. She didn't seem at all worried by the fact that my mother never did serve as her technical advisor and she appeared to be taking her Academy Award very much in her stride.

The Jewish Connection

Sibling rivalry was virtually unheard of when I grew up. Mainly these people were needed in the day in day out battle with parents. They were friends and allies. My brother Wolfe was a friend. Later, the only problem with most conversations with Wolfe was that after five or ten minutes of him being extremely intelligent and worldly wise, his astrology cut in, betraying the decades he spent in California. For example, I might be just about to bare my soul, feeling confident of his intelligence and sympathy, when he would say something that stops everything, like, 'Libras give good head.'

What do you say to that?

The kind of Jews we were is most colourfully expressed by my mother's remark about the second night of Rosh Hashanah. But years later, Neil Simon came up with a telling phrase. When I was directing *Brighton Beach Memoirs* at the National, I noticed that the evening meal, which the mother prepares throughout the first act, was set on a Wednesday night. I thought it would be a good idea to change it to a Friday and make it a Friday night dinner, celebrated in Jewish homes as *Shabbat*, with a fair amount of ceremony. I rang Neil Simon and suggested it. He was quite happy for me to do that. Then I asked if we might put in some prayers in Hebrew in addition to the business we had already added with the candles and the *Chollah* (egg bread). Neil didn't think it was necessary. He said, 'No'. He said, 'We were catch-as-catch-can Jews'. That is, the kind of Jews who don't say all the prayers, have probably forgotten them, and wouldn't have time anyway because they have baseball practice after Friday night dinner. It also means the kind of Jews who are aware of being Jewish and not denying it, but simply maintaining it in a particular American way, a very assimilated way.

In a similar way, I have always pushed for the characters in *Death of A Salesman* to be more obviously Jewish. When I first directed the play, at the Nottingham Playhouse, John Neville said to me, 'You're directing it'.

'Oh, great,' I said. 'Who's playing Willy?'

'I am,' John said. 'Is there some reason why I shouldn't?'

'No, not at all.' Pause. 'You realize he's Jewish.'

'Don't be silly.'

The first day of rehearsal, John turned up with a perfect mid-west American accent. I said, 'Why don't you try a sort of Jewish-New York?' He said, 'I don't think it's right.' The next day, he came back with the most beautiful deep New York-Jewish-European accent you've ever heard. His voice was like maple syrup poured over gravel. You would only hear that voice in New York, but never on stage. He became a noble but shattered human being from a definite place on Long Island and desperately seeking, through his son, the American dream.

Twenty-five years later, John and I would still tease each other about me making him play Willy Jewish. When he returned to the National Theatre to do *School For Scandal*, I sent him a note:

'Every Synagogue in England rejoices at your return. Good luck in Schul for Scandal.'

Dustin Hoffman

Dustin Hoffman is also one of these 'Catch-as-catch-can Jews'. This helped greatly when he was the centre of our Broadway production of *Death of a Salesman*.

Dustin tells the story of how he made his wife stop the car when she informed him that he couldn't have dinner with Arthur Miller the following night because it was *Yom Kippur*. He started screaming.

'Why don't you tell me? Don't keep it a secret. Why don't you tell me when it's a major holiday? You don't tell me anything. I have to have a warning about this kind of thing.'

Dustin's wife is very mild. She said something mild. Dustin screamed.

'Don't you know I was the kind of Jew who had a Christmas tree?'

Dustin sent me to the Plaza Hotel, during the four months we were spending on casting, to check out the actors in *The Cotton Club*. Coppola was directing it on location there. He had taken the entire second floor for filming and eating. He liked to give his cast a complete nosh every meal, and I arrived one morning at 8 a.m. to see them all digging into breakfast, while huge bowls of shrimp were being arranged for lunch. This may be one of the reasons why Coppola has happy actors.

Coincidentally, my father was staying in one of the tiny rooms on the second floor that wasn't occupied by Coppola. It was a very cheap room with no windows, the kind he preferred. So when Dustin joined me to chat to the actors and suggest that they might want to audition for *Death of a Salesman*, I asked him if he'd like to meet my dad. We knocked on the door. The Duke let us in, seemingly unimpressed. He had a wide selection of hats, most of them with feathers in the band, and Dustin tried on only six before they became friends. Fortunately, this took place before the rehearsals and gave Dustin and me a bond. He always knew that he was playing his father and he always knew that I was directing him to play my father, and somewhere in between there emerged a superb characterization.

Bud Shrake

But not all Texans are Jews. My brother Wolfe put me on to the now legendary Edwin 'Bud' Shrake. I met this tall, laconic, almost perfect Texan forty odd years ago in Austin where he was the centre of an artistic community.

Ever since meeting him, I was kept on the straight and narrow by his refusal to take anything too seriously, except for golf, an addiction which cured him of various other addictions.

With his other friend, Dan Jenkins, he constantly referred to my production of *Hamlet* in Central Park as *Helmet*, and this good humour helped me to withstand such moments as Joe Papp saying to me 'Five years ago I would have fired you'.

Once I was with my daughter Kate in New York, far too late at night for either of us, and Dan Jenkins related a tale of Bud Shrake.

'Bud was staying at our apartment with this junior leaguer (the Texas version of a Deb) from Austin who talked a blue streak. You couldn't shut her up. And she had this high-pitched voice. I don't know why he brought her up here in the midst of us sophisticates, but I knew he wished he hadn't. She just talked from morning 'til night. She couldn't seem to stop, and old Bud, he was getting more and more laconic. Anyway, one morning, Bud came down to breakfast and he was reading the paper. This damn girl was all pretty and sweet and talking like Chip 'n Dale. She was too young for one thing. Anyway, Bud just kept reading the paper and she was asking 'What are we doin' today?' and 'Didn't it look cold outside?' and 'Who was that weird man with the beard last night, and his so-called date and what on earth was she wearing?' and 'Can I have some grapefruit for breakfast?', and 'Do you like my hair like this?' And on and on.

Bud just sat there reading *The News*.

'And what are you doin', Bud? What do I have to do to get you to say somethin' to me? What's in the paper that's so interesting? What are you reading?'

'I'm readin' the horoscopes,' said Bud.

'Well, what does it say?'

'It says 'be nostalgic about your first wife'.'

Before we leave Texas, I think you might like to hear a little more about my mother, Josephine Davis Rudman.

When my daughter Kate was about to be born, Josephine appeared in Edinburgh to be present for this event and to make herself useful. Many Grandparents do this but none, perhaps, who demand so much attention.

I could see that it was all becoming rather a strain for Kate's mother, so I said, 'Mother, the baby won't be born for quite a while. Why don't you rent a car with Daddy and do some sightseeing. Scotland has wonderful lakes and rivers and even mountains. Scotland is beautiful. 'Lemme tell you something, Mike', she said, 'I don't give a shit about Scotland.'

Little did we suspect that this simple statement would become the basis of the policy of successive British governments towards that strange and beleaguered country.

Oberlin College

Interview For Oberlin College

Time	3.00 p.m.
Place	Oberlin College, Oberlin, Ohio
Date	March 1956
Post	Student for a Bachelor of Arts degree.

Two young men in jackets, ties and loafers sitting in front of a desk in the basement of a Victorian building in rural Ohio. Outside it is raining heavily. Sitting at the desk is a young man, only slightly older than the other two, wearing a jacket and tie and loafers, but also a lambswool pullover.

The two young men in front of the desk are Adams and Rudman. They are on a trip round the East Coast of the United States. They have had a series of appointments, looking at colleges and being interviewed by men called Deans of Admission. At Oberlin, they have found the most sympathetic, informal and welcoming of all the interviewers. At Princeton, for example, the strict, straight man in the striped tie behind the desk seemed very disturbed by the fact that Rudman's father had not finished his degree course at Oklahoma University and that Adams' father had graduated from a small junior college in East Texas. The man had even become nearly rude when it emerged that Adams' father was one-half Native American.

This Oberlin Dean seems only interested in the College Board (SATs) scores of the two applicants.

'You'll get into Oberlin easily with these scores.' And they did.

'Don't worry about the rain,' he said. 'It rains all the time, but you won't notice it.'

In fact, they didn't.

English Literature

An aerial view of Oberlin, Ohio would show two large squares dotted with brick buildings and five long straight roads radiating from the sides and the centres of these two squares.

The view from the ground is very much the same.

Oberlin is flat. Flatter than Norfolk. Many centuries ago, the glaciers receded after the ice age and those frozen rock mountains, when they melted, left in their wake a land scraped clean and covered with soft silt. This is a bland mid-western landscape. If there are any hills I didn't see them and none were reported. Most of us rode bicycles in the rain so we would have noticed a hill. Cars were not allowed. Neither was alcohol.

When I arrived at Oberlin, I joined a Freshman class of about six hundred. For no apparent or dramatic reason, this class shrunk to three hundred and fifty-seven at graduation four years later. Oberlin was the first academic institution in the world to grant a BA degree to a woman and also the first to confer that honour on an Afro-American. So, it is a liberal college in spirit but also, due to the lures of marriage and ordinary life, and the difficulty of its academic regime there, a college that loses a lot of its students before they have completed their degree courses.

The course that I most eagerly awaited in my first year at Oberlin was English Literature. Here I hoped to find inspiration and excitement. I sat with another twenty young students on the first day, waiting for our instructor.

He entered briskly. We knew that his name was Millet and we wondered if he might be by some chance related to the poet, Edna St Vincent Millay. Certainly we hoped for something exotic. But his looks were not promising. Middle-age, middle height. Light brown hair. Thick glasses. He walked quickly up the aisle, went to the blackboard and wrote with speed and in large capital letters M I L L E T.

'Millet', he said, pronouncing it like skillet.

'Not Millet' (like Millay) 'Just plain Millet.'

And that was what we got from this sensible, pleasant, intelligent mid-western man. Millet. He was very clear and very helpful.

Classes and Classifications

When I was at Oberlin, the student body was homogenous as was most of middle-west, middle America. But within the mostly white, mostly middle-class, mostly urban, mostly upwardly mobile student population, there were many who were unusual.

Once, in an introductory psychology class, Professor Turner was explaining the classification of highbrow, lowbrow and middlebrow to a class consisting almost entirely of middlebrows.

'Take, for example, salads,' said the Professor in a rare departure from his well-prepared lecture. 'The 'highbrow' would prefer a salad made in a wooden bowl. He might not even wash the bowl every time, but leave the olive oil and vinegar, and the various seasonings, to soak in. It might well be a salad made only of lettuce, of various kinds, with a sprinkling of mint and even some raw spinach. The vinaigrette sauce would be about four parts oil to one part vinegar, and he would mix in sugar and mustard and fresh ground pepper. Does anyone here prefer salad like that?'

Nobody answered.

'The 'middlebrow', on the other hand, would eat a mixed salad, consisting of lettuce and tomato and perhaps a spring onion. The dressing would be mayonnaise, or mayonnaise flavoured with paprika or tomato sauce or, in rarer cases, Roquefort cheese. Now, I imagine that most of us prefer that kind of salad, which is a good indicator of what we are, namely 'middlebrow'.

There was general assent.

'Now we turn to the 'lowbrow'. He would prefer a simple coleslaw.'

'Hey,' boomed a male voice from the back of the room. 'What's wrong with coleslaw?'

That voice belonged to a 'jock' or athlete, a rare but significant figure in the demographics of the college. More on them later.

Religious Discrimination

My first two weeks at Oberlin were spent going from one large building to another. There were four: (1) Wilder Hall, a four-storey building that housed the Student Union, canteen and all of the male first year students; (2) Dascombe Hall which housed the first year women and a dining hall where all the freshmen ate; (3) Peter's Hall where most of the first year liberal arts classes were held, and (4) the Gymnasium. We rose early, around seven, had breakfast in Dascombe, which was across a large lawned area crisscrossed by pavements, and went to classes, many of which began at eight.

I was shocked by the amount of hard work that was required. It was the general rule for a student to be given two hours preparatory work for each hour of class and there were fifteen hours of class per week. To do well you had to work harder than that and we all wanted to do well. We were highly motivated and competitive. But I enjoyed the meals and I was gregarious.

After only a few weeks, I had a large number of acquaintances.

These were people I knew well enough to call by their first names – Judd, David and Peter. And Alice, Susie and Debbie. I wanted to go into student politics, so my natural inclination to socialize was heightened by ambition.

About ten of the men were very nearly friends of mine already. After all, we slept in the same dormitory, had three meals in the same dining room, often contriving to sit together, and we went to most of our classes in the same building. We were doing liberal arts and, for the first two years, taking more or less the same subjects. Scientists and mathematicians mixed freely with arts degree students.

One late warm autumn evening, we were walking back across the lawn striped by pavements of concrete to Wilder Hall from Dascombe. There were about eight of us and we were chatting and joking and arguing as the September sun went down.

Normally, when we got to Wilder Hall, we would go up to the main stairs, have a bit of a chat, and then go to our rooms to take off the jackets and ties required for dinner. Then we would go in small groups to the main library for two or three hours of work.

But this evening, the others started to drift away. All of them. It seemed odd, so I made a joke.

'Where are you guys going? You got dates?'

Nobody laughed. I didn't know quite what to do. All seven of them were moving in one group towards the far end of Wilder Hall where the Student Union had it's meeting rooms. Not one of them answered me.

I asked again.

'You guys going to a meeting, or what?'

Nobody spoke. Suddenly I felt unwanted, excluded. These men were definitely going away from me to some single, unusual destination. And every one of them was almost my friend.

'It's just something we're going to do,' said Judd.

'All of you?' I asked.

'We're going over there. You wouldn't be interested.'

'I am interested,' I said. 'Very interested. Where the hell are you going? Where is 'over there'?'

It had become a joke to me, like so many of the jokes I had with these guys. It wasn't important but it seemed very odd and their reticence made me more insistent. And they weren't laughing. They were uncomfortable.

'What are you doing?'

'We're all going in there,' said David, gesturing towards the large meeting room on the right of the main floor of Wilder Hall.

'All going in there to do what?' I asked.

'It's a religious service, Michael,' said Pete. 'You wouldn't be interested.' They kept repeating that phrase.

'What kind of religious service? Why wouldn't I be interested?'

'It's the Jewish New Year,' said Judd.

'We're going to a service. It's called Rosh Hashanah.'

Of course. Oh, yes, I thought. Judd Kessler. Pete Kahn. David Sigman. They were all Jews. Every one of these young men that I had become friends with so quickly were Jews. And they all knew that they were and they all thought that I wasn't.

I was stunned and didn't speak.

'We'll see you later. Tomorrow. It's starting in a minute.'

'Michael, are you all right?' asked Judd Kessler.
'I'm fine. I'm Jewish, you know. I'm Jewish too.'
'Yeah, sure. See you later, Rudman. Happy New Year.'
And they went off to services. I didn't go. I don't know why.

Alumni

Oberlin revealed itself to me in an unexpected fashion years after I had left.

An agent in New York, Marion Seachinger, wanted me to meet another director. She wouldn't say why but I trusted her so I arranged dinner with him. Five minutes after we began talking, I could see why she insisted. This chap was terribly like me: similar background, similar interests, clearly talented and charmingly aggressive. The fact that he was black, merely highlighted our similarities. He had been to Oberlin, a couple of years after me. We had even dated the same girl. We became friends over that dinner and kept in touch for years afterwards.

He was called Gilbert Moses. Once he invited me to a production of his called *The Taking of Miss Janie* at the Hudson Street Settlement Theatre. He said to come early and have a drink with him before the show.

I arrived in good time, but Gilbert was in a flap. He had lost something and was searching all over the theatre. It is quite common for a director to lose things in the auditorium during rehearsals and to get into a panic about finding whatever it is as the audience arrives. I have often been in the same fix, haring around looking for cigarettes or spectacles, or handbag or jacket. It isn't easy because the director gets to every nook and cranny of a building and often in the dark.

I won't say what it was that Gilbert had lost, but I'll give you a clue: it's white, it makes you feel very good, it's slightly illegal, and he was desperate to find it. We tried to catch up on each other's news, professional and marital, while looking for this stuff behind every row of seats, in the prompt corner, even in the men's toilets. We were settling into our search and conversation when somewhere between the pass door to the auditorium and the door to the dressing room came a familiar sound.

'Hey, Gilbert.'

It was the unmistakable call of an actor in distress.

'I need to talk to you,' said the voice. He was good looking and African-American.

Gilbert was trapped. This was an actor in a nervous state three quarters of an hour before the curtain went up. He needed Gilbert so I stood aside, but not out of hearing. This actor was talking in a very loud voice and the following account of what he said is accurate even though it might appear exaggerated.

'Gilbert, man, I am laying down this shit and the audience, like they have their shit, man, and they are, like, there. Then she comes with her shit on the stage, which is like my shit, all right, but not my shit, and she is coming on strong with shit that is not real. And her shit, and my shit, and then the audience, like they've got their own shit and I don't know what kind of shit I should be laying down.'

That is what this actor said.

After the performance, which was, as you can imagine, very down home, and after the applause, which was prolonged because the show was excellent, I was waiting backstage for Gilbert. He placed me in the corridor and told me to wait until he had given the actors notes. I dreaded to think what he might be going through and I was anxious to tell him how good it had been.

After a long while, all the actors had gone as had all the people waiting for the actors, and I was alone in what looked like a small school building, I began to wonder if Gilbert had lost his you know what again.

Then I saw him. Not Gilbert. That actor. The one who had cornered Gilbert before the show. He was smiling. He was coming up to me.

'Hi.'

'Hi,' I replied. I was friendly, but guarded.

'I'm sorry we didn't get a chance to talk before.'

'No, well, I could see that you and Gilbert were busy.'

'Gilbert tells me you went to Oberlin.'

'That's right. I did.'

'I went to Oberlin.'

'Great.'

'Don't you find that the really wonderful and really unique thing about Oberlin is that it prepares one to deal with so many areas of concern and so many disciplines and so many levels of society? I mean it gives one a vocabulary, or the ability to acquire a vocabulary for almost any intellectual pursuit.'

I was speechless. But I agreed with him.

Sex and Politics

Oberlin is a small liberal arts college about thirty-five miles from Cleveland. When I went there, it was even more remote because as I've said students were not allowed cars or drink. And the rules were strict and puritanical.

One was difficult to follow. You could not, except in exceptional circumstances, have girls in your room. This did not, as you might imagine, produce a great deal of homosexuality. What it produced instead were young men who could and would do remarkable things.

There were two corollaries to the rule:

On the rare occasions that women were allowed in, the door had to be open six inches. This was known as the 'six-inch rule'. I'm sorry, but that is what they called it.

On the even more rare occasions when you were allowed to have a girl in your room and turn the lights down, the male student was actually required, and this was written down, to keep one foot on the floor. The nearest British equivalent would be found in the game of snooker.

Partly because of the six-inch rule and the one-foot on the floor rule, the men at Oberlin were filled with youthful high spirits. This was particularly true of the first year men, all crammed together into three floors of Wilder Hall, most of us in rooms no more than twice the size of a Pullman berth, sleeping one above the other in bunks.

My desire for political leadership had resulted in my being chosen head of my section, which numbered about thirty. Adams and I were sharing one of those tiny rooms. I wasn't sure what head of my section meant, but it was an elected office and I was proud of it.

One night, I became less pleased with the job.

Bob Fitch and several of the other 'jocks' had managed to find some drink and were roaming the halls in their underwear making a great deal of noise and unleashing their high spirits. It was a Sunday night. I had an exam the next day and so did many of the others. Oberlin professors were fond of the 'blue book', or regular heavy examination requiring a good deal of memorisation. I suppose it was a good idea. You had to either learn fast and write fast, or learn to make things up. But you couldn't do anything much if you had been up all night listening to yahoos prowling the corridors, slapping each other with wet towels. At two in the morning, I consulted with Adams.

'Should I go out there and quieten them down?'

'You could try,' said Adams.

'I am the section leader.'

'You are,' said Adams.

'It is the middle of the night.'

'I know,' said Adams.

'Some of us have a blue book tomorrow.'

'Most of us.'

I ventured out. I was wearing pyjamas.

Bodies hurtled by in the narrow passages. Some of them were carrying mattresses. Mattresses? I thought they must be very drunk. Certainly they were running fast and banging into the walls and into each other even more. I went into the communal bathroom. There were about ten young men in there, some from other sections, all wearing nothing but underwear, well muscled and some of them carrying mattresses. Two questions occurred to me, (i) why were they doing this? and (ii) should I try to stop them?

'Could you guys cut down the noise, please?' I ventured.

'What did you say?'

'I said could you keep it down. Most of us trying to sleep.'

'Go back to your room, bird turd.'

'Please stop it. It's very late.'

'Eat it raw.'

I went back to my room. I was shaken. I was terrified of the threatened violence, but I thought somehow it was up to me to bring it to an end. I was quite wrong, of course, but my fear of being a coward was getting the better of my fear of being hurt.

'Let's try to go to sleep,' I said.

Adams agreed.

The noise went on. I kept trying to sleep. The noise subsided. I got more nervous. The noise got louder. It got to be four o'clock in the morning.

'Should I go out there again?' I asked Adams.

'I'll go with you,' he said. 'I'll be right behind you.'

Adams' bravery fueled my fear of cowardice and out we went. The corridors were empty. We turned right. Adams was, as he promised, right behind me. We turned left. The corridor was dark. The last room on the right belonged to Fitch. Fitch was tough and, although a pre-med student, pretty much of an animal. He was about five-ten, heavily muscled, with light wiry hair all over his body but not much on his head. He wore thick glasses. He was mean.

All of the noise was now coming from Fitch's room. I knocked on the door. It opened quickly. All of the furniture was gone. The floor was covered with mattresses and seven or eight of the freshman football players were bouncing around on them. I went in. Somehow Adams was left in the hallway.

'What do you want?' asked Fitch. He was smiling.

'Could you all stop this and keep the noise down?'

My nerves caused me to say 'you-all', the second person plural in Texas.

'Are you blaming me?' Fitch demanded.

I didn't answer.

'Do you want a fight?'

Why on earth did he ask me that? I looked around the room. Strange people surrounded me. I was standing on a mattress with hardly a highly-developed muscle in my body. He rephrased the question.

'Are you saying that you want to fight me?'

'Yes,' I said.

Don't ask me why.

The others cleared away a little, but it was a small room. They had been hoping for this.

'Let's go,' he said.

'Take off your glasses,' I said.

As he took off his glasses, his head inclined a little to the left. Just as the glasses cleared his face, I hit him as hard as I could. I had always heard that the most important thing was to get in the first punch.

Several things happened. He went down. They pulled us apart. I pretended to want to carry on. They pulled us apart some more. He stood up. He was ready to stop.

'I quit,' he said.

I left the room. I told Adams what happened. Adams found it hard to believe. I told him about the glasses. Finally he believed me. Everyone went to sleep. Fitch flew to Illinois the next morning for serious dental repair work.

And for three weeks, everyone called me 'Rocky'. And the young ladies seemed more interested.

Francis Coleridge

But most of the students at Oberlin were not 'jocks'. Most were striving to become intellectuals. In fact, to be frank, Oberlin was half-peopled with intellectual snobs, young men and women who were on their way to solid and responsible careers as doctors, lawyers, civil servants and academics who looked down on anything that didn't smack of meaning and effort. Eventually, some of us found that to be a burden.

One day, Steve Swaim, a small but powerful history student, good at wrestling, helped me to invent a character called Francis Coleridge. We thought that the name smacked of effort and meaning and, most important, it sounded 'English'.

We stayed up all night writing a phony lecture. Then we made up the names of some books this 'Coleridge' had written like 'Revolution from the Right' and 'The Summer of Malcontent' and 'Red Flows the Humber'. We announced that he was coming to lecture at Oberlin and we booked a hall. Then we said that he had been detained in Antioch, the highly liberal and liberated college in Southern Ohio, and prevented from speaking there. If you were prevented from speaking in Antioch, then you must be wild.

I was particularly interested in how intellectuals like Andy Maguire and budding politicos like Jerry Rubin, would take to this hoax.

Rubin was eventually thrown out of Oberlin and went on to become head of the yippie movement and at least one of the Chicago Seven, but while he was there he managed to upset everyone, particularly the President of the College, by writing a poison-pen letter, which they traced to his typewriter. Rubin had a roommate called Murray Cowan, and they stood out from the beginning.

It was a tradition for the freshman girls, all scrubbed and hopeful, to serenade the freshman men, all housed in the same dormitory, about seven in the morning in the first week of term. Rubin and Cowan did not like this tradition. Halfway through the second verse of the second song, they put heads out of the window and screamed, more or less in unison, 'Shut up or we'll piss on your heads'.

But when Francis Coleridge came to the campus, Rubin was all ears and bonhomie. I don't know why he fell for the hoax so thoroughly. Perhaps because liars always believe a good lie. Rubin claimed to have known Coleridge and to have read 'all his books'. Andy Maguire, a young man with an inordinate amount of poise, recommended the lecture to his wide circle of friends and admirers, all budding politicians.

We found a graduate student of Theology who had spent some time in England and gave him our speech, a mishmash of John Stuart Mill, Plato, Hobbes, Kierkegaard and Ruskin, which made no sense whatsoever.

A typical paragraph went like this:

'We are told that Man is born to be free, yet everywhere is in chains and yet the State of Nature, nasty dull brutish, one might say British, and cold is nowhere to be seen. Man must grasp the nettle of his own being, ignore his nothingness, and choose to be free. Yet at the same time he must involve himself in the body politics. He must engage and see himself as both separate and equal. He must ignore the shadows on the wall. Let me give you an example....' And on and on. Pure crap. Two hundred odd budding intellectuals came and nodded and took notes. It was very long.

Then we went out into Tappan Square. We wanted to get our graduate student who had played 'Dr. Coleridge' out of there and back to his lodgings as soon as we could, before he could be found out. We were delighted, but apprehensive. Tappan Square is large with many trees and the walk back to the School of Theology was a bit too long. By the time we had crossed the square, our secret was out and reported in the College newspaper as a hoax, not a lecture.

Andy Maguire was stunned into silence for a day or so. Jerry Rubin pretended that he had known all along. Steven and I were very pleased. It was the first piece of original theatre that I had ever produced.

Theatre at Oberlin

I began acting at Oberlin, which was a very good place to begin. It is also a very good place to end because people there were more than willing to say you were dreadful. Once, I was crossing Tappan Square on a very pretty day. A chap called Ed stopped me. Ed wore trainers and khaki trousers every day and had a beautiful girlfriend. I had never met him. I knew that he wanted to be a writer. He had just seen my performance as Rakitin in *A Month in the Country*. He begged me to stop acting and to reconsider any plans I might have for going into the profession.

'Please don't,' he said. 'It would be wrong for you and for the business.'

I like to think that he is teaching English somewhere, still wearing tennis shoes, taking groups of students to see my productions in New York and London.

Oberlin had a theatre called Hall Auditorium, which had been donated by Charles Martin Hall, the man who discovered the particular process of electrolysis, which produced aluminium. He achieved this while he was a student there. Some professor told him, in his first year of chemistry, that if he mixed enough chemicals together, starting with whatever he could start with, then he would end up with this ideal synthetic metal. So he did. Legend has it that by the time he reached his final year, he was rich. Certainly it didn't take him long.

Hall Auditorium was beautiful. Large and modern and comfortable. Every year, students performed about thirty shows there. The French Club, The Drama Society, the Breakaway Drama Society, the Opera Club, The Gilbert and Sullivan Society – all these groups would produce one or two shows a year in this theatre that from a production point of view was very nearly of professional standard. In one term, you might see *Pirates of Penzance, A View from the Bridge, La Boheme, Dom Juan* (in French) and *He Who Gets Slapped*.

Or, even better, you could be in all of them, which meant, for one thing, that you didn't have to see them.

My acting career began in a musical called *Haircut*. Not *Hair*, *Haircut*. I played the part of the village idiot who wore overalls and spoke thickly. I was wonderful. I say this because (a) I was, and (b) I never was again. I sang a song, which is something that I cannot do, and it went like this:

> **Just pretend that you're a windmill,**
> **Or a monkey in a zoo.**
> **I'm an elephant with a splinter**
> **I'm a hopping Kangaroo.**

My actions were suited to the words and on the bit about the hopping kangaroo, I hopped across the stage. Lots of people cried when I died.

A blind man, who also wrote it, directed *Haircut*. His name was Danny Silverstein and he was the gentlest man I ever met. I went to the auditions, hoping to get a walk-on part, and he liked me and cast me as the village idiot. He had a girlfriend who was much taller than he was and who told him everything. She was, as it were, his eyes but he was very much his own ears. He was a tyrant. Gentle, but tyrannical. Not a word could be missed. Nothing could be changed.

After my success in *Haircut*, I was cast in a two-handed scene for one of the drama classes. Then it was thought that I had a strong voice, so I was cast as The Duke in *Measure for Measure*.

That was a mistake.

I found the part of The Duke impossible. Long speeches about death and no one to talk to. The director, a sweet man called Stan McLoughlin, didn't help me much. He used to drink a lot and call evening rehearsals. This practice is not unknown in the professional theatre. Stan used these evening rehearsals for strange behaviour. For example, he would dance around breathing fumes over you and slap you. Once he danced around to show me how much lighter I should be, then he slapped me and then kissed me. It didn't help much.

By the time I had graduated to these larger roles, I was eating all my meals in a place called The French House or *La Maison Francaise*. This was a dormitory and dining room for about thirty female students. The idea was that male students of serious French or, in some cases, students of the most interesting young women in the University, would eat lunch and dinner in a large room in which no language other than French was permitted. I think that if you insisted on talking Russian, they would let you, because they were so pretentious, but in the main we were to speak only French.

Somehow or other I had found myself at what was called the English Table. This was a table where mostly English was spoken. I think the theory was that the people seated there spoke French so well, that they didn't need to bother any further, that conversations would be more delightful if they were held sotto voce. It was a table for minor rebels.

One member of French House, who didn't sit at the English Table, was Harry Rolnick, the drama critic from *The Oberlin Review*. He did not like my performance as The Duke in *Measure for Measure*. He expressed himself clearly and without fear of contradiction. 'Mr Rudman does not so much act the part of The Duke as declaim it. And, in his ill-fitting Friar's outfit, he looks for all the world like a pontifical penguin.'

One week after this review came out, the only review that the performance got or was ever likely to get, I was feeling down-hearted and I was walking towards the French House quite late on a warm spring evening, when one of the young ladies shouted to me.

'Rudders,' she called me. 'Is that you?'

'Yes it is.'

'You've got to find Carol. She's at the Arboretum. There's a fire drill. They'll find out she's out of her room after hours and there will be real trouble. Please go and find her.'

Now Carol, whose last name I withhold, was a very affectionate girl who was often not in her room after hours. In this instance, she was going to be in real trouble because it would be discovered. She might even be expelled. There would be a head count after the fire drill. I went running down to the Arboretum, which was an area favoured by affectionate girls and their friends.

'Carol,' I shouted. 'Carol, there's a fire drill.' I felt a bit of a fool.

I walked for about a hundred yards and started shouting again, 'Carol, Carol.'

A sweet voice chirped, 'Rudders, is that you?'

'Yes, it's me. You've got to get back to French House immediately. They're having a fire drill. You'll be in real trouble.'

Without a word, Carol climbed out from under the spirited youth she was with and ran towards French House. Before I turned away, I recognized her companion. It was Harry Rolnick.

It is not given to many men to have such sweet revenge on a drama critic.

Professors

But not all our time was spent lying in the long grass, producing plays, snapping towels and concocting hoaxes. I worked hard, exceptionally hard if you compare it to what I had to do at Oxford, and we had some excellent teachers.

There was Frederick Artz, the history professor, author of the widely read *The Mind of the Middle Ages*, and a charismatic teacher known for his witticism including 'You can lead a whore to Vassar but you can't make her think.'

Artz was also known for an incident that occurred in one of his classes. An attractive co-ed was sitting on the first row and laughing generously at all his jokes, smiling at him and, most people thought, being flirtatious. Suddenly he stopped mid-sentence, looked at the young lady for a moment and said 'Would you mind crossing your legs?' She was very embarrassed and did what he asked. 'Now that the gates of hell are closed,' said Artz. 'We may proceed.'

There was George Lanyi, a fiercely anti-Communist Hungarian who taught politics, especially international politics. He said many memorable things like 'The problem is not that the Americans and the Russians don't understand each other. The problem is that they understand each other too well.' And he taught us, and this proved helpful to me later, that the Labour Party in England is very conservative.

Then there was Professor J.D. Lewis, the Head of the Government department who, in one paragraph, explained the separation of powers in the American Congress. It went something like this:

'There is a cup of hot coffee. That is the will of the people as expressed in the members of the House of Representative who are elected every two years. Then there is the saucer, which represents the Senate whose members are elected every six years and who are therefore not so sensitive to popular opinion. What we do is to pour some of the hot coffee into the saucer and let it cool. Then we pour it back into the cup and then we have drinkable coffee. And we have a reasonable compromise between impulse and experience.'

Also, we had Professor Clive Holbrook who taught Christian existentialism with such zeal that many of us nearly joined up.

But the most inspiring was a quiet, unassuming man called Andrew Bongiorno. He was a specialist in both Milton and Dante and the most dedicated scholar I have seen at the five universities I have attended. I should point out that at three of those five, I only did a short course.

Bongiorno was a small, slim Italian American with a gentle demeanor and a razor sharp mind. He never made a joke. He never reprimanded a student. He never seemed to do anything except read Milton and Dante and lecture about them. Even Milton, in his hands, was fascinating and we listened carefully. His illuminations of Dante were mind-boggling and never to be forgotten.

But, in our last year, some of us were lucky enough to be accepted into his small seminar on 'The Principles of Literary Criticism.'

Of course, we thought, we are ready for this. Haven't we worked hard and read into the night for years? Don't we sort of speak French? Aren't we questing for knowledge? Finally, we thought, Mr. Bongiorno is going to become expansive and share with us chosen few the secrets of literary criticism.

Not at all. We were to go away and design a table.

A what? A table.

At our first meeting, he gave us an assignment. We were to imagine that there was no such thing as a table, but there was a need for something that does what a table does like hold plates and typewriters. It had to be a certain height, have legs and so forth. We were to write down what those needs were and what we had provided for each requirement and, more importantly, why we had chosen each feature instead of other alternatives.

We left, not inspired and delighted with insights and poetry as we had expected, but puzzled, worried and bewildered. However, it was Bongiorno and we did it. The following week we handed in the essays. He thanked us, put them in a small pile, smiled a little and then gave us our next assignment.

We were to go away and write a short story. He would provide the plot, which would be the same for all our stories. We could create the characters, the dialogue, the descriptive passages – everything – but we had to stick to the plot.

Wow, we thought.

Then he added that at every point in the story, at every choice we made, we were to write it down on a separate document and explain why we had made that choice. For example, why is her hair blonde? Why does he work on Wall Street? Why is she five feet five? We were to hand in both pieces of work the following week.

Are you beginning to get the idea? Artists make choices at every turn and to appreciate their work you need to know why these choices were made, especially if you don't like something or don't understand it.

This way of thinking is particularly helpful if you are directing a play when often, for one reason or another, you or a producer or an actor, thinks something could or should be cut. You have to think about it hard and try to work out why it is there. And, quite often, you don't cut it and when the play opens you are very glad that you didn't.

So, thank you Professor Bongiorno. Thank you Oberlin College.

I was sad to leave Oberlin but I looked forward to a life afterwards. I had read a lot, played a little, laughed occasionally and, as John Edward Williams, another Texan would put it, fallen in love with English literature.

Oxford, where I ended up next, was different from Oberlin in one significant way. Whereas at Oberlin the other students were more than reluctant to praise artistic ambition, at Oxford everyone seemed delighted to praise and encourage theatrical endeavor of any kind. Perhaps they were more confident of themselves and I certainly was.

Alphabetical Order by Michael Frayn, Hampstead Theatre 1975
with June Ellis, James Cossins, Bernard Gallagher, Billie Whitelaw
and AJ Brown. (Photo by John Haynes)

Clouds by Michael Frayn, Duke
of York's Theatre,
1979 with Felicity Kendal
and Tom Courtenay.
(Photo by John Haynes)

Schweik in Second World War by Bertolt Brecht, Nottingham Playhouse 1966 with Chris Hancock, Maggie Jordan, Vivien Heilbron, and Harold Innocent.

Donkey's Years by Michael Frayn, Globe Theatre 1976 Michael Rudman with A.J. Brown.

(Photo by John Haynes)

MB Rudman and Mrs Rudman, Dallas, TX, USA 1950.

MB Rudman entertaining troops 1942.

Amanda Shorthouse and Kate Risebero, Michael's daughters,
celebrating Tottenham Hotspur's win over Arsenal in the
1991 FA Cup semi-final at Wembley.

Felicity Kendal, Michael Rudman, Wolfe Rudman and Tara Rudman
circa 1984.

Oxford

Interview For Oxford

Time	3.00 p.m.
Place	The stairway outside the Principal's office of St Edmund Hall, Oxford.
Date	November 1960
Post	Student for a Bachelor of Arts Degree.

A young man in a jacket and tie is sitting on the stairs outside an office reading *Aesop's Fables*. A much older man opens the door.

'Who are you?', asked the Reverend J.N.D. Kelly, Principal of St. Edmund Hall.

'Michael Rudman,' says the young man, putting away the book.

'Should that mean something to me?'

'I have applied for entrance to the college. I have written to you several times and you have replied once.'

The young man is invited in. Questions are asked. Many of these questions touch on the life experience, particularly the sexual experience, of the young man. More surprisingly, before his eyes, the Principal goes through the young man's formal application to the college. He leafs through carefully prepared scholastic records. He casually reads out letters of reference, which, until now, the young man had thought sacred and secret.

'Michael Rudman is not a brilliant student, but he is a very good student indeed.' That from Professor Bongiorno, Head of the English department at Oberlin.

'I'll offer you a place to read PPE,' says the Principal.

'But I want to read English Language and Literature.'

'Yes. Then you'll have to take three years. And, at the end of it, you will have a second BA which will become an MA.'

'I only wanted to do two years.'

'Then it will have to be PPE.'

'I want to do English.'

'Then you'll have to see Dean Midgely. I know that he will like you. I like you.'

And the young man, after an interview with Dean Midgely and several hours of written examinations, is admitted to read English Language and Literature at St. Edmund Hall for the academic year beginning 1961.

For three years.

Paris

Between the time I was accepted by St Edmund Hall and October 1961 when I took my place, I had nine months to prepare. Nine months. Like all putative American exiles, I went to Paris where, for the most part, I played pool at the American Students and Artists Centre on the *Boulevard Raspail* and I spent a lot of time with the early DW Gottleib pinball machines all over the Left Bank.

France was my preparation for Oxford.

I was hanging around the Cannes Film Festival in 1961 watching Alan Ginsburg, very smart in a blue suit, hustling meals off wealthy film producers. I was getting to know people, especially the people who were around and about the Beat Poets. I became friendly with the actors in the film of *The Connection*. As a result, I was offered a job in Paris with the Living Theatre. I was an unpaid stagehand and for a week I worked in whatever capacity Judith Malina or Julian Beck thought necessary. They ran the company. I did a bit of hammering and I used a saw. I did some prompting and a great deal of going out for food and drink.

The Living Theatre insisted on presenting three productions in one week at the Theatre Des Nations and the last was the most complicated. It was Brecht's *Jungle of the Cities* and, along with Julian's highly complex set, came a sound plot that syncopated with most of the movements on the stage, no matter how small. There was a lighting plot to match. Julian also took the leading role.

Doing three plays in one week was difficult enough for a bunch of Americans five thousand miles from home, but Julian's set for the Brecht play made everything more difficult. It was made up of thousands of bits of wood, which we had to piece together in two all-night sessions. By the time we got to the technical run-through of this last play, the cast and staff were exhausted. The technical director, a young woman called Lee, was especially exhausted as she had fallen in love with one of the actresses. Her exhaustion took the form of a nervous breakdown and I was appointed technical director. I thought this strange as I had only been in the professional theatre for six days, but I took the job.

My principal task was to station myself in the lighting booth with a ginger-haired Frenchman who spoke no English and tell him the lighting cues, as they were handed down by Julian, when he wasn't working on the set or acting. This all went reasonably well. My French improved quickly. But at nine o'clock, an hour after the time announced for the opening performance, it was decided to abandon the technical run-through and go ahead and give a performance for the audience, most of whom were sitting in the auditorium already. It meant that there was no technical work possible on the second half and that we would all have to play it by ear. In my case, it meant playing it by eye as well because I was, suddenly, not just the helper to the operator of the lights, I was now the lighting designer.

There was a terrific fuss with the audience demanding that the show begin while we were still working on last minute things behind the curtain. Finally, someone went out and apologized on behalf of the technicians of the Vieux Columbier Theatre. Then someone had to go out and apologise for the apology because the stagehands had gone on strike as a result of certain slights to them in the first apology comparing them unfavourably they thought to workers at another theatre. When this was over, it was about nine-thirty and the audience was in no mood to receive a play about the evils of capitalism in Chicago.

I asked Julian what I should do about the lighting in the second half as nothing was planned and the electrician didn't speak English. He said that I should always read two or three pages ahead so that I knew what was coming and let the chap know generally what he should do. I should signal to him whenever the next effect occurred and he would probably be able to do it.

About half way through the second act, however, as I was leafing through the pages, staying about three ahead of the show, I came across the word 'Fire'. Never, I think, has that word had such an impact in a lighting booth. The stage direction read 'The entire city of Chicago bursts into flames'. How was this going to happen with ten minutes notice?

I started speaking French with my hands. I said '*Dans six pages* there has to be *un feu*'. The ginger-haired man didn't even blench. He said to tell him when. I said I would tell him. We were getting on very well by this time. He seemed to know exactly what he was doing. When we got to the appointed page, I said, '*Maintenant. Feu!*' and suddenly this man's limbs began to fly in all directions. It was an old fashioned lighting board with levers that pushed up and down in semi-circles. He managed to get one foot on one lever, and another foot on another, one hand on another and the other hand on yet another. I think that if he could have used his nose, he would have. The left arm went up, the right arm went down. The left leg went up, while the right arm went up with it. Then the left arm came down, the right arm went up. Then he put my left hand on one lever and left foot on another and gestured to me to push them up and down. I did.

After about two minutes of this, I looked out onto the stage from our position, which was on the side of the auditorium. 'My God,' I thought, 'the entire city of Chicago is in flames.' The next morning when we were at the airport getting ready to fly to Frankfurt, someone picked up a copy of *Le Monde*. The review was a rave. In particular they praised the lighting and in particular the fire in Chicago. Also, they announced that the Living Theatre had won the award for the best Dramatic Ensemble at the Theatre Des Nations.

When I got to Oxford, my experiences in Paris, especially the work with the Living Theatre, helped me to get productions for the O.U.D.S. and the E.T.C (Experimental Theatre Company). I rose quickly in those groups and by the middle of my second year, I was President of the O.U.D.S.

One of the first people to make himself known to me when I took over the OUDS was Jeffrey Archer. He seemed to be around every corner in his first year at Oxford. He was meeting people, running hard and fast, and he wanted to become an actor. At every opportunity, and there were several, he would ask me if I could possibly fit him into one of the OUDS plays. I said I couldn't find a way. but Jeffrey is persistent. Finally, I offered him the part of Mark Antony in a reading of *Julius Caesar*. This was the annual Michaelmas Term reading for the President to assess freshman talent. Jeffrey was delighted with this excellent role. He was less delighted when he learned that he would only be reading Mark Antony in the second half of the evening. But he was undeterred. He was certain that he would make his mark.

And, indeed, he did. As we drew to the end of a very long evening, Jeffrey cleared his throat, paused for a moment over the imaginary body of Brutus, and said in that loud clear voice,

'This was the roblest noman of them all.'

Roald Dahl and Patricia Neal

In the Spring term of my year as President of the O.U.D.S., people who were active in the real world of cinema and theatre contacted me for the first time. Roald Dahl and his wife, Patricia Neal, had enjoyed my production of *A View from the Bridge* and had been very impressed with the quality of the acting. They wanted to meet me. They lived in Great Missenden which, you might not be surprised to hear, is very near Little Missenden and every year Roald and Pat were active patrons of the Little Missenden Festival of the Arts which was based in the church.

Neil Stacy, who had played Alfieri in *A View from the Bridge* and I were invited to tea. We ate cakes and listened to glittering talk of Broadway and Hollywood and received many compliments on our fine ensemble work and our youthful talent. We were impressed. We were especially impressed when, having suggested a play for our visit to the Edinburgh Festival, Roald went to the phone and dialed 'Eli' in New

York. Eli Wallach and his wife, Ann Jackson, had done this play, *The Scarecrow*, off-Broadway recently and Pat and Roald were certain that it would be perfect for us to take to Edinburgh. I was grateful because I was desperate to find something good or, even, something that we could do.

Eli and Roald had a nice chat. It seemed long and expensive. The script was on its way. I was pleased. Then Roald got down to business.

He and Pat wanted us to produce the play that they were commissioning for their festival. It was a play about the life of St. Paul and it was to be presented in the church. Roald, it seemed, was a committed Christian.

A highly respected local writer, Ian Roger, was writing it now. What Roald and Pat wanted, and certainly Pat agreed with everything that Roald said, was for us, the same actors and the director whose work they had seen in *A View from the Bridge* to stage this play about St. Paul following on immediately from doing *The Scarecrow* at the Edinburgh Festival. We had only had a couple of cups of tea and some cakes, but already our entire summer was planned.

We agreed, in principle, and were invited to the European premiere of Pat's latest film, *Hud*, which took place for some reason in Aylesbury. Soon the script *The Scarecrow* would arrive sent by Eli. Soon after that, the script about St. Paul would arrive from Ian Rodger and we would cast it, hopefully rehearsing it during the day at Edinburgh while we were performing *The Scarecrow*.

Boy, what a mistake.

No one liked *The Scarecrow* except JC Trewin in the *Illustrated London News*. It was a strange, dated play, which read well and played badly. Then the St. Paul script arrived from Ian Rodger.

It was all duologues. The language was stilted. It was a chronological account of the life of St. Paul told by the character of St. Paul to his jailer. It was dire. It read like an interview in the Church monthly. Also, it was going to be impossible to stage in the Little Missenden Church, which had huge pillars. At least one third of the audience would be masked from the action at any given time.

I told all of this to Roald on the telephone, also saying that none of the actors wanted to do the play for all the above reasons and more. I was hoping that he would let us out of it. He was furious. I was apologetic.

He said that I had promised to do it myself. I said that I would of course keep my promise, but I couldn't force a group of amateur actors presently sleeping on the floor of a drafty hall in Edinburgh, performing in the evenings a duff play that he had suggested, to carry straight on, for no money, and rehearse another duff play for one performance in a church. He said they could all have five pounds. He said they had promised to do it. He told me in no uncertain terms that I had better go back to them and get them to agree. I said that I would find different actors. Anyone that he would care to choose. Local actors. I would keep my promise. He said that was impossible, that he wanted those actors, the ones had seen in *A View from the Bridge* and that I had better get them. I said that I would try.

I went back to them. I said that we could rewrite the play ourselves. Ian Rodger was more than willing. I said that we could change it in all kinds of ways, especially for the shape of the building. We could perform some scenes all around the church so that everyone could see something. I said that we had more or less promised and it was for a good cause. I mentioned the five pounds.

For some reason, when they heard about the five pounds, several of them agreed to do it.

We rehearsed in a ballet school far out on the Cromwell Road. Ian Rodger was more than cooperative. As we hacked his script to bits, making a fluid and fluent play for eight actors out of a static seated duologue, and tarting up the life of St. Paul, Ian went out for sandwiches and biscuits, absolutely delighted that this work was going on and, even more so, that his play was being done. He was a very sweet man. Also, he had read the script.

We rehearsed for a week, then all we turned up in Little Missenden for a working run-through in the churchyard at teatime on the day of the only performance.

As might be expected, *The Life of St. Paul*, in this version, was tending rather towards the sensational. We had decided to go for the evangelical side of his character and two scenes took place in noisy churches, the action spreading, with considerable shouting, to all parts of the 'auditorium'.

As we rehearsed the end of the play, which we had turned into a passionate argument between Paul and The Voice of God, I noticed that across a low fence from us, was a graveyard. In the dusk, I saw a tall stooped figure coming towards us. I turned back to the action and the dialogue, which we were now rewriting. I huddled with John Watts and Paul Howes, who were playing, respectively, The Voice of God and Paul. Then I asked them to do it again. This is what they rehearsed, at full tilt.

> **VOICE OF GOD: Saul, Saul, why doest thou persecute me?**
>
> **PAUL: No, No. My name is Paul.**
>
> **VOICE OF GOD: Saul, why doest thou persecute me?**
>
> **PAUL: No. No. No. My name is not Saul. My name is Paul and I HAVE BUILT THY CHURCH.**

I looked round in satisfaction after this very dramatic ending had been put in place.

'That's good, isn't it? Everyone?'

The actors were all pleased. The ending had panache and style and it made its point in a dramatic way. I looked further round. The tall figure in the graveyard was now near the fence. It was Roald Dahl and he was moving away and he was unhappy. He was stooped over a lawn mower, and he was pretending to mow the graveyard in the fading light.

After the performance that night, he never spoke to me again.

Joan Littlewood

It was the custom and practice of the two major dramatic societies to invite prominent theatre practioners, mostly directors, to speak for an hour or so in an informal setting and answer questions afterwards during which many of us tried to impress enough to possibly get a job after graduation.

We had George Devine (committed, straightforward and inspiring), Peter Brook (boring and not helped that the RSC insisted on the talk being tape-recorded), Michael Elliott (brilliant and charismatic) and William Gaskill (very interesting).

Then we had Joan Littlewood.

Joan, as she insisted we call her, mesmerized us for maybe an hour and a half. It seemed like twenty minutes. She told us about her childhood, her relationship with Gerry Raffles, her ways of working, her political convictions – not all doctrinaire – her disastrous experience with Peter Hall and the RSC – and her hopes and dreams. It was said of her in her heyday that actors would have followed her over a cliff if she asked. We would have done the same.

After the talk, some of us went to the Luna Caprese, our favourite restaurant. We were unaccountably happy and overstimulated. We talked about Joan without the slightest bit of undergraduate skepticism. We all wanted to be her.

Then she came into the restaurant.

Most of us sat there in awe and talked very quietly, but not John Heilpern. John was and is of the journalistic persuasion. He was not burdened in any way by awe and respect for his betters. He had an enquiring mind and an even more enquiring tongue. He wasn't afraid of anyone.

You won't be surprised to know that he has been until recently a drama critic in New York City.

After quite a bit of wine had been drunk at both tables, Heilpern leaned across to Joan and said, very loudly, something to the effect that her latest film, *Sparrers Can't Sing*, was crap.

Without a pause, Joan got up and came over to our table and sat down. She was intrigued by his criticism and the way it was made.

We all ended up at John's large house on the outskirts of Oxford. We stayed up all night. We told Joan our hopes and dreams. I attempted to impress by saying that both the RSC and the Royal Court had offered me jobs and I was trying to make up my mind. We told her everything. She had the gift of getting people to talk about themselves and we certainly all did that. Even though for three years we had all been together, worked together and slept together, that night we learned things about each other that we never could have imagined.

Then it was dawn and Joan had to go. We drove her to the station and waited with her. We had all run out of things to say and she seemed preoccupied. Eventually, the train arrived.

A small and now unprepossessing woman went up the step and into the carriage. Surprisingly, she turned and looked straight at me.

'Do your own job,' she said.

I am glad to say that, whenever possible, I have followed her advice.

PART 3

Success and Failure

The National Theatre

Interview For The National Theatre

Time	6.10 p.m.
Place	The corner office in the National Theatre with a good view of St. Paul's.
Date	March 1979
Post	Director of the Lyttleton Theatre at the National Theatre.

Peter Hall is wearing a black suit. The interviewee is wearing Chelsea boots, dark slacks and a cashmere pullover. The secretaries are wearing jeans.

There is some good-humoured conversation. Compliments are exchanged. Then.

'Why don't you come here and run one of these three theatres?'

A challenging question to be sure.

'I don't like the Olivier. I've never been in the Cottesloe. I love the Lyttelton. It's a great comedy house.'

'Then it had better be the Lyttelton,' concludes Sir Peter.

And it was. In a matter of minutes, my life changed so much that I am only now, thirty-five years later, beginning to realize how much.

When I got back to Hampstead, I sent Peter this poem by William Butler Yeats, which he had enlarged, printed, framed and hung on his wall:

The fascination of what's difficult
Has dried the sap out of my veins, and rent
Spontaneous joy and natural content
Out of my heart. There's something ails our colt
That must, as if it had not holy blood,
Nor on an Olympus leaped from cloud to cloud,
Shiver under the lash, strain, sweat and jolt
As though it dragged road metal. My curse on plays
That have to be set up in fifty ways,
On the day's war with every knave and dolt,
Theatre business, management of men.
I swear before the dawn come round again
I'll find the stable and pull out the bolt.

The Meetings

Before I tell you about the aims and ideals, the triumphs and the disasters, the stars, the directors and the writers at the National Theatre, you have to read about the meetings.

Yes, the meetings.

The first meeting I can remember was about the third that I attended. The Box Office manager and the Press Officer weren't there, so there were no big arguments. No, this was that select band of directors of the three theatres and, of course, the usual complement of secretaries and 'assistants'.

An assistant was a secretary who had been there for more than three months.

We were all provided with charts. Long charts with lots of little squares in different colours, signifying dates of rehearsal and dates of performances. With three theatres and over twenty shows in a year, you can imagine how complex these charts were. They covered eighteen months of planning, rehearsals and performances.

Harrison Birtwistle took a look at one and said, 'I know a bloke who can play this.'

At the early meetings, I was extremely busy. I was still running the Hampstead Theatre; I had two shows running in the West End and I was trying to plan my first year as Director of the Lyttleton. Six shows. Sometimes I left my charts at home.

Christopher Morahan didn't like it. He was a BBC man and a National Theatre man and he knew, and I think he was right, that it was impossible to keep up with the intricacies of, for example, allowing Paul Schofield two nights off every week when he was in two plays, and 'dark nights in the Cottesloe' and two press nights, and split previews and touring, and twenty-two week lead-in for the workshops, if one did not have one's chart.

At this particular meeting, Christopher asked me twice if I had my planning chart. The first time I smiled. The second time, about half an hour later, I looked at Bill Bryden as hard as I could. Then, ten minutes later, he asked again, rather like a headmaster, I thought.

'Michael, did you forget your chart?'

'No, Chris. I thought it was secret so I memorized it and ate it.'

Most of these gatherings were held in the Conference Room and most of them began at 9.30 a.m. They were called Early Morning Meetings. I couldn't understand why they were called that when to succeed or even stay in this business, you have to get up around seven and start work at 7.10. I learned later that they were called EMMs simply to distinguish them from Morning Meetings (casting, budget, programme, set, costume and planning) and from Evening Meetings (Associate Directors and long term planning).

Once, during an Early Morning Meeting, someone asked what Peter Hall thought of a particular subject. Peter wasn't there. Often he would be doing something else while the problems were being chewed up and solved, or indeed, created at the Early Morning Meeting. I had seen Peter by the lift at about eight-thirty and I said so, thinking that someone might go and find him.

'Hour dropper,' said Michael Hallifax.

The various characters that attended the EMMs had some things in common, like an ability to subsume their own aims and dreams to the collective aims and dreams of the National Theatre, and with that ability came a fierce loyalty. Most of us also had complicated personal lives, which were simplified and even purified by being inside a concrete artistic bunker for twelve hours a day.

One day, people were whipping themselves up into a kind of frenzy about the lack of loyalty of a particular actor who was causing a tremendous amount of trouble to the chart-makers and decision-discussers, which was that Early Morning meeting, which were us.

Michael Gambon was going to Stratford to play King Lear instead of staying with us to play Corialanus, as we thought he had promised. 'How could he do this to **us**?' and 'Where is his loyalty?' and 'Didn't he make a commitment?' and so on. The fact that we changed our minds on actors and directors and plays several times a week didn't occur to the communal mind that morning. The meeting-beast seemed almost to be moving towards some punitive act on the hapless Gambon, who was probably asleep, somewhere, happy in the thought that he would not have to struggle with Coriolanus. Voices were raised in anger, even in condemnation. 'How could he break his word?' was heard, and 'Doesn't he realize what *Galileo* did for him?' 'He made a commitment.' All heard amid the jangle of coffee spoons.

'Hang on a minute,' I piped. 'Didn't everyone around this table get married? Didn't we all promise to 'love, honour and obey'?'

The meeting-beast was diverted and went to devour some other subject, but soon returned to the hapless Gambon who was, of course, forgiven within weeks because of his talent, his hard work, and probably for keeping his word, for the most part.

Somewhere at the centre of the upset over Gambon, but never voiced, was our knowledge of how hard Peter Hall had fought and how many voices he had silenced for Gambon to play Galileo the previous year. That was the role that had lifted him to the top. Of course, it was Michael Gambon who actually played the part, so really he did it himself but at every meeting for weeks before rehearsals, months actually, many people said many times that Brecht was not 'box office', that Gambon was not a star, that it wouldn't pull it's weight in the repertoire and that people wouldn't come. And they kept asking Peter why. Why do it? Why not do it in the Cottesloe? Don't you know that Brecht is box office death? And the answer came back every time 'Because I promised him and because I think it will do well.' And he was right on both counts.

It would be wrong to describe Peter Hall as the 'Claudius' of the

National Theatre and only in a Peter Hall production would Claudius have the charm and intelligence, and indeed the talent that Peter Hall has, but one regular at our meeting was very like Polonius. His name was John Russell Brown and he was our in-house academic.

He was Head of the Script Department and the chief literary advisor. He had been an eminent Shakespeare scholar and had praised Peter's work very highly.

One morning, all the directors met in Peter's office, supposedly to discuss plays that we might do, but it turned out to be a session on Peter's current production of *The Orestia*. This was a magnum epic encompassing three tragedies by Aeschylus, performed in masks by an all male cast, translated from the Greek by Tony Harrison.

Peter was worried about one of the leading performances. He didn't think that the actor was going to 'get there' and he was seriously considering asking him to leave.

'But its going to be marvellous.' JRB had launched himself. 'It's going to be a great success. The tone and the muscularity of the production throughout and indeed each detail will simply ride over any weaknesses that you, at this stage, might see and indeed the rest of us, and I have seen it three times...'

'Three times?' we all thought. 'My God.'

'...and each time the whole becomes more and more clear and at the same time more complex, and I honestly believe that it is a production that will reclaim these plays for today and it will certainly be received, at least by anyone who gives it even a moments thought and, I daresay, even by the critics, as a kind of testament to Greek theatre and a moving *raison d'etre* of the subsidized theatre itself.'

'You're fired,' I said. Quite loudly.

I don't think that I have ever heard Peter Hall laugh so much. After all, I hope that I was a making a joke at my own expense as well. What were we all but borderline sycophants? Someone had to lead, and that was Peter, and the rest of us had to follow in our various ways, or leave.

Eventually, I left.

Unproduced plays, the ones that never make it to the starting gate, tell you a great deal about a theatre. For years, *Guys and Dolls* was one of these. Laurence Olivier nearly got it off the ground, then it languished. I got it to budget stage, which was also unfortunately heavy memo stage:

> **TO: MR**
>
> **FROM: MICHAEL ELLIOTT (ADMINISTRATOR)**
> **We can't afford it.**

I even had it cast. Warren Mitchell and Peter Straker were keen. No commitments of course. Then I went on a short holiday (four days) and came back to find that the official view had changed and that another director was doing it. Then I got another memo:

> **TO: MR**
>
> **FROM: MICHAEL ELLIOTT (ADMINISTRATOR)**
> **We can't afford not to do it.**

I didn't mind. Of course if I had known that Richard Eyre was going to cast it brilliantly with people who I thought were unsuitable and said so (big mistake, I was very wrong), and if I had known that he was going to have one of the biggest successes that the National had ever known, then I would have minded but not much.

Director of the Lyttleton

As Director of the Lyttleton, I was busy. One day I remember was particularly full:

- Filming starting early morning in Rickmansworth for the television version of my production of Maugham's *For Services Rendered*;
- Telephone calls all day from Peter Hall's office in which I was resisting a proposed revival of *The Caretaker*, which would actually be a stage version of a television production now in rehearsal.
- Getting back from Rickmansworth in time to meet Lillian Hellman's agent about *Watch on the Rhine* at the interval;
- Avoiding an Associate Director's meeting.

I managed all but the last. If you think that Peter Hall always gets what he wants, then you really should have tried Harold Pinter.

By the time I got to the Associates Meeting, the Associates were well oiled. I had been overdosing on coffee and Perrier, and I was wearing a suit one size too small due to the huge breakfasts that I was getting on the film set. I had managed to charm Hellman's agent a little and it looked like we were going to be able to have the cast we wanted without going to the Supreme Court. I was in a good mood. I was feeling successful. I was wrong.

When I say well oiled, I mean that some of them could fairly knock it back. Bill Bryden wasn't averse to a bevy. The Peters, Hall and Wood, liked a glass of wine. Gillian Diamond could be relied upon. Harrison Birtwistle did not drink tea, and Harold Pinter insisted on having a bottle of whisky. Of course, he didn't drink at all, but he insisted on having it at the meetings.

My being Director of the Lyttleton was a problem to them. I was doing things like *The Elephant Man*, *Translations* and *Measure for Measure* set in the Caribbean, and even a new play by an unknown writer. Also, I was refusing to do things like a Peter Nichols play about middle-class, middle-aged marriage and sex, a Doctorow play about the same thing and now I was resisting this television version of a revival of Harold's play *The Caretaker*.

Harold was sitting silently when I arrived. His silence was nearly as eloquent as one of the pauses in one of his plays. Most of the others were talking loudly at the same time. There was a good deal of 'I didn't join the National Theatre to be...' and 'I don't think that anyone around this table...' and 'Yes, I'd love another glass of red wine.' This was before tight road traffic laws and tight entertainment budgets. I think it was Peter's idea that a little buffet, a little wine and the ideas would flow, and indeed the criticism, which, let there be no mistake, Peter thrived on. He used it well.

Soon the attack shifted onto me. Why weren't we doing this production of *The Caretaker*? What possible reason could there be? Wasn't Kenneth Ives a marvelous director and wouldn't it absolutely pack the Lyttleton? And wasn't Warren Mitchell, Ken Cranham and

Jonathan Pryce a dream cast? And wouldn't it be already rehearsed because of the television production? And wouldn't that be marvelous for the budget? And wasn't the play a modern classic? And wouldn't it pack the Lyttleton? And on and on.

I listened to all this, making very few comments, but being reluctant enough for the others to get more and more agitated. They were surprisingly unanimous, probably because this was something that both Harold and Peter wanted, and surprisingly vocal.

Harold said nothing.

Then the others started up again. I got slightly cross and nervous but I stayed quiet, nodding a lot.

Then Harold spoke.

'Are you going to do this play? Are you?'

I answered at length. Being Harold and being impressive, he required an answer. I said, respectfully, that it was, of course, a fine play, probably it was a minor classic. But, I said, it had been revived many times and quite recently in London, with Leonard Rossiter, directed by Christopher Morahan, who was here tonight and that, of course, the cast was excellent and the director excellent, and it was a wonderful play, but wasn't it wrong for the National Theatre to present what amounted to a stage version of a television version of a play that we had all seen many times? Wasn't it a bit early for a major revival?

There was a long pause. Finally, Harold spoke.

'I don't give a fuck what you think.'

That was pretty eloquent and Peter Hall was even more eloquent when he invited me into his office early the next morning and told me I was putting up too much of a barrier to writers who were important to him and to the National Theatre and *The Caretaker*, in a new production, would do extremely well at the box office. I said it wouldn't. I was wrong.

The next morning I caved in. I rang in from Rickmansworth and the production went on.

Harold and I became quite friendly later when I extended the run of the play beyond the dates those heavily committed actors were willing to do. We replaced them with Norman Beaton, Oscar James and Trey Foster; three black actors who were at the Lyttleton in my Caribbean

Measure for Measure. I know Harold was pleased. On the night the critics came to it, he asked how I thought it would go.

'I think it's too good,' I said. That time I was right.

The Actors

Some actors were reluctant to join the National Theatre. They had reasons: some political, some artistic, some financial. They had to be lured.

John Alderton is a complicated chap. He and I had a long meeting before he joined us to play Estragon in *Waiting for Godot*. I had been frank with him. He had a reputation as a leader and I wanted to direct the play. He was agreeable to that. He told me that the only reason he often took over projects himself, as well as being the star, was because that was the kind of show he was usually involved with, especially on television, but with this, a great play and a company show at the National Theatre, of course, I would be the director.

That isn't how it turned out. Always in directing a play you reach a point where you have to start directing it, instead of merely presiding over the rehearsal. That is, you have to say something like: 'This is the play we have, you are the actors we have, and, after all the different things that we have tried, I now know that what is going to make this combination work is such and such.'

Then you have to start persevering with 'such and such', encouraging 'such and such' and increasingly often, insisting on 'such and such'. This makes some actors cross.

It didn't make Alec McCowen cross. Alec was playing Vladamir. He had been directed many times by good directors, so he went along with it. It didn't make Colin Welland cross. Colin was playing Pozzo. He is a writer himself and he knows. But it made John Alderton cross.

He began to flinch every time I spoke. He would say things like 'Can't you wait until the end of the scene?' and 'We haven't learned the lines yet. Can't you wait until we have learnt it before you start telling us what to do?'

I pointed out that Alec and Colin had learnt it and none of us wanted to wait. He got even more cross.

Finally, one afternoon, when he was being especially touchy, I suggested that we change directors. I said that I couldn't replace him because he was a big name and people had already booked but that being at the National Theatre, we could, after all, get another director.

That seemed to stun John Alderton.

Years later, people tell me that he rang them at midnight, or came round to their office after rehearsals that day, and said, over and over again, 'He says he will get another director. What do I say to that?'

Apparently most of them advised him to get on with it because he did. And he was marvelous. Good reviews and everything. He even kept the beard. On the first night, he said 'Thank you for casting me in the part.'

Warren Mitchell

But not all actors have to be lured to the National. Warren Mitchell was anxious to go there and, contrary to all expectations was fairly easy to direct. Before he played Willy Loman, we met. I told him that I thought the man and his family were Jewish. Warren disagreed. It was the first of at least one hundred good-humoured arguments. This one took place in his garden in view of his tennis court and his swimming pool. It was pleasant. He conceded.

Then we met at the National Theatre. He was impressed. Warren rebels against the British establishment, but loves having a place in it. I asked him for three assurances before I finally offered him the part: (1) that he would never complain about the money he was being paid; (2) that he would do what I asked without argument; and (3) that, in playing the part, he would never shout. He readily much agreed to all three.

For the few months in rehearsal and on tour, he (1) constantly referred to how low his salary was; (2) argued with everything; and (3) shouted on practically every line. Until the first performance in Leeds, when he was excellent and stopped complaining.

I gave Warren a great deal to say about who played his sons. In fact, he really did the casting of Stephen Greif and David Baxt, both of whom he had worked with, just as later when I directed the play on Broadway, Dustin Hoffman went out and got John Malkovich for Biff, whom he rightly saw as a future star.

Whereas Warren wanted to shout all the time, Stephen would hardly ever raise his voice. We looked for a way to accommodate that reluctance into the scheme of things, but sometimes he had to shout, I thought, and so did the others. One scene climaxed with a short row between Biff (played by Stephen) and David Bext. David was shouting and upset. Stephen remained almost comically calm. Finally, in frustration, I told Stephen that he was going to have to shout the last line of the scene, and then rush off. The line was 'Help me, Hap. Help him' He had to do it. The scene and the play needed that button.

He said that he wouldn't. He couldn't.

I said that he would have to. And he could.

He said that he wouldn't.

I asked why?

'I just wouldn't do that. I just wouldn't shout in a situation like that.'

'But this isn't you, Stephen. This is Biff Loman, son of Willy Loman.'

'I don't care, Michael. I just wouldn't shout. I wouldn't do that.'

'But Stephen,' I said. 'No one has ever written a play about you.'

That seemed to work.

Warren and I knew each other well enough before we did *Death of a Salesman* together, and afterwards we became close friends. He introduced me to Tottenham Hotspur, a subject on which we never argue. We did, however, have a further disagreement.

We played tennis together often and were fairly evenly matched, depending on fitness and work schedules, and we never had a dispute over a line call. Until one day.

Warren had his own court and he was very bossy. It had to be swept and the lines marked before and after each match. Warren prepared the lunch and you had to eat it. Usually, it was very good. Certain bathrooms were not to be used. Fine. He was house-proud and it was his house, his court. And he was generous and hospitable.

But one day it went wrong. I arrived on time. I changed in the proper bathroom. I went onto the court. We swept it carefully, especially the lines. Then we started to knock up. I thought I was hitting the ball particularly well and I started going for the baselines. I noticed, with satisfaction, that Warren was rushing to the net in the knock-up. On days when he was feeling frisky and rushing the net, I could rely on winning two extra games. Then he retreated to the baseline. I tried a few topspin forehands. I thought they were better than usual and I noticed Warren frown. Then I hit a beauty into the corner. No comment. He didn't go for it. Remember, this was the knock-up.

'Warren?'

'What?'

'Was that good? Wasn't that good?'

'No.'

'No? It wasn't good?'

'It was out.'

'I'm sorry, but I know that was good.'

'It was out.'

'No.'

'Yes.'

'No, it wasn't.'

'It bloody well was.'

We didn't speak for three months. Then he invited me to a Christmas party. We never quarreled again, but then we never played tennis again.

The Writers

The writers whose plays I direct are usually the people who I get to know best. With Samuel Beckett it was only a slight acquaintance, but I felt close to him.

Because I was directing *Waiting for Godot* at the National, I met him for one hour in a hotel bar in Paris one morning in September, the year that he died. My memory of him is fragmented.

1. The first impression was coloured by what I had been led to expect, but it also became the lasting impression; an extremely courteous Anglo-Irish gentleman, living near the centre of Paris near several hospitals, and meeting old age with grace and irritation.

2. The two things he seemed most interested in, to do with me, were my son, about to be born, and my interest in sport. Whenever I mentioned Jacob or tennis or golf, one of the

warmest smiles you have ever seen broke out on his face. It was almost a grin and almost audible.

3. In his youth, his family had their own lawn tennis court, and in the summer he spent 'all day playing golf by myself with two balls, one ball competing with the other...'

4. Hmm, I thought. *Waiting for Godot?*

5. His eyes were of the brightest blue with what I could swear were black crosses in the middle of them.

6. Just as the play, *Waiting for Godot*, seemed to want to break dramatic moulds, so he seemed resistant to any conversation about accepted theatre practice such as actors delving into the biography of characters, or costume representing the history of a character.

7. He displayed a surprising acting ability when he quoted lines from the play or sang either of the two songs. I suspect that like many playwrights, he was an actor manqué.

8. He remembered well the Abbey Theatre in the late twenties and thirties. Apparently, he would go once a week and sit in the one-and-sixes, which were just to the right or left of the three shilling seats in the balcony. He was full of praise for the Abbey's history.

9. I am more and more convinced that the play is like one man's dialogue with himself, rather like the two Byzantium poems of Yeats. A dialogue inside a poet's head.

Arthur Miller, I got to know much better. In my opinion, our production of *Death of a Salesman* in 1979 contributed to a major revival of interest in his work.

I believe that all playwrights have two ways of behaving. One, when their plays are being done in the commercial theatre, and another, quite different, when their plays are being done at the National Theatre. I won't dwell on the way they behave in the commercial theatre. None of us, I think, are seen at our best when there is money on the table. But, I can tell you that Edward Albee, Alan Aykbourn, Arthur Miller, Neil Simon and Bernard Pomerance behave like angels when they are given

National Theatre budgets for sets, enough time for rehearsal, enough consultation on casting, enough interviews in *The Independent* and all the other 'enough's' that they get at the National. The only exception was Lillian Hellman who spent at least two thousand pounds of everyone's money screaming down the phone at me.

'Trust? Goddamnit, I hate that word. Don't talk to me about trust.'

'We're giving you the best actors we can find, Lillian. Peggy Ashcroft is a very good actor.'

'I want STARS! I want Maximillian Schell.'

'He's in Germany. He's German.'

'No, he's not. He's Swiss. Get him. Get Maximillian Schell.'

'I can't.'

I couldn't. But, eventually she was won over by an enormous set, Susan Engel, Peggy Ashcroft, David Burke and tea with Mike Ockrent.

If my theory about the behaviour of playwrights is correct, which it is, and if it is accepted, which it could be, then we have another strong argument for the existence of major subsidised theatre. There are roughly four principal participants in the production of a play: the play-wright, the director, the producer and the leading actor. If the playwright is behaving sweetly, then you can be pretty certain that the others will and you are on your way to a well-ordered and successful production.

Arthur Miller, for example, arrived at the National rather apologetically, said a few words to the cast, watched a few previews, gave a few notes and left. It was nice. He had, of course, made his views on casting well known a few months before. Neil Simon was the same, except that he, perhaps more worried than Arthur about his reputation in *England*, came to some early rehearsals as well as a preview of *Brighton Beach Memoirs*.

One morning, Neil did not like one of the actors, especially in one particular scene, which was not a very good one. I won't say which. He made it quite clear that he didn't like the performance, both in notes and unhappy looks to me. What happened taught me something important.

After Neil had done a lot of 'This isn't the right way to play this' and I had done a lot of 'Maybe we could lose a few more of the lines,' all in whispers, and he had done a bit of 'Maybe it's just that the actor isn't

American,' and I had found out that there was always trouble with this part and that, in fact, the first person to play it had been sacked in a car park, then we came down to a kind of confrontation in the rehearsal room, with the entire cast watching and pretending not to watch. It was a very quiet confrontation but that is what it was. Neil, with his glasses in one hand and a script in the other and me, desperately wanting a cigarette. We were close together at a table, far enough from the others for Neil to speak without being heard.

'I don't think this is going to work out.'

I thought that I knew what he meant. I looked at him.

'She'll never get there.'

I said nothing.

'I know that you don't fire actors in a place like this, the National. I know you can't do that.'

Again, I said nothing.

I didn't say 'Yes'. I didn't say 'No'. I didn't say 'Can we discuss this over a drink?' I merely looked at him with what I hoped was an agreeable expression and said absolutely nothing. It seemed like five minutes. Then the conversation moved on.

What I learned was that it is sometimes possible and also very useful to keep your mouth shut. I was able to do so for two reasons: (1) I was terrified, and (2) I knew that the actor was going to be good in the part. It was a hard part to play and it needed time and care taken and, indeed, when the production opened, there was no doubt that her performance was one of the best in the show.

This happened only because we were working at the National where there was plenty of time and a good atmosphere and where the playwright was a little bit in awe of and grateful to the organization itself.

The Directors

Working at the National Theatre also meant working with other directors on a more or less equal footing. Although I was Director of the Lyttleton, I was more alongside the others than over them. For one thing, they were senior to me, many of them, and certainly better known. It was refreshing to have lunch with them, the ones who weren't on special diets. Directors seldom get a chance to socialize with each other. Bogdanov was once very nice to me during a difficult period when our paths crossed in Washington; and Frank Dunlop magically appeared in the seat next to mine during the third act of a West End flop just to tell me that I had done a good job. But, generally we don't meet.

At the National, however, we would find ourselves standing behind each other in the queue in the canteen, meeting together every Monday, Wednesday and Friday morning about planning, and every Thursday morning about plays and generally would be in each other's way at almost every turn. We even started dressing the same; trainers, jeans, pullovers and longish hair. I suppose if we had been in the city, it would have been bowlers and pin-striped suits.

One day I was enjoying the opportunity of asking another director about the more pedestrian problems of our work. I was chatting to Peter Wood, a prickly character like most of us, and I was saying how difficult I found it to answer an actor when he asked on the first day of rehearsal if he could go to the dentist at, say, three o'clock on the Thursday of the third week of rehearsal.

Peter said, 'I always say they can go and they still think I'm a cunt.'

At this point the curious reader will want to ask a question: 'Why ever did you leave the National with all those people saying and doing funny things including you? Why?'

I can explain.

Peter Hall never used to say anything important outright. I don't mean that he hid things. Far from it. He is an honest man. But, if it was important enough, then it came out in dribs and drabs. It would be mentioned in a director's meeting, mooted in an Early Morning Meeting, budgeted in a planning meeting, chewed over in an Associate Director's meeting, and so on. By the time it came out completely, you thought it had already been going on for three years and it was time to congratulate everyone.

But when he began to change the system at the National from one different director running each of the three theatres to one of streams or companies of actors moving among the three theatres, I caught on quickly that I was about to lose the best job in the English speaking theatre. I didn't need to see forty-three budgets, two-hundred memos, or to be taken to dinner twice to understand what he was doing. Once was enough.

I began to question the wisdom of change. I wrote to him. He wrote to me. He invited me to his office. He was nice. That didn't worry me. As Nancy Meckler said of someone, 'I've seen that side of her before.'

He said that he wanted to change the system. I said that I liked it very much the way it was and thought it was right for everyone. He said that he didn't have enough flexibility. He didn't like the possibility that I might not do a new play by one of his favoured playwrights. I said that I understood that and it might happen, but not often. He said that the actors wanted to move among the different theatres. I said that some actors didn't and that all good actors resisted any system they were in, and that if they didn't they would be soldiers or accountants or even directors. He said that I could be Deputy Director. I said that I didn't want that. I asked him to think about it. Then he said something really good:

'This is what I definitely want. And I don't mean definitely. I mean definitely.'

It isn't the same without the gestures showing the different meanings of the word, but you get the idea.

And so I left.

Eventually . . . .

Broadway

Interview For a Broadway Production of *Death of a Salesman*, May 1981

This consisted of lunch with Robert Whitehead, the producer, Arthur Miller, Dustin Hoffmann, the leading actor who was also, with Arthur, the principal producer, and myself.

Arthur and I wore casual clothes, Robert wore a suit and Dustin was in a dress, pretending to be a woman. He was filming *Tootsie* at the time and wanted to practice his womanly wiles and see if he could fool the people who worked in the restaurant. He knew them quite well and dined there often in his normal clothes.

They didn't recognize him.

The conversation was lively and pleasant. This was the first time I learned that in America acting is a competitive sport. Dustin said that on the opening night in New York he wanted to be so good that every actor in the City would hate his guts.

Death Of A Salesman

Once you have arrived on Broadway you and your show are already almost certainly a success. Then you collect awards, give interviews, drink Harvey Wallbangers and either date or avoid dating. But getting there, convincing all the necessary people that you deserve to be there, sometimes requires several months of hiring and firing, long nights in provincial hotel rooms, three or four hundred doughnuts and a fair amount of shouting.

After a fairly sweet rehearsal period, mainly taken up with compliments being hurled back and forth, and long lunch breaks, the Company of *Death of a Salesman*, our playwright, a large technical staff and I arrived in Chicago. We were all in the hotel and ready to work on the stage when we found out that the set, consisting mainly of a small wooden house placed on a turntable, was not fitting onto the stage. Apparently the stage at the Blackstone Theatre in Chicago slopes down at the sides and none of our highly trained and highly paid technicians had known this. To this day, I wonder how that could have been but I never dared ask. As Katy Woodhouse says 'Don't complain about it; deal with it.' That's what directors do.

So we decided to have a run-through without scenery on the mezzanine of the Hilton hotel near the theatre in one of those banquet rooms that even Willy Loman would have avoided. All of us, except for our leading lady, who had not been able to recover from the one hour flight from New York and had repaired to her hotel, a much nicer hotel, The Ambassador East, which film buffs may remember from *North by Northwest*. It was sort of uptown. We were midtown old Chicago: seedy, uncomfortable and no bright lights.

The run through didn't go too badly, considering, but one of my notes to Dustin Hoffman afterward triggered a response that could only be called extraordinary.

I suggested that he should pause and look at a suitcase with a tennis racquet strapped to it before asking, pathetically, about a family that had their own tennis court. I knew that it would get a good laugh and prick any bubbles of sentimentality, as it had for Warren Mitchell at the National.

Dustin didn't like the idea.

I asked him to try it.

He thought the suitcase was in the wrong place.

I said that we could move it.

He said the furniture was in the wrong place.

I said that we could move it; a little bit.

Then he exploded.

'You are trying to turn us into a bunch of fucking English actors.

What are you anyway? I can't stand this. I can't stand it. We are American actors. I'm not John fucking Gielgud. You can't do this to us. I won't put up with this. You need therapy. Your sex life is a mess. We are American actors. I will not turn my head like some little dancer to some fucking suitcase at some fucking count of one-two-three. This is insane.'

This and more for about six minutes. Then there was quite a pause. Then a couple of others joined in.

I was calm. I tried to explain what I was after and why. The other actors were on different sides of the issue. John Malkovich was on both sides. I can't remember what they said, but they all talked a great deal.

Then, Dustin exploded again with more of the same. Then, after a further tirade, there was a long pause after which Dustin apologized. He said he was sorry. They were all in a state because the set didn't work and we couldn't get onto the stage and we opened in two days, and because the leading lady was in her hotel room probably drunk. He was sorry.

'Don't worry,' I said. 'Forget it. It's a great play and it brings out great emotions.'

'No,' said Dustin. 'I do this on shit.'

We all laughed together.

On tour we had arguments and screaming and even humiliation, but we also had a good time. The rehearsals on the road were superb. As Dustin and Malkovich mastered their roles and as Dustin relearned stage acting (he had been away from the theatre for thirteen years) he grew in confidence and his sense of humour returned.

One Friday night in Washington, I went to see the show without telling the actors that I was in. I was appalled. Since the Tuesday, Dustin had changed almost every move. Every inflection was different. He was crying wherever possible, shouting far too much, and all this to a packed house at the Kennedy Center. The response was lukewarm. Fearing the worst, I slipped into his dressing room afterwards. I forget which film director was in that night. I think it was Cimino. I approached him cautiously. 'Hi, Dustin, the show was…'

'Oh my God,' he said, 'were you out there tonight? Oh, no. It was

The Changing Room by David Storey, Long Wharf Theatre, New Haven, USA 1972 with Michael Rudman, John Lithgow and cast.

Morosco Theatre, NYC, USA 1972.
(Photo by Martin Schaffer)

Harlequinade, The Browning Version, Lyttleton Theatre 1980 with Alec McCowan and Geraldine McEwan.
(Photo by John Haynes from the National Theatre Archives)

Brighton Beach Memoirs by Neil Simon, Lyttleton Theatre 1986 Neil Simon and Michael Rudman in rehearsal.
(Photo by John Haynes from the National Theatre archives)

Death of A Salesman by Arthur Miller at Lyttleton Theatre 1979
with Warren Mitchell and Stephen Greif.
(Photo by Michael Mayhew from the National Theatre archives)

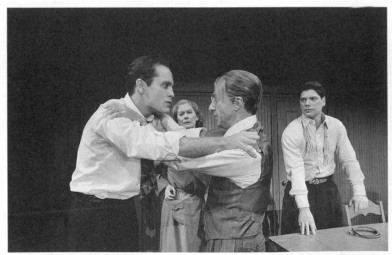

Death of a Salesman, Broadway, NYC, 1984 with Dustin Hoffman,
John Malkovich and Steve Lang.
(Photo by Inge Morath © The Inge Morath Foundation/Magnum Photos)

Fathers and Sons by Turgenev, adapted by Brian Friel, Lyttleton Theatre
1987 with Ralph Fiennes and Robin Bailey.
(Photo by Michael Mayhew from the National Theatre archives)

Jane Eyre Sheffield Crucible 1993
with Jack Shepherd and Emma Fielding.
(Photo by Gerry Murray)

Measure for Measure, Lyttelton Theatre
set in Caribbean.
(Photo by John Haynes)

Grapes of Wrath
Sheffield Crucible 1992
Charlotte Cornwall,
Neil Stuke and cast.
(Photo by Gerry Murray)

Old Masters by Simon Gray at Long Wharf Theatre, New Haven, USA 2011 with Sam Waterston and Brian Murray.
(Photo by T. Charles Erickson)

Jake Rudman and Fred Washington, 2012.

Chin Chin by Francis Billetdoux, Theatre Royal, Windsor 2013 with Simon Callow.
(Photo by Robert Day)

terrible. I hated that audience. They hated me. I did everything wrong. I hated them. How much of it did you see?'

'All of it.'

'Oh my God. Come back tomorrow. You'll see. Come tomorrow afternoon.'

The next afternoon, at the matinee, Dustin was perfect. The difference was astonishing. Everything was as we had rehearsed it and better. Afterwards, in his dressing room, relatively empty because it was a matinee, he embraced me. Dustin is probably the best hugger in the western world.

'Was that it?' he demanded.

'Oh boy, yes,' I murmured, still glowing from the performance and the hug.

'That's what you'll get on the first night in New York,' promised Dustin.

And that is what we got.

Dustin was beginning to relax and enjoy himself in Washington and it is no exaggeration to say that he loved feedback. Also, he liked meeting young people.

He had a nephew in Washington who was sort of working for him. Dustin had a knack of getting people to work for him. Of course, he paid them, which is a help.

The Kennedy Center is a long building containing three theatres. The foyer is huge and for *Salesman*, the queue for returns was so long that it stretched to the very end of the building.

'Get out there,' he said to his nephew. 'Go right down to the end of the line and find somebody who is waiting for a ticket and tell her that we have picked her out to come backstage and watch the show from the wings and have a drink with me afterwards.'

So the nephew went into the foyer and went right down to the end of the queue and found a young woman who was hoping for a return. She was German and spoke English very well and the nephew explained what he was offering her. She was delighted.

That evening she watched the show from the prompt corner and at the end she was ushered into Dustin's room for a chat.

But there was a problem. She was from a small town in Germany that didn't have a cinema. She had never seen a film and she had never heard of Dustin Hoffman. I have often wondered whether or not she enjoyed the play. Certainly the conversation afterwards was brief.

Hamlet and *The Changing Room*

Broadway never had any problem being Broadway until the movies came along. Then Broadway was no longer 'the cat's pyjamas' or 'twenty-three skidoo'. Now, in some ways, it became just another stepping-stone to a film career. This has meant a gradual weakening of the seed, especially where playwrights are concerned and, yes, directors, and of course actors, who can make as much in two weeks on a movie as they can in a good Broadway run.

I had a difficult evening the night after my production of *Hamlet* opened at the Lincoln Center. We had some very good reviews, including *The New York Post*, which called it in a big headline 'The Best US *Hamlet* Ever' and I was feeling pretty smug. David Rabe and Jill Clayburgh had invited me to a party in an apartment somewhere downtown, so I squeezed into my brown velvet suit and went. I was hopeful of meeting lots of *glitterati* and talking to them about the problems of putting Shakespeare on Broadway. Unfortunately, there was no one in that golden crowd even remotely interested in talking about me, or Shakespeare or England, or any of my current strong points. They were talking deals, and where to live on the coast, and agents and everything that movie people quite rightly talk about. There was no one there that I even recognized, let alone knew. Jill Clayburgh wasn't there. In my zeal, I had arrived too early. So I left, feeling rather depressed.

I was staying at the Royalton, then a cheap hotel across from the Algonquin that Audrey Wood had put me onto when I did David Storey's *The Changing Room* a few years before. She lived there and preferred it to the Algonquin for price and security. I liked it too, but it didn't have a restaurant and the Algonquin buffet, a delicious collation of stuff, was always guarded by a long line and a headwaiter who looked like a well-dressed Hungarian drill sergeant. That night, I had a look inside the Algonquin lobby, glanced at the long queue, considered bribing the headwaiter, thought better of it, and left, but then I changed my mind and turned back. Damnnit, I was hungry. I was wearing a suit. I had just directed *Hamlet* on Broadway. I decided to wait my turn in line and took my place about halfway along the lobby behind some very strange people from Seattle.

I was alone in New York. I was ten pounds overweight. I didn't know anyone below 72nd and 2nd. No one wanted to know me because I wasn't in films, and I couldn't even get a table at eleven o'clock at night in the most famous theatrical hotel in the world. I was dejected.

At this point, the Maitre'd came up to me and asked 'Are you Michael Rudman?'

'I beg your pardon?' I asked, hoping to hear it again.

'I think you are Michael Rudman and I would like to show you to one of our best tables.'

Fairly calmly, I followed this adorable man past the admiring glances of the strange folk from Seattle and the others in the queue, to the best table in the centre of the famous dining room. 'I must explain,' said the Maitre'd. I thought that he spoke a little too loudly, but not nearly loudly enough for me. 'The grandson of our owner, the owner of the Algonquin, is a student at Princeton and he is doing a dissertation on your work, beginning with *The Changing Room* by David Storey and he has asked me to seat you at this table and...'

At this point, I wanted to ask him to start again because I was sure that there was this young couple in the corner who had not quite heard all of this, but as I was having a hard time believing it I let him go on.

'Because he is such a devoted student of your work, he would be grateful if you would let him sit with you for a few moments after your meal and ask you some questions.'

'Certainly,' I said and ordered cold roast beef with a Waldorf salad and a very nice red wine.

Really, I was having a hard time focusing on this but it seemed possibly, remotely plausible and the chap did have quite a few facts right. I enjoyed my meal tremendously and it was only spoiled, although not entirely, by the grandson when he did arrive. What he really wanted was information about David Storey, Christopher Hampton and NF Simpson, three Royal Court dramatists on whom he was indeed writing a dissertation. Mainly what he wanted was their telephone numbers and he was quite right to choose me as I had them all, since we were all members of the George Devine Award Committee. He seemed very nice and I gave him the numbers.

After *Hamlet* had been on Broadway for a while, I thought I had better go back and see it. There had been a couple of cast changes and I was worried that Walter Kerr, the only important critic to dislike it, would have too much effect on Sam Waterston, our *Hamlet*. He had written, at length, that Sam was too angry and not lyrical enough.

I was right to go, though wrong to try to make the trip over and back in one weekend to return for rehearsals of an improvised musical at Hampstead. I drank too much on the plane and I was hungover and in a bad temper when I arrived at the Lincoln Center the next day for the matinee. It was awful.

Sam's verse speaking had became noticeably beautiful, at Mr. Kerr's urging, and a few gentle words to Sam seemed to sort that out. But, like some directors, I vented my irritation on the crowd.

Why were they so low-keyed? Why couldn't they bring excitement to the play scene? What was wrong with their costumes? I managed to control my temper, but I was discussing the problem at length with one of the small part actors who liked talking to directors. He was sympathetic.

'I just don't understand it,' I said. 'I leave here for four weeks and this is what happens.'

'I know, Mike. It's terrible.'

'All of the activity is gone from the first play scene. Everything we did at rehearsal has been cut in half.'

'I know.'

'And what on earth is going on just before they burst in on Laertes's re-entrance? What are they shouting out there?'

'Where, Mike?'

'Outside in the corridors. When they are meant to be shouting '*Laertes* shall be King. *Laertes* King.' What is going on?'

'You really want to know?'

'Yes. I want to know.'

'You want to know what they're shouting?'
'Yes. Please tell me.'
They're shouting '*Laertes* shall be King. Burger King.'
No wonder it sounded wrong.
Directing can be humbling, after all.

Auditions

The auditions are the first step in trying to get to Broadway.

For *Death of a Salesman*, we auditioned for four months. Yes, four.

For *The Changing Room*, Arvin Brown at the Long Wharf, cast most of the company for me and the rest of the casting took place with a few auditions and many telephone calls. One actor, diminutive and wiry Jake Dengel, rang me about the part of the burly masseur played in England by Brian Glover.

'Look, Jake,' I said. 'You sound great on the phone and Annie Keefe (the stage manager) says you are super to work with, but if you are only five feet six and thin, how can I cast you as a man who makes his living massaging people and is bound to develop huge muscles?'

'Yes, but I'd be an interesting item in the locker room.'

I cast him. He was wonderful. He made John Lithgow (who won a Tony Award) look even bigger and even better. He was always busy but never distracting.

For *Hamlet*, which I did twice for Joe Papp, the auditions were more normal. If seeing sixty girls for 'Ophelia' in one afternoon is what you call normal. I rebelled at that and the next afternoon there were only twenty. One of them, downstairs, afterwards, in the lobby of the Public Theatre, came up to me. I knew her from England.

'I'm sorry about that,' I said. 'Such a crush.'

'Well, Michael, am I going to get the part?'

'I don't think so. No. I really want someone dark and serious.'

'I suppose a fuck is out of the question?'

She wasn't joking.

Wanting someone dark got me into trouble of a different kind, the kind of trouble you have with yourself when you realise ten years later that you have made one of the biggest mistakes of your life.

There was this girl: tall and blonde. I thought maybe I had met her before, but couldn't place her. Joe Papp kept going on about her. 'She's going to be a star. She's going to be a star.' They say that all the time, I thought. But I wanted someone dark who could be strong and, when she goes mad, frighteningly intelligent. I wanted her to stage Polonius's funeral with dolls and look as subversive as possible, as subversive as Hamlet. Really, it would be better if she were dark.

But Joe Papp kept on at me. I met the blonde girl. She read for me. Quite good, I thought, but not complex enough. I went to see her in a play. She was good but still not right for Ophelia. Papp was furious. She's a wonderful actress. She can play any part. Papp's assistant casting director was furious. She's going to be a star. Still, I held out and refused to cast her. I was proud of being strong. I said 'No'.

Her name was Meryl Streep.

Many years later she offered me a part in a film (see 'Cinema Blank' chapter), but people close to me said I shouldn't do it. I don't know what they were worried about. I have proved that I can't act. I thought it was very gracious of Meryl, if I may call her that, and it is only one of the reasons that I see every one of her movies.

I do have a good memory, but the name of this next chap escapes me, and you would never have heard of him. But, his story should be told.

I was auditioning the crowd for *Hamlet*, the supers, the actors who were paid one hundred and ten dollars a week and would virtually be walk-ons. They would swell the numbers in the play scene and play *Fortinbras's* army. American Equity allowed you to have about fifteen of these people.

One afternoon, I was seeing scores of them. I don't know how many. They would come in, do a bit of Shakespeare, maybe an improvisation, and go off, never to be heard of again. But every once in a while you would meet someone good. This chap was certainly the best.

I said to him, after he had recited his pieces and messed around a bit, that he was excellent.

'Thank you, Mr. Rudman.'

'I have hardly ever seen a better audition.'

'Thank you. I thought your production of *The Changing Room* was terrific.'

'You read that scene really well. Really well.'

'Thank you.'

'I can offer you the job right now, right here. I have no doubts.'

There was a pause. I thought we were all a little hushed by the dramatic impact of my gesture. I imagined this actor's brain was swelling with the thrill of being offered a part on the spot by an eminent, transatlantic director in a Shakespeare play.

Not at all.

'I'm very sorry, Mr. Rudman, but I won't be doing it.'

'Why not?' Was I a bit sharp?

'I'm a school teacher, you see, here in the city and I couldn't manage most of the rehearsals and some of the performances.'

'Oh well,' I said. 'That would be difficult. Missing performances.'

'I guess we'll just have to forget it.'

'I guess so. Do you mind if I ask you a question?'

'Not at all.'

'If you aren't free to do the job, why audition in the first place?'

'I like acting. It's the only acting that I get to do. You see?'

I saw.

The Producers

Getting to Broadway, the difficult bit, means dealing with a particularly American phenomenon: the Broadway producer.

It isn't easy to do Shakespeare in America. The actors are torn between being English, like the Royal Shakespeare Company which they admire, and playing the parts downright American. It is important to urge them to be American and to find a framework to enable this.

When I directed *Measure For Measure* (with Kevin Kline and Andre Braugher) in Central Park, we set it in an Americanized Caribbean island country. That worked well. With *Hamlet* we had a non-specific military state with hints of Nixon and Dean Rusk. It wasn't wonderful, but some of the acting was special; especially that of Sam Waterston as Hamlet and John Lithgow as the Player King.

But the *New York Times* review was excellent, especially for me and Sam. And, Joseph Papp, who was known for his quick, incisive decision-making (ha ha), deliberated for two months, including a two hour long distance phone call with Sam, before finally taking it into Lincoln Centre where it received respectful notices. I see no need to mention that one critic wrote, 'Mr. Rudman has elevated miscasting to an artform.'

That the show worked at all was a minor miracle. Joe cut two thirds of the set six weeks before rehearsals and Santo Loquasto, the designer, and I had to do a lot of scenic tap dancing to come up with anything halfway decent. Joe said the cuts were because the musicians' strike on Broadway had severely cut Box Office receipts for *Chorus Line*, but I think it was because he couldn't make up his mind what he thought of the production.

But Joe was passionate about the play. He was in love with it. He believed that *Hamlet* should be done every year on Broadway. And he had some unusual ideas including doing it with a female actor playing the lead and giving her the line *It is I, Hamlet the dame....*

My first experience of Joe came at a matinee of *A Midsummer Night's Dream* in the Forum Theatre at the Vivian Beaumont in the Lincoln Centre, where he was Artistic Director for a few years. I was about to direct *Hamlet* and I'd been invited over to do some casting, and of course I had to see his company perform *A Midsummer Night's Dream* in the afternoon. There was a delay in starting for the single reason that Clive Barnes, the all-important critic for *The New York Times*, wasn't there. Joe and his co-producer Bernard Gerstein were dashing round looking for Mr. Barnes. There was a tremendous amount of whispering and gesticulating, quiet shouting, and ringing Trish, Mr. Barnes's wife, and asking if anyone knew where he was and why he was so late. Then it became apparent that Barnes was not going to appear for this Sunday matinee, especially organized for him, and that his review would not appear in *The New York Times* as was hoped and planned but rather there would be a review by Mel Gussow, the dreaded second-string critic who, even if he liked it, couldn't make it a hit.

Finally, everyone went into the auditorium except Mr. Papp and myself. I was hiding behind a pillar. In his agitation, he went to two of the coffee ladies and said something about the way they served the coffee. I couldn't hear what he said, but it was quite intense and powerful. They looked at each other, amazed that this great man should speak to them on this subject. Then he rushed into the auditorium. The doors shut behind him and the coffee ladies were left. One turned to the other and asked, 'Do we have to take this shit?'

That is what many of us ask about many producers.

Producers are an ever more numerous sector of Broadway. As the years pass, their numbers increase in inverse proportion to the number of plays produced. *The Changing Room*, my first Broadway show, had four producers, three of them women. Now they could number ten or twelve.

The sole male among *The Changing Room* producers was one Charles Bowden who was last heard of producing a phone-in joke service, and who had one supreme virtue. He knew Tennessee Williams very well. One night he invited David Storey, our playwright, and myself to dinner to meet Mr. Williams. Tennessee told us a story. He told it towards the end of dinner in a lazy, sweet southern accent:

'Well, I was in London and of course it was arranged that I should meet Rudolph Nureyev. I was invited to a cocktail party and sure enough he was there and I was delighted to meet him. When I was about to go home, Rudolph said to me 'would you like to go home in a taxi or would you like me to give you a ride?' I said I would very much like for him to give me a ride. When we were in the car, Rudolph asked if I would like to go back to my hotel or if I would like to go to his apartment. I said that I would be delighted to see his apartment. When we got to his apartment, he said to me 'would you like to sit here in the living room or would you like to go into the bedroom?' I said that I would very much like to see his bedroom. As soon as I sat down, Rudolph took off all his clothes whereupon I said 'Rudolph, you have the most beautiful body I have ever seen, but I do not wish to make love to you.' Rudolph seemed very pleased and he sat down too. Then I said that of all the novelists I admired, I most admired the Russian novelists. That Dostoevsky and Tolstoy were my favourite writers of that genre. And I said that Russian music was the music I liked most of all and that Tchaikovsky and Shostakovich were particular favourites of mine. And that of course the playwrights were the very best I knew. Indeed, no dramatist in my opinion, could compare with Chekhov, Turgenev and Gorky. And he said,

'What about the painters?"

David Storey

David Storey is a remarkable man. I choose that adjective carefully. It is a word he often uses to praise work. It is reserved, enigmatic and low key.

When he saw our production of *The Changing Room* at the Morosco for the first time, he said it was 'remarkable.' We didn't know if that meant he liked it very much, but we were pleased. After he had been with us for a while, we began to realize that, although he could never be anything but loyal to Lindsay Anderson's original production at the Royal Court, he found quite a lot about our work to admire.

Most of all, he liked the energy bordering on desperation of the American actors. Like the characters of the play, who were impecunious working men in a small town in the north of England, playing a dangerous and violent game for some scraps of money to feed themselves and their families, the American actors were not far off the poverty line themselves. And for these actors, there was no regular television work, as there was for English actors of that period, and, most important, there was no welfare state. No safety net for serious illness or even pregnancy. Many of our actors were married, but few could afford to have children. The process itself was too expensive and the wife couldn't afford to give up work.

So, David saw in our actors and the way they were playing their roles, desperation similar to that of the characters in the play.

But, the rugby songs that our people were singing in the bath worried him. In England, they had sung *My Way*, which of course they would. But in New York, for all kinds of reasons, they were singing bawdy songs we had found in a book of rugby songs. The bath was offstage but, for the sake of reality, I had insisted, as had Lindsay in London, that we build an actual communal bath with hot water offstage just as Rugby League players would have. This contributed a lot to the spirit of the scene and the bawdy words, some of which the audience could hear, helped to make the scene energetic and enjoyable.

For example, they sang one familiar childhood song with very different lyrics.

Instead of singing:

They're changing the guard at Buckingham Palace
And Christopher Robin went down with Alice

Our men sang:

They're changing the guard at Buckingham Palace
And Christopher Robin went down on Alice

David wasn't at all sure about that but he let it go. It was permissible, but not 'Remarkable'.

David didn't spend all of his time in New York watching his play. He did socialize quite a bit. Sometimes I took him to *Elaine's*, the fashionable and enjoyable water hole on the Upper East Side frequented by writers, artists, actors, politicians and policemen. Surprisingly, he liked it a lot.

One night, after the show, we were at a big round table peopled by all kinds of arty types. After about half an hour, I noticed that David had changed seats. And then, a little while later, he had changed seats again.

He was working his way around the whole table asking questions, getting everyone's life story and everyone's hopes and dreams. I think that's what real writers do.

I'm glad to say that I have remained friends with him. Every year we send each other a Christmas card and we used to have an annual dinner at a small Italian restaurant in St. John's Wood. Unfortunately, David has had health problems recently and the dinners have stopped. But, the card he sends is always amusing and, quite often, complimentary.

Nudity

Before rehearsals of *The Changing Room*, I had foreseen only one problem. The nudity. The play requires fifteen young men to take off all their clothes. There is no way round it. It is the changing room of a Rugby League football team and not only must they be nude, they must flounce around, as men do in those places, with no modesty false or otherwise.

I wondered how I would approach this issue with the cast. I had heard that Max Stafford-Clark had once come to rehearsals completely nude himself. I sincerely hoped that I wouldn't have to do that.

In the end, I didn't even have to mention it. The first character in the play to undress completely was positioned downstage left and played by Rex Robbins, a character actor of considerable repute, with a very deep voice, five children and huge testicles.

When we came to run the first Act, which was early on in rehearsals, Rex knew all his lines, as did most of the others, and he simply undressed completely. The others followed suit as it were. They took off all their clothes, moved around with no embarrassment, and put on their rugby uniforms. But George Hearn forgot one of his moves and never got upstage to where his uniform was placed so he was stuck downstage centre, bollock naked. He didn't flinch. He stayed there for about twenty minutes until he found a way of reaching his clothes.

There was never any awkwardness after that. Indeed, towards the end of the rehearsals, when the actors were coming out of the bath completely naked without a trace of modesty, they would hang around waiting for their entrances, throwing a rugby ball around.

I believe that being nude on stage liberates an actor and gives him confidence. After all, what they want most of all is to be accepted for what they are.

However, one small issue came up.

An actor called Steve who played tennis, replaced John Cazale who had left the cast to do a movie, so we arranged a match at an indoor court about half an hours drive from New Haven. He played quite well.

When we are changing, Steve said he had a worry and it was to do with Annie Keefe, the stage manager. Annie was a very attractive, hard-working young woman with a terrific sense of humour. She was the only woman in a room filled with testosterone and bawdy humour and appeared unfazed. I'm pretty sure that she was enjoying both the work and the nudity, but she was cool. Apparently this made her even more attractive, especially to Steve.

'What if I get a hard on?'

I said I didn't understand.

'Annie is gorgeous,' he said. 'And I'm standing there naked right near her. What if I get a boner?'

I suggested that he cover it with a towel, as he would do in the circumstances of the play.

Death Of A Salesman Again

Producers can be a big help, when pushed.

Dustin Hoffman and Arthur Miller tried to fire me. Yes, imagine that.

Two weeks into the casting of *Death of a Salesman*, Dustin and Arthur rang up the producer, Bob Whitehead, and told him that they could no longer work with me. I had shouted at Arthur Miller.

What?

Yes, I did. A little.

An actress called Martha, I think, had just recited one of the speeches from *Death of a Salesman* as if we were her therapists. It went on for forty minutes. It was dire. It was slow. There were terrible pauses. We were all in a foul temper. It was hot in New York City. There were four of us trying to cast a play. We had already seen ten unsuitable actors that day. Then Arthur said that what we really should do is look at a tape of Mildred Dunnock playing Linda in the original production. I shouted at him that we had enough on our plate. Dustin had been shouting all week, but not at Arthur Miller.

Next day, they rang Bob and said they wanted to get rid of me. This was three and a half months before rehearsals. But Bob said 'no'. I couldn't believe it. He was the producer, but he only had ten per cent of the show.

Bob said 'I'm not gonna fire Rudman. I've seen Rudman's production of *Death of a Salesman* and so have you. Dustin saw it twice.

If you get rid of Rudman, then I go too.' This was the producer talking. Do you believe it?

They didn't fire me. Dustin's lawyer was brought in from California. We had a meeting. Dustin gave a long speech that would have worked well at General Motors or ICM. We were all buddies again and actually did rather well.

The Changing Room Again

Now to end this chapter, I'm going to return to the production of 'The Changing Room' for a cautionary tale.

The play opened on a Thursday night in New Haven. The all-powerful critic for *The New York Times,* the aforementioned Clive Barnes, was there.

His review, which came out on a Sunday morning began with 'The best in American theatre was to be seen last night at the Long Wharf Theatre in New Haven.' Within minutes, at least ten Broadway producers and those pretending to be producers were on their way to Connecticut. The theatre had performances on Sundays.

This review meant that I was in a strong bargaining position when my agent was doing the Broadway deal. Her name was Phyllis Wender. She was a tough lady, who, it was said, wouldn't cross the street to see a play but would drive through sleet and snow to Maine in the middle of the night to read a good contract by candlelight.

I was in my tiny office at the Traverse earning £20 per week, when I had a brief conversation with her on the phone about the deal. She said they were offering a fee of $2500 (a reasonable sum in those days) and two and half percent of the gross box office takings. I said, 'Fine and billing the same as the author.' I hadn't really thought about it. That was the phrase that I remembered from a contract I had once read. It was pretty standard in England.

There was a slight pause and Phyllis said, 'I'll see what I can do.'

We now cut to a few months later. It was about two in the morning and I had been playing some night tennis indoors in Brooklyn with Bob Steinman, an old friend of mine from Dallas AZA. He brought me back to the hotel, The Piccadilly, which I had chosen because it was next door to the theatre, The Morosco, and cost only $12.50 a night.

As I got out of the car, Bob said, 'Look at that' and pointed up to the Morosco marquee. There, in letters about three feet high, it read 'The Changing Room' and right below that, in letters the same size, it read 'DIRECTED BY MICHAEL RUDMAN.'

What had happened was that the producers had no stars to bill in a cast of mainly journeymen actors and beginners and the only 'name' was David Storey. On the other side of the Marquee, in the same lettering, it read 'BY DAVID STOREY.' This was pleasing at the time, especially in front of a boyhood friend. But I had a lot to think about and I never even noticed it again until months later when I was in the city putting replacements into the cast.

I had been in Ma Bell's, a café in Shubert Alley across the street from the Morosco. On my way out, I saw A.J. Antoon and Jason Miller, the director and author of *That Championship Season*, which was at the Booth theatre and had won most of the awards that year. I knew these two guys from a party in London.

Thinking I was being funny, I sidled up to Jason and whispered to him, 'Are you the pothead who won the Pulitzer Prize?' But, he had no time to answer. Before he could speak his wife, looking up at the marquee of the Morosco, said, in what I thought was a very loud voice, 'Who the fuck is Michael Rudman?'

The Collected Play of Michael Rudman

I was on holiday from a busy schedule at the National. I was in an extremely good mood one morning and I had an idea for a play. I thought I would write up the ideas in a few minutes and give it to Mike Leigh. He could then improvise it into a play like *Abigail's Party*. But the person I was on holiday with tended to sleep late and I tended to wake up early, so after about five days and a lot of coffee and cigarettes, I had written one third of Act 1. I decided to write the play myself.

It was called *Short List* and it was about a committee that meets regularly to choose the most promising playwright of the year. It was a subject I knew a great deal about having been on at least three of them myself. Also, I knew about committee meetings; from the National, from my B'Nai Brith Youth Organisation in the States, from Hampstead and the Traverse. I knew about meetings.

I wrote the first act easily and enjoyed it, especially the revisions and the cutting, which I did with relish and contempt as I was throwing out, as I saw it, the work of a vastly inferior writer who could not complain.

Then I put it on David Aukin's desk at Hampstead Theatre. I put the first act in a brown envelope, addressed to him with a note: 'I thought and thought what I could get you for your fortieth birthday and I decided that the one thing you needed and wanted was the first act of a new play by an unknown playwright.'

The next day I had a message from David.

'It's very good. You are a playwright. Where's the second act?'

Of course, I had already written the second act. I was keeping it back (i) to give David a shorter read, and (ii) because it wasn't as good as the first act. I had, after all, learnt some tricks from playwrights at the National. I gave him the second act, immediately, hoping to impress him.

Normally, David takes an eccentric position on anything important.

For example, when I reached the first nadir of my life in 1993, I outlined all my problems to David: financial, marital, and professional. He asked good questions sometimes helpfully interjecting. But mostly he listened. After about an hour, he stroked his beard and said with a faraway look in his eyes:

'Well, Michael, I suppose you'll have to make the ultimate sacrifice.'

'What's that?' I asked.

'You'll have to take up smoking again.'

Being David Aukin he had lots of criticisms of the second act of *Short List* and gave me a beautiful piece of advice: I should listen to his criticisms, follow his lead, but not write a thing for three weeks. Most playwrights either rush off and rewrite too much, too soon, or rush off and find themselves unable to follow the producer's suggestions. Three weeks is a good period of time to assimilate criticism and a useful gestation period. After two weeks, I actually looked forward to working on the second act and I improved it greatly, though probably not enough.

What is it like to temporarily switch from being a director to being a writer?

It's like what I imagine it might be like to change sexes: it certainly isn't worse, but it is very different. Whereas the director is a powerful person whose opinions are noted, the writer is someone that the actors attempt to ignore and often do, with some success. It's almost a necessary part of the actor's function, to get away from the playwright and to let the director help him to find what it is in him that can be joined to the writer's creation and brought to the stage in an exciting combination. The playwright, on the other hand, usually wants the actors to be, as much as possible, vessels in which he gives his original, and sometimes personal, thoughts and feelings and experience to the audience.

So, there is a healthy tension between actor and playwright. It's more than puzzling if you are used to being always listened to, as I was, and suddenly find that no one, not even the director, seems to have the time to hear anything you have to say.

One day, near the opening at Hampstead, I had rewritten huge chunks of the second act, for the third time, and was still waiting, as far as I knew, for anyone to read them, let alone tell me what they thought of them. My heart beat quickly when Mike Ockrent, the director, came up the aisle during a technical rehearsal and said:

'Michael, can I talk to you outside?'

I rushed outside with him and waited. Did he like the new stuff? Did Ian McKellan like it? Was it 'in' or 'out'? He said,

'You know that Italian play that Ralph Richardson is going to do at the National?'

'Yes,' I said. 'I turned it down.'

'I'm doing it.'

'Good luck.'

'How much do you think I should ask?'

Nothing about my precious rewrites.

Mike Ockrent, and two of the actors, Ian McKellan and Bernard Hill, were honest in their criticisms to say the least. I had been going to rehearsals as much as they would allow, which wasn't very often but on one occasion I wormed my way in and I was trying hard to look and sound like a playwright.

There was a tremendous amount of discussion about one particular section of the first act, and the result of it was that Mike took me aside and said, 'Look, Michael, Ian and Bernard don't think it's funny enough.'

'What isn't funny enough?', I asked, affecting the stern, implacable manner of Bernard Pomerance.

'This section,' said Mike and he pointed to it. It was quite a big section and it was very early on.

'It seems pretty funny to me,' I said, trying to sound definitive and yet co-operative, like Arthur Miller.

'They don't think it's funny at all and they want you to rewrite it.'

'Fuck 'em.' I said, trying to sound like Harold Pinter.

'Just go away and make it funnier, Mike,' said Ockrent. I hate being called 'Mike', even by a 'Mike'.

So I did go away and I thought how on earth can I do this? This isn't fair. Who are these people? I went back to my flat, which was 365 yards from the Hampstead Theatre and got into a bath. Immediately I got this wonderful idea. The idea was so good that I put some of it into verse. And it was much funnier.

I saw far too many of the thirty odd performances of *Short List* and every time I saw it, there was a playwright next to me or behind me. They all came to have a look. Playwrights whose work I had produced, playwrights whose work I had not, famous ones and aspiring ones, male ones and female ones. None of them liked it very much.

I was surprised as I was clearly no threat to them. The more successful playwrights were nicer.

Harold Pinter said 'Rich text'. Michael Frayn wrote me a complimentary note. I rang him.

'Thank you for the sweet note, Michael.'

'It's really very good, Michael. I am most impressed.'

'Reluctantly impressed?', I asked, quoting from his favourite play *Clouds*, by Michael Frayn.

'Not at all. I am thrilled. And Claire loved it. We were delighted.'

'Well, thank you. Thank you very much.'

'Are you writing another one?'

'I've already written it.'

Slight pause.

'Really?'

'And I've got Felicity to play the lead.'

'I'm coming round to break your fingers.'

I knew it was a joke.

I learned a fair amount about writers in my brief sojourn as 'the playwright'. I learned, for example, to be nice to them and to take them out to dinner a lot and not to talk about myself as much. And, as a result, they have been nicer to me.

But mainly I learned about actors. I learned that Ian McKellan is good because of his voice and his talent and his brain., but also because he gets the other actors together twenty minutes before every performance to 'get into' the situation of the play for each show. And he puts up with no rubbish. Also, as the play takes shape, he is the one you tend to write for because he can learn and perform text that is dense and funny. And he does it quickly.

But most of what I learned about actors, I learnt on the night of the final performance of *Short List*. I knew that they were planning to call me up before the audience and I pretended to discourage it but I made damn sure that I was there and in a good position to get onto the stage.

Ian organized it. And I did go up and I gave a little speech. It didn't get a very big laugh. But then the audience started clapping, all smiling and looking at me. I was bathing in a pool of warmth and congratulations. One hundred and fifty-eight people were smiling at me and clapping for me all at once and I was there in the middle of it.

'Oh my God,' I thought. 'Imagine getting this eight times a week. This is why they do it.'

At that moment, I understood actors a lot better.

Cinema Blank

The world of cinema has to had to wait a few decades for my first film and is still waiting, not counting the ever so slightly filmed version of my National Theatre production of *For Services Rendered*.

The principle reason for my career in the cinema being a blank is my inability to communicate with these communicators. Put more simply, the men and women who run film companies never seem to like me very much. I have met them on the beaches and in the taxis. I have eaten curry with them, played ping pong with them, served them tea in my home, dined with them at Elaine's and even Manzi's, although in that case the guy didn't show up.

Once I was introduced to David Beagleman in Elaine's.

'This is Michael Rudman. He's directing *Hamlet* at Lincoln Centre.'

'*Hamlet's* been filmed eight times.'

What kind of answer was that? Later that night, I introduced Mr Beagleman to one of his nieces, whom he had never met.

I once, and only once, got into an argument with Arnold Schwarzenegger and his wife. One of them would have been enough. It was in Elaine's at the favourites table and I was holding forth. I hadn't had a drink, but I was holding forth. I was maintaining that it was not 'tragic' that a young man had failed to ice-skate to the best of his ability in the Winter Olympics in Canada because his sister had died of cancer. Someone said it was 'tragic'. It was very sad, I said, but not tragic. Mr and Mrs Schwarzenegger said that it was tragic. Mrs Schwarzenegger became more than angry with me when I said that 'tragic' events involved a great man (or woman, for goodness sake) who, through some major flaw in an otherwise excellent character, had fallen to his or her ruin. I pointed out that Aristotle had said nothing about teenage ice-skaters.

She was livid. How dare I explain such a thing to her? The implication was that she had probably got three A's for Aristotle in Humanities 237 at Yale. Then she stopped talking and Arnold got up. Now, when Arnold Schwarzenegger gets up, he truly gets up. This man is as big as a house and he isn't all that tall. He said that they had better go to another table. For the rest of the evening, people bought me drinks for my bravery, I think, and because I did not get up.

I've never had the diplomacy for the film world. I believe they call it 'schmoozing' now. In theatre, generally, they like you to be honest, as long as it is about their work. (While being honest, it is best to steer clear of questions of beauty or romance.) Even Dustin Hoffman, who must have hated me at times, used to say 'The thing with Rudman is he's always right.' It was like some kind of illness. But, it doesn't work well with film people always to be right and I hope that all aspiring cinema directors will take note. You cannot stop short at an ordinary amount of flannel and flattery. You've got to keep shoveling all day long until you reach the top, and then you'd better shovel even faster.

Clouds

Money was a big problem with my best film idea, which was Michael Frayn's *Clouds*. I had directed it twice on stage. I thought it was a great idea. Small cast. Perfect material for the cinema. The only trouble was that it was set in Cuba. Cuba? How on earth does one get a camera into that strange, fortress of a little country? Even a brownie? How does one film there? I tried and failed. I didn't fail as badly as others who became so committed to their 'project' that they tried to build Havana elsewhere, but I did fail.

My trip to the Cuban Embassy was an omen.

After long telephone conversations and a great deal of 'research', I managed to get a lunch arranged with the Cuban Cultural Attaché to the London Embassy, Snr H Ricardo. Apparently, he liked Chinese food, which seemed fair enough, so I booked a place in Victoria for lunch in order to begin the long process of getting permission to film in Cuba.

The film was all about Cuba. Even more, it was about people writing about Cuba. It really had to be done there.

My secretary arranged a car and a driver as there is nowhere to park anywhere near the Cuban Embassy. Also, I thought I should impress Snr Ricardo even if he was a Communist. The driver arrived at precisely 12.30 p.m. wearing a grey suit. He was a tall, good-looking, bespectacled man who looked familiar. I asked him, politely, if I knew him. He said, 'No, sir'. We walked down the Mews to the car. The car was also grey and rather handsome, not too grand, and there was a copy of *The Independent* on the back seat. I was impressed. A cheap but classy car.

Partly by way of conversation, I asked the driver again if I might have met him somewhere. After all, I do get around quite a bit.

'No, sir,' he said..

Then, as we pulled away and we drove past Panzer's, the delicatessen, about one hundred yards from my office, I said to this chap.

'Look I'm awfully sorry but you look just like the man that works in there…'

'I am that man,' was the reply. 'I am, in fact, your greengrocer, Mr Rudman.'

Of course, everyone in the movies tells lies. And why not? We are not paying them all that money to be truthful. We are paying the writers to make things up. The actors pretend to be someone they aren't. The producers pretend that they have the up-front money when they don't. The distributors say they will pay up-front money when they won't. And the directors and the producers pretend they don't know that the others are pretending.

No wonder the drivers lie.

Lying is the necessary lubricant of the film business, and the weird thing about people who do it is that they always assume you are lying too.

I was once in a sauna with a man we shall call Sam who says that he 'produces' movies. Now this a fairly straightforward lie because virtually anyone who can pay for lunch and smoke a cigar can 'produce' a movie in the sense of putting a deal together or putting up some money or getting someone else to do that and then selling the deal on to some other producers.

Sam and I had been in this sauna together for four and a half minutes and we began to talk and he said that he had been to see *Clockwise* that night. I said, 'Oh, I had dinner with Michael Frayn last week.'

'You know him?' asked Sam.

'Yes, very well. I've directed three of his plays.'

'Really?'

'Yes.'

'Do you remember the names of any of them?'

Harry Saltzman

I had two meals with Harry Saltzman, who was one half of the producing team of Broccoli and Saltzman who were responsible for the early Bond films.

The first meal was at Langhan's Brasserie and was not remarkable for anything except for an observation I made on leaving the restaurant. I noticed that Harry's car was parked very near the restaurant in an extremely non-parking zone, on double yellow lines in fact, but that it had not received any attention at all from the Police or from the Traffic Wardens who were normally predatory in that part of Mayfair. I didn't think any more about it, until after my second meal with Harry.

The second dinner was a delicious one at the Brasserie Saint Quentin. Ishmail Merchant apparently had a motto, which is something like 'Never waste a mealtime'. If that is a maxim in Hollywood, then Harry was a believer.

On this occasion, I was to eat with Harry and Jay Presson Allen, a formidable woman who had adapted a French farce that Harry was wanting to do on Broadway. They wanted me to direct it and wanted to know what I had thought of the script, which I had read the day before.

I had some trenchant criticisms of the play and the translation and the conversation went something like this:

I pointed out that the English version wasn't very French, whereas the events of the play, which mainly involved a family business and a mistress, were very French indeed.

Jay and Harry said that could be fixed.

I pointed out that the leading roles were not attractive enough to get stars to play them and it seemed to me that stars were a *sine qua non* for a Broadway production.

Harry and Jay said that could be fixed.

I pointed out that whereas the original French play must have had witty dialogue to accompany all the farcical behaviour in the script, this version had none.

Jay and Harry said that could be fixed.

Finally, I said that until all these improvements had been made, I couldn't possibly commit to doing the play. I said that only then should they send me the script again.

Jay said that they would have another director by then.

But the evening was not a total loss. I got to learn a little bit more about mendacity among movie folk.

Jay, a tough woman from Texas, regaled us with a story of how she got *Cabaret* made into a film by telling the producer she was half-Jewish.

'Are you?' I asked.

'Not at all,' she answered.

Then, as we left the restaurant, the following dialogue ensued:

'Gosh,' I said to Harry.

'What?' said Harry to me.

'There's your car again, parked on a double yellow line.'

'Yeh,' said Harry.

'Oh, look', I said. 'It's got an invalid sticker on it.'

'That's right,' said Harry.

'Is that how you can park it anywhere you like?'

'That's how,' said Harry.

'Sorry,' I said. 'Are you an invalid?'

'Oh, no,' said Harry.

'Then how come you…'

Harry answered me straightaway.

'My chauffeur's a diabetic.'

Then I thought.

'Oh.'

When I have been out of work or out of hope for immediate work, or both, my attention has often turned to films. All of these efforts have been hopeful, cheerful and unsuccessful.

Once, I asked around for an American agent who would help me get going. Everyone recommended CAA. They were big. They represented Dustin and Meryl Streep and just about everyone. Writers, directors, you name it. Mike Ovitz, their leader, had been a key figure in putting together our production of *Death of a Salesman*. He had been nice to me. I decided to make overtures through a young man who had a close friend working there. This young man mentioned my interest to a slightly less young man who was high up in their organization. A conference call was arranged whereby I would speak from London and they would be in California and we would discuss the very real possibility of me being represented by the most successful agency in Hollywood, thereby furthering, or to be more accurate, beginning my film career.

I sat, or rather stood, at the appointed hour in my study in Maida Vale sounding and, I hope, looking presentable. I had brushed my hair. Eventually, about twenty minutes late, they called.

We talked about what I had done, where I had been, what the possibilities were of me spending more time in California. Soft, beige American voices came to me by satellite. These two men were reassuring, competent, business like, beautifully assimilated grandsons of Irish and middle-European grandfathers. They said practically nothing of any substance, but they implied that if I were willing to move to Hollywood and go to interviews with lots of studio executives with my ideas and their ideas, then I would almost certainly become a film director and they would be my agents. I remembered something Bert Fields, the high-powered Hollywood lawyer who represented Dustin and Michael Jackson had told me:

'Anyone who has one idea and is willing to lie a little, can direct a movie in this town.'

I was dubious about that. My lying is third-rate at best. And I always perspire. I conveyed my doubts to the two grandsons in this conference call. I said that I wanted to stay in London. That I had many children here. I said that I didn't think that Hollywood was my kind of place. I asked them, collectively, why they were interested in me? One of them answered slowly, but in one memorable sentence. I wrote it down. I thought that, translated into Latin, it could be a good motto for a Hollywood studio.

'The thing is, Michael, you are very, very talented at the moment.'

Movie Stardom

I have, in fact, come closer to being a movie star than I have to the director's chair.

I had a strange friend called Bobby Zarem, a press officer in Manhattan. Bobby is the man who created the 'I Love New York' campaign and helped to launch the Hard Rock Café as well as the careers, or some part thereof, of many stars of the cinema and sport. Bobby would get on his exercise bicycle for several minutes every day, but as he eats several meals every day, he never reduced his corpulent shape. He was jolly and he worked hard and he travelled a great deal, so he did well.

One night he invited me to dinner at Joe Allen with Alan Alda and Meryl Streep. Meryl was in London to work on *The French Lieutenant's Woman*. We chatted. Alan and his wife were pleasant. Meryl seemed preoccupied, as indeed she was because after about half an hour, she left to feed her new baby. Before she left, she reminded me that I had been nice to her close friend, John Cazale, when I was in New Haven rehearsing *The Changing Room*. I had released him from the play so that he could be in the film *The Conversation*. I remember being very loathe to do it, but very pleased when even though he knew he was out of the play and that we were replacing him at any moment, he threw himself completely into the run-through we had scheduled. Then he followed me around for a few days, being very nice and very grateful. He was always with a tall, blonde girl in a trench coat. That must have been Meryl Streep.

The result of this apparently casual dinner was that Patsy Pollock, the casting director of *The French Lieutenant's Woman*, began to ring me two or three times a day. It was one of my busiest times at the National so I didn't return all of the calls. I was editing a television special of *For Services Rendered* and attempting to guide a production of *When we are*

Married for the Lyttleton. I was also rehearsing a new Alan Ayckbourn play, *Taking Steps* for the West End.

When I did manage to speak to Patsy, she had astonishing news. I was being offered the role of Meryl Streep's husband in *The French Lieutenant's Woman*. Karl Reisz wanted me to play it. Meryl was very keen. Would I come and meet Karl?

I said that I couldn't. Number one, I wasn't an actor. Number two, I was very busy all of my waking hours, and number three, I thought it was a crazy idea.

Patsy said that I should let Karl and Meryl be the judge of my acting. It would be a doddle, said Patsy. There were only two locations, one across Waterloo Bridge from the National in the Savoy Hotel, and the other in Englands Lane, very near my home, and crazier things than this have happened in films, she said.

When film people want you to do something, there is only one thing that moves them on from mere desire to an absolute need to get you at all costs. You have to not want to do it. Pretending isn't good enough. But a straightforward refusal with no poncing about will positively inflame them. This is what happened with Patsy. Her phone calls increased in frequency. Weekend filming was promised. High wages were mentioned. Eventually, I agreed to see Karl. After all, his office was only two blocks from my flat. I put on a tie.

Karl Reisz was a very nice man. I saw a poster of *The Gambler* on the wall and complimented him on that excellent film. He was genuinely pleased.

'Please sit down,' he said, very nicely.

I sat down.

'Now this part, Michael, that I want you for, that Meryl wants you for…'

'Do you want me to read for it?' I asked.

'Oh, no,' said Karl, getting even nicer.

'Great,' I said

'The character is about forty. He is American and sort of intellectual,' said Karl, smiling and talking at the same time. 'He's over here with his wife, who is very attractive and a successful actress making a film in London. He is quite jealous and, well, he's a little boring.'

'Well, Mr. Reisz, that's not a thousand miles away from me.'

'Please, call me Karl.'

'Karl.'

'Now, it isn't a very big part,' Karl went on, smoothly, 'but of course it is very important.'

Then Karl started to leaf through the script, which although written by Harold Pinter, was bloody long. It must have been at least one hundred and fifty pages, but nowhere in those pages could Karl seem to find the character of Jimmy, which was my part, if he offered it to me and if I accepted. Jimmy was hard to find. Both of us began to wonder if Jimmy had any lines at all.

My heart went out to Karl because he was doing what I had done a few times. He was trying to keep talking while searching a script for a part so small that it might never be found. He really was very nice.

'Here it is,' he said, with some relief.

'Ah,' I said, trying to encourage him.

'No, sorry. This is where he is mentioned. Now let's see. Ta, ta, ta, ta, here we go, it should be about here.'

Finally, he found it. It was about six lines, all to do with answering a telephone in a suite at the Savoy.

'Here we go,' he said, and handed the huge script across the desk to me.

'Do you want me to read it for you?' I asked again. He was so nice, I would have done almost anything.

'Oh, Lord, no,' he said. 'Just take a look at it.'

I took a look at it for as long as I thought was proper and I handed it back to him.

We talked for a while longer and then I left. The next day I got two calls from Patsy even though it was Sunday. I began to relish the whole business. What a lark, I thought. I'll be able to do it at the weekends, slot it in , as they say, and probably learn a great deal about film. And everyone at the National would be impressed.

I was pretty well determined to do it and the next day in the canteen at the National, I told Alec McCowen.

But Alec McCowen didn't warm to the idea at all. The more I talked about it, about what fun it might be and how much I might learn and how nice they were being, the more Alec's fact seemed to frown. Frowns are not what you expect from Alec McCowen.

It transpired that Alec didn't think it was a good idea at all. He didn't say so in so many words, but I got the impression that he didn't want any director-laddies having a lark doing acting when directing was their job. Acting was his job. He didn't like the idea of me swanning over there to do it and swanning back with all kinds of amusing stories about what was, after all, his life's work. Also, he didn't think it was good for me as a director, who expects to be taken seriously, to be doing things like that. He didn't say all this, but he said some of it and with the frown it was quite enough for me.

I rang Patsy and told her I couldn't/wouldn't do it. She was very nice. They cast a French actor in the end. He was extremely good looking, but not at all American, boring, jealous or intellectual.

And that's the closest I ever came to doing a film.

Felicity Kendal

Some of you, patient readers, will have heard of me before buying this book or, to be more accurate, before receiving it for Christmas. Others will, by now, have googled me and most of you will be wondering why on earth I have barely mentioned Felicity Kendal. The reason is, it is difficult to write about a relationship that has gone on for over thirty years and included friendship, laughter, marriage, tears, a child, divorce, reconciliation and a considerable amount of work.

But I will try.

The first time I saw Felicity was in a matinee of *Table Manners* by Alan Ayckbourn. Everything about that show was delicious. All of the acting was truthful and comically energetic. The writing was accurate, complex and eloquent, and, for me, the direction by Eric Thompson was sublime. But, mainly, I was struck by the young actress playing Annie. I can't say that I fell in love with her that day, but I certainly felt differently about her from the way I felt about Tom Courtenay and Michael Gambon.

Not long after that I saw Felicity again at Eddie Kulukundis's Christmas bash in the circle bar at the Drury Lane Theatre. At first I didn't recognize her, but as soon as I did I resolved to chat her up. Before I could work up the nerve, she was making an early exit. She did look back, wistfully I thought, but not at me.

A few months later, when I was driving back to Hampstead Theatre after playing tennis, I heard an attractive voice on Radio 2. I remember exactly where I was. It was the corner of Buckland Terrace and Fitzjohn's

Avenue. An actress was being interviewed and she was saying that what she really wanted to do next was a comedy on stage. The interviewer called her Felicity and I thought immediately of Michael Frayn's *Clouds* that we had done a couple of years before and, for a variety of reasons, failed to get into the West End.

When I got back to the theatre, I said to David Aukin that I thought we should try to get Felicity Kendal for *Clouds*. I spoke loudly so he could hear me through the thin wall that separated my office from his. He shouted to me, 'Do it. Do it now.' So I called her agent who was receptive to the idea and we sent a script. The word came back a few days later that she wanted to do it with Tom Courtenay. They were a couple at the time and wanted to work together.

We met at her tiny house in Putney. All three of us were pretty charming and we went on to do the play and have a big success.

Success often forms a bond. All of us in that Company had a very good time and most of us went on to do more plays together, and play golf.

I don't now why, but I was surprised to learn that Felicity was very wise and gave good counsel. I had a huge shock when the first play I directed at the National was on tour. One of the leading actresses, Jane Hylton, became very spiky and withdrawn after one performance and so I scheduled a private note session with her for the next day. When she didn't show up, I went to her hotel and we learned that she hadn't been seen that day. Eventually, I went to her room. A security man forced open the door and we found the lady slumped over her desk. She was dead. It turned out that since her husband, the love of her life, had died she had stopped wearing her pacemaker.

I went to London. The only person I wanted to talk to was Felicity. We went to dinner at Joe Allen and she reassured me and convinced me that it wasn't my fault. She was very understanding and supportive. I was grateful.

Quite soon after that we were dating and we decided for all kinds of reasons, we would keep it a secret.

This was quite difficult. We were both at the National and we both had children. My two daughters spent every weekend with me and

Felicity was at my flat all the time. I swore them to secrecy. I was quite tough about it and they seemed to understand that they were to tell no one.

But, occasionally, if there was a preview or a dress rehearsal, I had to get them a baby sitter. Rebecca, Warren Mitchell's daughter, sometimes looked after them for an evening. Now, I had told Warren, who could tell that I was getting serious about someone, that I was seeing a schoolteacher. I suppose it had always been a fantasy of mine and it seemed to work. I wasn't sure that he believed me, but he didn't say anything.

Then he rang me one morning.

'I think I know who this schoolteacher is, Rudman.'

'That's impossible.'

'Ask me how I know,' said Warren.

'Okay, Warren, how do you know?'

'Because when Rebecca came home from babysitting last night she told us that Katy, your youngest, asked if she had ever seen anyone famous naked. Rebecca asked her if she had. 'Yes', she said. 'Well,' said Rebecca, 'who was it?' 'I can't tell you,' said Katy, 'but she's the short one in *The Good Life*.'

I was quite high up at the National and very well observed and so, of course, was Felicity. I was Director of the Lyttleton Theatre and responsible for the programme and the casting. I had cast Felicity in *The Second Mrs. Tanqueray*, which I was directing, and we had been on tour for a few weeks. We were about to open on the South Bank and we were having some last minute rehearsals.

Very few people knew, but quite a few had guessed, that she and I were having an affair. But it was never mentioned. There had never seemed to be an appropriate moment to bring it up.

We were rehearsing a scene with a strong curtain line. In her fury with her husband, Paula Tanquery shouts at him *'We'll see.' Curtain*.

But we were having trouble getting the right amount of intensity. I kept urging Felicity to be more fierce, but decorum (or something) was holding her back. We rehearsed this moment over and over, but it still wasn't reaching the right pitch. Several members of the company had drifted into the auditorium to watch this, to them, very interesting rehearsal. Finally, I said 'Felicity, I don't understand why you won't play this part after all you did to get it.' It got quite a big laugh, especially from her, and the end of the scene worked very well after that. And so did we.

Working with Felicity

People often ask me what it is like directing the person you're living with. Is it difficult? Are there conflicts? The answer to both questions is 'no' and, as they say in Scotland, 'quite the reverse.'

Felicity likes to be directed. Of course, she tends to work with the very best directors like Peter Hall, Peter Wood, Trevor Nunn, John Caird and Lindsay Posner. But, even if she is working with someone who is not wonderful, she never complains. She just gets on with it.

We trust each other and we are confident that the process will work. It has certainly been successful both commercially and artistically. Anthony Sher and Greg Doran, who are partners, have told us recently that when they are doing a play together they never discuss it outside the rehearsals. Felicity and I try to follow that rule and, on the whole, we succeed. Once, I even moved into a flat near my office to avoid even the appearance of collusion.Once in a while though, after a few glasses of wine, there can be a discussion about a lighting cue that goes on until three in the morning.

And there is one argument that has been going on since 1979 about some impromptu dancing (Cha Cha) that I wanted Felicity to do with Paul Chapman and Olu Jacobs in *Clouds* by Michael Frayn.

The play is set in Cuba. The three of them come back from a swim. Felicity's character, a female journalist who is flirtatious bordering on promiscuous, is having a laugh with these two attractive men while Tom Courtenay's character, Owen, is seething with impatience and jealousy. He is also a journalist, but a very male and English one. When and if he sees her dancing with two other men, he stands at one point and says with venom '*It's so unprofessional*.' This line gets a big laugh and gives the play a bounce if there is Cha Cha dancing before it. If not, it only gets a chuckle.

Felicity was reluctant to do this dance, which is strange considering her later work on *Strictly Come Dancing*, but she did it and it worked very well and we still argue about it occasionally.

The best thing about the director and a leading actress being together while doing a play is that the director gets to see how hard the actor works. Felicity fills pages writing down not only her lines, but also all the possible thoughts, moods and motivations she might have at any given moment in the play. Seeing all this is good for a director who normally only sees the fruits of the labour and not the process.

And it helps a lot that we admire the same kind of actors so she is always pleased with the people I cast and works well with them. It's surprising how many leading actors or stars, as they are sometimes called, find fault with the other actors especially the younger ones and even want one or more of them fired.

Also, it is handy if you have directed a play in the West End with one of the leading actors who can tell you how it is going and, from time to time, let you know if some things are getting slow. Felicity is almost always right, even though I sometimes have to ask her to speed up a bit as well.

One nice thing about not discussing the play outside of rehearsals is that there can be some big surprises. One time we were doing a difficult play that had a scene requiring great intensity, anger and passion. We had discussed the scene many times. None of us were happy with it, but we didn't know what to do. The other actress in the scene was helpful and agreed that there was a problem, but she couldn't come up with anything either. Then, there was a run-through and at the climax of the anger, Felicity, who is, after all, quite a small person, picked up a chair and threw it halfway across the room. Everyone was amazed and everyone liked it. Now that I think about it, it was never mentioned again.

Marriage

When we got married – was that too quick for you? It seemed quick to us – many things went very well. One of them was our parents. Geoffrey and Laura Kendal loved the fact that I was a director and they especially loved it when I cast them in a play at the National Theatre. And I loved it when Geoffrey got a round of applause at every exit. And my mother adored Felicity, partly because she was famous and also because they both loved shopping. And my father was thrilled that whenever he met any English people on his travels, he could casually drop into the conversation, after about three minutes, that Felicity Kendal was his daughter-in-law. He went on doing this well after we were divorced.

As for my mother she was, as they say in Texas, in hog heaven. One day she and Laura went to the matinee of a play that Felicity was in and I had directed. After the shedding of coats and hats, after the opening of the chocolates and the tweaking of make up, my mother suddenly turned completely around to the people behind her and asked, 'Do you mind if we tell you who we are?'

And then we had a baby. A lovely boy.

Jacob was born at eight in the morning. Felicity called to tell me. She had excused me from watching and worrying and waiting. I rushed to the hospital. I looked at him. I looked at her. We were all smiles and hugs. And then I asked if she would mind if I went to my rehearsal. She said, 'Of course not.'

I was directing *Waiting for Godot* with Alec McCowen. The week before, Alec's lover and, later, close friend had died of AIDS. The funeral was at noon. I asked him if he wanted to rehearse later that afternoon. He said that of course he would.

So it seemed the least I could do was to turn up for rehearsal at eleven in the morning on the day that Jacob was born.

And Alec and I discovered something together about the play. Birth and death. Death and birth. That's really what it's about. And, for the first time, I have to confess, we knew that we were going to love doing *Waiting For Godot*.

A few days after his birth we held a *briss* for Jacob. This is the ceremony in the Jewish religion in which a baby boy is circumcised. As it is a religious ceremony, there has to be a *minion*, which is ten men. This meant that, in addition to our family and womenfolk, I had to find ten adult Jewish men who were available on a working day, at noon, for a short service, drinks, and a cold lunch. This wasn't easy.

There were the usual suspects: David Aukin, Mark Eisenthal, the family solicitor, Warren Mitchell and others but we were having trouble making up the numbers. So I invited Michael Winner. He accepted, as they say, with alacrity.

At that time Michael's girl friend was Jenny Seagrove, a classy, attractive actress with great self-confidence and a strong voice. While the men were upstairs, doing the business with the Rabbi, the women waited downstairs and sipped wine.

Earlier I had asked Michael Winner if he had prepared Jenny for what was to happen, especially all the screaming and yelling. 'Oh, yes,' he said, 'I have briefed her fully.'

When the deed was done the men trooped downstairs for a welcome glass of wine and a little celebration, when we were nearly all in the sitting room, there was one of those lulls in the conversation that seldom happen anywhere but on a stage. And into this lull came Jenny Seagrove's voice, loud and clear.

'When do we eat the foreskin?'

The house where we lived was, in a very real sense, paid for by Dustin Hoffman. I bought it with the sizeable royalties I received from the tour and the Broadway run of *Death of a Salesman* and I was grateful. I still am. But, frankly, I earned every penny.

The rehearsals, in New York, were long and sometimes grueling. Dustin, who was one of the producers of the show, insisted on working every hour that Equity, the Actor's Union, would allow. We only had one day a week off. But, we did take a holiday on New Year's Day. So, so as not to waste time, Dustin invited me and my bride, as he called Felicity, for a lobster dinner on New Year's Eve.

Murray Shishgal was there with his partner and there were a lot of anecdotes and laughter and a considerable amount of high quality white wine. After the main course – there was no dessert – all of them started to reminisce and the subject of the previous New Year's Eve came up.

'Do you remember that?'

'That was so funny'

'What was that terrible play?'

Lisa, Dustin's beautiful and dutiful wife, was sent to get the photographs. There were quite a few of them and they were passed around. There was more laughter. But not from me.

A year ago, to the day, this group had had their photograph taken outside the Strand Theatre in London during the second act of the play. Dustin had a habit at that time of sometimes leaving plays at the interval and that is what they had done. Unfortunately, the play was called *The Real Thing* and Felicity had played the female lead.

There was a little embarrassment, but not much, when this fact emerged. Someone noticed a large photo of her behind the group in the front of house display. There were one or two muttered explanations. Felicity made light of it, as only she can do, and the conversation soon returned to anecdotes and jokes.

Now we cut to three months later in a limo in Washington. Dustin was taking Felicity and me to dinner after the show. Again, not wanting to waste a minute, he asked us if we knew a play called *The Real Thing*.

I said that we did.

'Whadya think I oughta do? They're auctioning the film rights and some guys want me to agree to play the main man for them? Whatdya think? Is it a good play?'

'Well,' I said, 'there's a very good speech about a cricket bat in the second act.'

Later, at the hotel, that seemed very funny.

I know it all seems very jokey and lovely and for a long time it was but, regrettably, to say the least, the marriage hit the rocks. It is only fair to warn you that there is some description of those rocks in the next chapter, the one about the Chichester Festival Theatre where, I'm sorry to say, almost everything went very wrong very quickly.

Chichester

Interview For Director of The Chichester Festival Theatre

Interview 1

I was in a hotel near Marbella, getting fit and trying to write a screenplay, which I don't recommend. Having done about ten minutes on it one afternoon, I decided to take a nap. I was woken up by knocking. A telegram from Peter Murphy had been slipped under my door saying that Robin Phillips had suddenly resigned as director of Chichester, and they were interested in me and would I meet the chairman who happened to be in the Marbella area?

The chairman, Kenneth Fleet, was a financial journalist with a sports car, a mistress and a strange haircut. We agreed to meet in the buffet area of Los Monteros, a fashionable hotel.

He was forty-five minutes late. He didn't apologise.

We talked for a long time. It was enjoyable. I said, prophetically it turned out years later, that there was a place for a third major Theatre Company in Britain and Chichester could be it.

Fleet and I parted on friendly terms. He more or less offered me the job and I accepted on the condition that there be no interview. He agreed.

About three weeks later, there was a formal interview with the board.

Interview 2

The candidate, in late middle age, is wearing a wool suit on a hot July day. Having jogged in the theatre grounds in the morning, he is feeling fit and well. This feeling doesn't last long.

The entire board is there. The men are wearing suits. The woman is well dressed. She is wearing a silk suit and heels.

The questions are mainly directed at finding out which famous actors he has worked with, which ones he knows and how many of them he could persuade to work in West Sussex.

The answers are a little vague, with a considerable amount of name-dropping and some amusing anecdotes. He probably mentions Dustin Hoffman three times.

They offer him the job on the spot and stress they are looking forward to meeting Felicity Kendal.

What Happened?

At the end of the last chapter I indicated that, after the power and the glory of the National, after the fun and frolic of Hampstead and the Traverse, after enjoying a wonderful personal life, when I took the job at Chichester, my life started to go downhill at considerable speed. Largely, I blame myself. Of course, the economy going to hell didn't help.

For the following Christmas, after a year and a bit at Chichester, I received five Christmas cards from lawyers, which will give you an idea of how bad things got. They were from:

1. Julie Scott Bayfield, my solicitor for my libel action against *The News of the World*.

2. Mark Eisenthal, our family solicitor, who was helping me to sell my house and advising me on my divorce.

3. Hilary Browne-Wilkinson, my divorce lawyer.

4. Peter Curnock who was dealing with my severance agreement with Chichester.

5. Geoffrey Shaw, QC who was advising me on the libel action.

Mistakes

1. The biggest mistake I made was taking the Chichester job without enough time to plan my first (and last) season. I was in the middle of directing a terrible play for the West End and thought wrongly I could be like Peter Hall and do three things at once.

The corollary to that mistake was not realizing how important star casting was at Chichester. I started with the directors and the plays that would be right for them, instead of starting with the stars.

Of course, I got some top drawer directors: Peter Wood, Paul Kerryson, David Leveaux, Annie Castledine, and Peter Hall.

One morning, I was talking to David Leveaux about how much I was enjoying my job and I asked him 'Who else gets to talk to three good directors before lunch?' He answered, 'Richard Harris.'

2. I failed to make Felicity an integral part of my plans. I think I wanted to do it all on my own. The board, with some justification, expected that she would be part of the package and she expected it too. I offered her two parts, but neither of them were major leading roles. She turned them down, preferring to do a new Simon Gray play.

3. I thought I could deal with the board with charm and jokes. (See title.) Indeed, I made them laugh a lot at board meetings until we got into the middle of the season when there was a board meeting every Saturday morning about finances and nobody was laughing at anything.

4. Even more wrongheaded was my assumption that I could produce ten plays in one summer and direct three of them. Whenever I think about this, which is quite often, I literally shake my head in amazement.

5. After realizing, too late, that there weren't enough stars in my season, I turned to Peter Hall, probably the biggest name in British theatre, to do a big musical. This extravaganza not only shattered the budget but put unbearable strain on the entire staff, including me.

The name of that musical was *Born Again* and it was adapted from *Rhinoceros* by Eugene Ionesco.

6. Thinking I could plan the summer season while directing the Christmas show the year I took up my post. *The Wizard of Oz was,* and this is a favorite phrase in Chichester, 'great fun.' We worked hard on it and the first night was wonderful. I remember walking around the grounds after the show and getting that special feeling that only comes when you know you have done something good. That feeling didn't last long.

My main problem was that I was arrogant and optimistic. I had, or so I thought, saved the Traverse and Hampstead theatres, helped the National get back on its feet, had hits on Broadway and in the West End, and won a few big awards. I thought that this now relatively obscure provincial theatre would be a piece of cake.

It was more like trying to push treacle up a flight of stairs.

The Chichester Festival Theatre consisted of two theatres, an administration building and a rehearsal shed. The theatres were the Festival Theatre, a 1400 seat amphitheatre with an open stage, and only seems to work when the house is full. The other is the Minerva, which is small, modern and works for almost everything no matter how many people turn up.

Leslie Evershed-Martin

I was in my office early the morning after the first night of *The Wizard of Oz* and the first call I got was from Leslie Evershed-Martin, the founder of the theatre and the chairman of the trust, which was one of the two governing bodies of the theatre. He didn't say much except that he thought the production was 'stunning.' I was delighted.

That was the last nice thing he ever said to me.

Leslie was a large man, powerful even. He looked strong and he was, for the most part, silent. But, when he spoke, everyone listened. Also, his thoughts and dreams were big. He was an obscure optician when he founded the theatre. But he raised many thousands of pounds to build it and he managed to get Laurence Olivier to be the director for the first few seasons, which were a huge success. It is worth mentioning that he was twice Mayor of Chichester and active in amateur dramatics.

The Season

The Wizard of Oz was my first production as a director but the first show I produced was *Therese Raquin* in the Minerva. It was directed by David Leveaux and had a terrific cast: Neil Pearson and Joanne Pearce played the two lovers and, not only could they act, they were both athletic and brave.

David staged their lovemaking scene with great energy and without restraint. For several minutes we watched the two of them writhing around on a big kitchen table and looking for the world as if they were, in fact, copulating. It was amazing.

In my role as director of the theatre I had seen a run through and approved of the production although I did worry about how the Chichester audience would react. They were, after all, considered to be 'sober, steadfast and demure' and many, if not most, were seriously religious. But, I wasn't about to censor David's work.

During the first preview, I became more and more apprehensive. Finally, we got to that scene. Neil and Joanne got together. They went onto the table. They began to writhe and moan and, even more than in rehearsal, they, as the saying goes, got into each other.

The audience went completely quiet. The only sound was the simulated lovemaking. Then utter silence.

Pause

The lady in front of me said, loudly, in a cut glass accent: 'I hope that table's strong enough.'

What I learned that night about the Chichester audience was that yes they wanted to be entertained and yes they were straitlaced, but mainly they wanted it to be good and if it was, they would enjoy it, even love it.

There were only a few tickets sold in advance for *Therese Raquin* but after the first couple of previews the entire run was sold out. We did five plays in the Minerva that season and there was hardly a seat to be had. Two of them, *70 Girls 70* and *Scenes from a Marriage,* transferred to the West End.

West End Transfers

Because everyone is always interested in anything that transfers to the West End, although many shows that don't transfer are better, I will tell you something about *Scenes From A Marriage* and *70 Girls 70*.

Scenes From A Marriage is Ingmar Bergman's coruscating study of marriage. The beginning, the love, the intertwining, the tension, the adultery, the battle, the divorce, the sex after divorce and quite a lot besides. Alan Howard and Penny Downie played the couple brilliantly and Simon Higlett designed an excellent minimal set. It played to packed houses in Chichester and transferred to the Wyndham's Theatre.

70 Girls 70 was a Kander and Ebb musical that had briefly been on

Broadway. It was about the lives and loves of a group of men and women in their seventies. The main theme was that these funny, attractive people were not about to give up on life: In one number two of them actually sing that they are still *'doing it'*.

Perfect, you might think, for the Chichester audience and you would be right. Paul Kerryson brought it to me, and I had been impressed by his production of *The Rink* in London. He cast Dora Bryan in the lead and it was a success from the moment we announced it. Michael Codron took it to the Vaudeville Theatre where it did well. The wit and the music of the show were appealing but the signature moment was when Dora, then 68, did the splits. Nobody could believe it.

The Main House

But the Minerva was the sideshow. The five productions in the big theatre were the main event and the fact that they only played to sixty-five percent of the possible box office takings was the main reason I was fired.

Oddly enough, the two that I directed did well: *The Merry Wives of Windsor* with Penelope Keith and Bill Maynard was a success and *Rumours* by Neil Simon was greeted with great enthusiasm.

One of the problem shows was *The Power and The Glory* based on Graham Greene's novel. In the frantic casting and cross-casting of the season, we had tried hard to get a big name for the leading role of the whiskey priest. It was a serious play for a summer theatre festival and needed some glitter.

Ed Woodward, whom I knew well from my Nottingham days, was seriously tempted. On the day we reached the deadline for announcing the season, his agent gave the impression that he would commit. But he didn't. I often think that if he had done, my whole season would have looked quite different. He was a big name and a wonderful actor.

But we were lucky enough to get Edward Petherbridge. He was extraordinary. Mesmeric. But, we didn't sell enough tickets.

The Board of Directors

The board began calling meetings every Saturday morning mainly to fret about the box office and chide me about my plans and decisions.

They would begin with the budget, especially expenditure. They had many concerns but the main thing that bothered them, especially Leslie Evershed-Martin, was *Born Again*, the musical Peter Hall was directing and which, from the beginning, was way over budget.

Peter tended to spend every penny available and demand quite a few more. He did that at Stratford with great success and he did it at the National and probably he did the same thing on operas. The producer always had to make a choice with Peter, which went something like this.

'Do I let him go on spending and hope that it will be a huge hit and hope and pray that it will make up the over expenditure when it is a hit, or, do I curtail him and risk him quitting?'

Peter regularly threatened to walk out. That was his main tactic. Finally, on *Born Again* I had to see him early one morning in my office and tell him that if he threatened to quit again, I would have to let him. I told him that it was demoralizing everyone including me. He was sweet and said he wouldn't do it again, and he didn't.

Born Again

Wordsworth advises us to 'recollect in tranquility' and I am trying to do so, with this chapter in general and with this terrible musical in particular.

There were many problems. For example, the script was banal. But I wanted Peter involved in Chichester. He was far and away the biggest name I could inveigle to work there that summer. Also, he is a wonderful director and a lovely man.

Peter made some mistakes, too. Also keen on names he cast, in a leading role, Jose Ferrer, who was a marvelous actor but not a singer, and he chose Gerald Scarfe as his designer. Gerald, a brilliant artist, had very little experience of designing for the theatre. Anticipating that, I hired Paul Farnsworth as assistant designer on the production to guide Gerald. Paul was not only gifted but had a lot of experience at Chichester. The arrangement worked well up to a point.

Even so, an error of judgment was made during the previews. The play was about people in a small town being turned into rhinoceroses. In the first act you saw them as the people they were and shared their bewilderment and fear when they saw other people becoming rhinos. In the second act you saw them all as rhinos themselves.

It was meant to be a satire on conformity.

When the characters became rhinos they had huge costumes, which were like gorilla suits only much larger and more bulky. But, in the first couple of previews, in addition to the rhino suits each character had a distinguishing piece of costume: frilly knickers, for example, or a necktie or a bowler hat.

The audiences loved these little embellishments. For one thing, they could identify the characters who were now rhinos and there were a lot of laughs as a result and, believe me, laughs were welcome in that show.

But, Gerald Scarfe decided that these distinctions were wrong, that the play was about conformity, that in the second act everyone should be the same. The costumes were changed for the opening night.

Many of the laughs were gone. The applause was muted and the reviews were lukewarm. Then the board was really on my case.

And I made a major miscalculation. I allowed myself to think that we could raise enough money, around £100k, to pay for the projected overspend on the budget of *Born Again*. When we made the budget for the season, being arrogant and optimistic, I convinced Michael Lynas, the administrator at the time, that we could find the cash from investors and producers. He seemed to agree. In the end we only got forty thousand. Some from Duncan Weldon, some from Michael Winner and £10k from Simon Cryer, my accountant.

Subsidy

Evershed-Martin had a few blind spots. One of them was government subsidy. He had built a successful business without any, and he thought he had built a theatre that was entirely self-made and self-supporting. He never took into account the fact that the first few seasons were actually subsidized by the National Theatre through Olivier, who was also the director of the National.

For example, in the first season, the sets for *The Broken Heart*, *Uncle Vanya* and *The Chances* were stored in huge pantechnicans paid for by the National and parked in the large car park. The Chichester Theatre was small backstage and there was nowhere else to store them. Many of the plays moved with Olivier to the National so, in effect, Chichester was working in tandem with the most subsidized theatre in the English-speaking world.

Leslie did not accept these facts and was unalterably opposed to his theatre receiving any money from the government. This led to a big conflict with me because I realized that without Arts Council support the theatre wouldn't continue for very long.

Newcastle

Towards the end of the season, I thought I had found a way of solving Chichester's financial troubles.

I was encouraged to apply for and was offered a job running a big theatre company in Newcastle along with Chichester. My idea was to open shows there, mostly paid for by the Newcastle grant, and bring them to West Sussex already built, and played in. I accepted that job thinking that many problems had been answered. I had, of course, cleared all this with Kenneth Fleet, the chairman.

But, Leslie put a stop to it. He wouldn't accept Government subsidy in any form.

It is interesting for me to watch the growing success of the Chichester Theatre over the past few years and applaud Jonathan Church and his colleagues for getting a fair amount of Arts Council subsidy. Of course, the main reason for their success is their flair for programming, organization and producing, but a cash injection doesn't hurt.

Other Problems

More and more that summer, I felt that I was in a downward spiral. What with the shortfall in income, the daily hassle from the board, the stress of directing three of the ten plays we were producing, not to mention the constant parties, I had enough on my plate.

Around that time, Felicity decided to leave me. And she had good cause.

There was a young actress in the company called Joanna Riding. She was doing three plays. I am glad to say that she has become very successful. One reason I am glad to say that is because when we were casting *The Wizard of Oz*, it was up to me to decide between two unknown actresses for Dorothy. I chose Joanna. The other girl was Catherine Zeta Jones.

Unfortunately, *The News of the World* decided they would print a story claiming I was having an affair with Joanna. I still don't know, over twenty years later, where or how they got their information but it was completely wrong. They claimed that I was guiding her career and that I had given her a lift home one night and all that that implies. According to them, their story was based on some anonymous letters. They later learned in an expensive (for them) libel action that I was having dinner that evening with two friends in the theatre restaurant, which was open on all sides.

I had never even had lunch alone with Joanna. Once I had dinner with her and her fiancé. That was it. The only time I saw her alone was one morning at about eight when I was working in my office and she asked to see me.

But *The News of the World* printed their story and someone had sent Felicity an anonymous poison pen note saying that I was fooling around in Chichester and my life went into a tailspin.

I was seeing life on a split screen. One half was my daily life in Chichester – budget meetings, rehearsals, script conferences – and the other half was my terrible personal life.

But it was not all doom and gloom.

Rumours by Neil Simon

Neil Simon is not very funny.

Many, indeed most, of his plays are marvelous and hilarious but as a person Neil is serious, steady, nice, deliberate. He never makes a barbed remark and, although I'm sure he could, never makes cutting derogatory statements about the people who have crossed him over the years. He doesn't even criticize the critics, a favorite pastime in theatre.

Also, he gives good advice. When I was directing his play *Brighton*

Beach Memoirs at the National he said, 'You should never count the laughs. You should count the coughs.'

Once, during rehearsals for that play, I was talking to him on the phone and I brought up the subject of an extraordinary line in *The Odd Couple*. I said it was one of my favorite moments in the play.

Oscar says to Felix, during a big argument in the second act, 'And one time you left a note for me on my pillow and it said 'We are out of corn flakes, signed FU'. It took me ten minutes to work out that FU stood for Felix Unger.'

Neil said, 'Yeah, I wrote that without thinking it was funny or anything and then when I went back and read that section I saw that line and I thought 'Oh, my God.''

Neil Simon came to Chichester that summer like a cool breeze on a scorching desert. He had adapted his play, *Rumours* to be transplanted from London Island to Haslemere and he had enjoyed doing it. Robert Butler, our dramaturg had helped alot, but it was mainly Neil's work.

He arrived with his wife and a huge car with a driver. They checked into the best hotel in the area. He absolutely refused to let us pay for anything. He is very generous.

The first evening he was there we did a run-through of the first half of the play for him. I don't think I have ever enjoyed a rehearsal more. He and his wife giggled and laughed and guffawed through the whole thing. They were full of praise afterwards and throughout their stay they were charming and helpful even when they found out that they didn't like the second act nearly as much.

Years later Duncan Weldon asked me if I would consider directing a revival of that production. I couldn't find my script so I rang round the actors. Because she is conscientious, Polly Adams had kept hers. I told them why I wanted the script and John Quayle said, 'Oh, you must do it again. When we went out there every night at Chichester we were greeted with a wall of laughter.'

But, sadly, that production was the only out and out hit we had and, as Pieter Rodgers once said to me at Hampstead. 'Every season you need two hits.'

My typical day

Here are some to the things I might do in a day in the middle of that terrible Summer:

1. Rise early. I always managed that.
2. Work out on the exercise bike in my cottage. I usually managed that.
3. Get to theatre and greet as many people as possible, partly so they knew how early I got in.
4. Look at box office receipts from night before and projected sales for rest of season.
5. Check phone messages at London office.
6. Check faxes.
7. Read reviews of play that had just opened.
8. Read scenes I was rehearsing later that day for the play.
9. Ring Peter Hall to check on casting for *Born Again*.
10. Search for an Administrator to replace Michael Lynas who had taken another job.
11. Speak to one or two directors of the plays in preparation.
12. Field phone calls from Board, especially Kenneth Fleet.
13. Rehearse from 11.00 to 1.30 p.m.
14. Sandwich in office.
15. Try to get Felicity on phone.
16. Stodgy lunch with Evershed-Martin.
17. Genial meeting with Paul Rogerson, the General Manager about winter programme.
18. Give notes to director on last night's preview.
19. Talk to my London assistant, Patricia Michelson
20. Make three fruitless phone calls to raise money for *Born Again*.
21. Go through new version of *Rumours* with Robert Butler.
22. Return to rehearsal.
23. Walkabout to see audiences coming in, eat a bag of dry roasted peanuts, drink a Perrier.
24. Try to find my father for our weekly phone conversation.
25. Check ticket sales for that evening.

26. Try to get London agents on phone to discuss casting for next season.
27. Talk to press officer, Lucinda Morrison, and find out which critics were coming to press night that week.
28. Avoid *News of the World* woman stalking me in car park.
29. Field more phone calls from board.
30. A few phone calls about transfers to West End *of Scenes From A Marriage* and *70 Girls 70*.
31. Go to preview of show opening that week.
32. Look at designs for set of next play I was directing.
33. Look at proofs for programme.
34. Get Chinese takeaway.

Reader, I could go on an on. It was a nightmare. But at the time I was enjoying being so busy. I had no idea how badly I was doing. Kenneth Fleet kept trying to tell me but I still had just enough of the arrogance and optimism I started with to keep going.

More on the Board

I had regular lunches with Leslie Evershed-Martin and Chinese dinners with Hugh Cudlipp, the legendary former Fleet Street editor and now a Lord, who once drank an entire bottle of white wine in my office before dinner and forgot what we were doing that evening. Also, there was a man called Max who insisted that I play golf with him and there was Henny Gestetner who gave a lot of dinner parties. At one of them, I was stung by a wasp.

All they wanted to know was how and when the finances were going to improve. Of course, I couldn't tell them.

I realize now that I was utterly unsuited to that job. I wasn't at all the kind of person they wanted working for them or to even have lunch with. I didn't go to church. My marriage was breaking up. *The News of the World* had printed that I was a philanderer. I didn't drink all that much. I didn't know enough stars. I made a lot of jokes. (See title.) And I hardly ever wore a suit. Also, and I hesitate to say this, I don't think they liked the fact that I was Jewish especially the two Jewish ones.

I don't want to dwell on the production of *Born Again*. As a matter of fact, I think everyone would rather forget it, but it was the cause of an emblematic conversation I had with Evershed-Martin.

After the weeks of badgering me about how expensive the production was going to be, about how far over budget it was, how it was stretching all our resources, how this Peter Hall was a terrible man, how I should never have engaged him, how he was ruining the theatre – after all that, on the opening night Leslie took me aside and insisted that I introduce Peter to him and his two sons. Why? Because Peter was a star.

At every board meeting, there was an intense, blond young man who was our accountant. He was always negative about our plans and seemed to delight in pointing out where and how we were losing money.

Early one morning, after seeing a particularly raunchy play the night before, this painfully shy accountant asked to see me. When he came in, we chatted for a while. I could barely hear him and I couldn't work out what he wanted. Then he pulled out a bible and began reading scripture to me very loudly, as if I were in church. I couldn't stop him. He went on and on, louder and louder. He had chosen a long passage.

I think he was trying to save my soul.

Next Season

During all this I was trying to put something together for the following season. I didn't have much time, as I was doing all of the above and more.

I had one good idea. I had gotten to know Don McLean (*American Pie, Vincent, Till Tomorrow, Castles in The Air*) when I was at the National and I wanted to do a musical based on his songs. My plan was that somebody could write a book tying the songs together. This was before so-called jukebox musicals, but that is what it was going to be.

Don thought it was a great plan. He was half in love with Broadway. He brought his bride to Chichester to see a show and have dinner. Chichester loves musicals and the songs were good, popular and, above all, well known. We were excited about it and Simon Higlett had agreed to design it and had come up with a brilliant overall concept.

Alas, it never opened.

I think it's fair to say that the cards were stacked against me. I repeat,

I was ridiculously busy trying to produce and/or direct ten shows. I wasn't well connected with stars and their agents. There was no producer working alongside me. And we were running out of money.

My predecessor as director of Chichester, if you don't count Robin Phillips who lasted only a few weeks, was a man called John Gale. He had been at Chichester for many years. He was an experienced West End producer, a local resident, a regular churchgoer and a man of strong views about the Chichester audience. Put simply, he believed that a famous play or musical with a star name – let's say Susan Hampshire or Keith Michell – would do well regardless. And he was usually right but even so, he and I disagreed on almost everything.

My dad used to tell a joke all the time: 'I remember my first day of school. I remember my last day of school. Same day.'

It was a bit like that for me at Chichester. I managed to get the Don Mclean musical going and I had plans to do some excellent new plays in the Minerva. It was possibly unfortunate that two of them were Jewish. One was *The Immigrant*, about a Russian Jewish family that emigrates to America, landing and staying in Galveston, which is on the coast of the Gulf of Mexico. Another was about an Israeli artist and an American woman living in Israel.

Here was my plan. Based on the success of *Rumours*, which was written by a famous writer and had a cast of excellent British actors, I thought it would be enough to let the known quantity, the selling factor of a show, be the play or the musical, coupled with a high quality director and excellent actors.

Unfortunately, I didn't get a chance to find out.

One big problem was the way Chichester had always announced it's season. In those days, a brochure had to be printed in early spring so that the patrons could book in advance. The money from this financed the season. But actors were not committing that far ahead any more. So by the time it came to a announce the second season, it didn't have enough stars. I didn't think it looked too bad – we had Alec McCowen in a Somerset Maugham play, Elizabeth Spriggs and Rosemary Harris in *Arsenic and Old Lace*, an early Noel Coward play about adultery with Sara Kestelman, a new play with Henry Goodman, *The Three Musketeers* and the new musical featuring the songs of Don McLean – but, apparently, it wasn't good enough.

It was around this time that the Board summoned me to a meeting. I knew it was going be bad, but I couldn't have imagined it being as awful as it was. The meeting was held high in the boardroom of a modern office block overlooking Trafalgar Square.

The Chairman said that we would go round the room allowing every board member to state his objections to the way I was working. One by one, each one of them voiced their criticisms. None of it was pleasant. Some of it was nasty. Finally, one member summed up by saying that I had not cast enough stars in my first season. Why, for example, was there no famous leading man in *The Silver King*? I said, with what I hoped was dry wit, that I had tried several big names and finally, when we got down to Michael York and he said no, I plumped for Alan Howard, the best actor in England.

I don't remember much else about the meeting.

Cut to a couple of weeks later, a Sunday night, about 8.30, I was in my study reading a book by Jake Eberts about the film industry in which a hell of a lot of people were fired. I was alone in the house; Felicity and Jacob, our son, had moved to Chelsea. The phone rang. It was Kenneth Fleet. Could he come and see me; he had something important to say. I knew what it was about. I said okay and rang Peter Murphy. Peter, who is almost always right, said that whatever I did, I mustn't resign because it would cost me a lot of money. I had to wait until they fired me.

Fleet came round about half an hour later. He was just getting past the friendly stuff about how much he liked and admired me when the phone rang. It was Felicity to talk about our relationship. I had to say that I couldn't talk as Kenneth Fleet was there and was about to fire me.

That speeded up the process quite a bit.

So, I didn't resign. I was fired. One reason he gave was that I had lost the confidence of senior staff. I have always hoped that he didn't mean the General Manager, the lovely Paul Rogerson, who still sends me a Christmas card every year and still calls me 'Maestro.'

A Selfie

Sometimes I imagine myself being interviewed about my time at Chichester. It goes like this:

Q. Was it your fault?
A. Yes.

Q. Was the result inevitable?
A. Yes.

Q. Did you learn a lot?
A. Yes.

Q. Are you glad to have learned so much?
A. No.

Q. If you had it to do over again, would you?
A. No.

Q. Did you try as hard as you could to make it work?
A. Yes.

Q. Would you advise another director to take the job?
A. Now, yes.

Q. Can you sum up the experience in one word?
A. Exhausting and debilitating.

Q. That's two words.
A. Now you're beginning to see the problem.

Footnote

21/5/1991 – *The News Of The World*'s STATEMENT READ IN OPEN COURT

'Defendant's Solicitor

My Lord, on behalf of the Defendants I accept that there was no truth whatsoever in the allegation that Mr. Rudman was having an affair with Miss Riding. It was not the intention of my Clients to give credence to the contents of these anonymous letters. However, they recognise that they may have done so be revealing their existence and I apologise unreservedly to Mr. Rudman on their behalf.'

PART 4

Back on Track

Sheffield

Paul Allen

I don't know the ins and outs of Sheffield Theatre politics all that well, but I'm pretty sure that Paul Allen has been the main mover in finding and hiring artistic directors of the Crucible since the late eighties.

I know he got me there. Also, Michael Grandage. Also Sam West. Also Daniel Evans.

I call him the *Eminence Rose* of Sheffield Theatres.

When I was there he couldn't get to board meetings because he was doing *Kaleidoscope*, the BBC radio arts programme, as a presenter, editor and critic. Both took place on Thursdays. But, as far as I could tell, nothing of any importance was ever done without consulting Paul and he initiated many of the decisions.

I first encountered him when I did *Henry IV* at the Sheffield Playhouse, the precursor the Crucible in 1968. He was the critic for the *Sheffield Telegraph*. He liked the production a lot and, over the years, we met occasionally through *Kaleidoscope*, especially when I was at the National and at Chichester and I always enjoyed being interviewed by him. He seemed to bring out the best in me.

So, when he approached me about the Crucible in the foyer of Hampstead during the run of *Making It Better*, I listened carefully and, bruised as I was from Chichester, I was tempted. I said I was interested, but that I would not agree to be interviewed. Paul, who was speaking for the Board said that would be fine. No interview.

So, there were two interviews: one with senior staff and one with the Board. Of course, interviews can be helpful because the applicant tends to make policy statements, which in many cases are later fulfilled. This had happened to me at the Traverse.

Interview 1

The now clearly middle-aged interviewee meets with senior staff: the Chief Executive, the Accountant, the Casting Director and the Marketing Manager.

It is pleasant and good-humoured. The Accountant and the Marketing Manager drink a lot of wine. The Chief Executive has one glass.

The interviewee talks a lot. He makes them laugh, but not too much. He had learned his lesson in West Sussex. He tells them that the thrust stage, with the audience on three sides, requires a great deal of energy going back and forth over distance. Of course, with the right actors, you can achieve this with two or three but from time to time, quite often in fact, you need to fill the stage with actors and movement. That is the way Tyrone Guthrie worked and it was he who popularized the thrust stage in Minneapolis.

The senior staff seem to agree.

Unfortunately, in order to get large casts, the interviewee agrees to only three weeks rehearsal. This is the only way, they said, that the budget could work.

Interview 2

The full Board. Very nice people.

The interviewee wears a suit, as do all the other males....

I don't remember much about it except that I made the same mistake about budgeting that I made in interview 1.

I think I took the job at Sheffield for two reasons; (i) Hoping that I could recreate the joy of working at the Nottingham Playhouse, not only for myself but for everyone else and (ii) to get away from the mess of my divorce.

I didn't achieve either.

But, on balance, my time in South Yorkshire was a success. Certainly several of the shows we did were excellent and I had the joy of working with Wendy Spon, our brilliant casting director, who is now at the National Theatre. At least three of the shows would have never made it to the stage without her.

The Board

Dealing with the Board at Sheffield couldn't have been more different from Chichester. The Chairman, John Cornwall, was always supportive and good-humoured. The moneymen were pleased with the upturn in box office receipts and, those members who were interested in the quality of productions, were pleased.

Something typical of my time at Sheffield happened on the first night of our first production, *A Midsummer Night's Dream*, which I directed. It had a terrific cast including Anthony Brown and Alex Kingston. It had a lot of merit.

Probably, truthfully, it was only a little better than average but whenever anyone works on that crazy, wonderful play, they come away believing that they have tapped into the genius of Shakespeare and that it has brought out the very best in them and, of course, they are right.

It was a complicated set to put on the stage and when they were building it there were problems with the floor as it had been designed with little mounds everywhere. But there was quite a bit of dancing in the show, which would be impossible on a bumpy floor. I realized this at about four in the morning, got up and went into the theatre where they were doing an all nighter. I got there in time and the production manager, Rob McKinney and I solved the problem by levelling the floor.

All this was made worthwhile by a conversation I had with the Chairman and one of the carpenters on the opening night. It was that kind of a theatre, very democratic. Everyone talked to everyone.

We were talking about the show and how well it had gone and suddenly the carpenter grabbed the Chairman's arm and said, 'John, you should know Michael has worked bloody hard on this damn thing.' It was one of the highest compliments I have ever been paid.

The Board meetings were short, infrequent and low-key; very South Yorkshire. My favourite line was from one of the lawyers. When we were debating the merits of us having lots of meetings about something and setting up a sub-committee or letting our accountants do it, he said 'You don't buy a dog and bark yourself.'

Jane Eyre

When I was planning my first season at Sheffield, Paul Allen suggested strongly that we do *Jane Eyre*. Never being shy of asking for advice, I rang John Gale, my old sparring partner in Chichester, to ask him about it.

'Schedule it immediately,' he said. 'Don't hesitate. Three weeks after it was in the Chichester brochure it sold out and we had to do extra matinees. All the posh young women in England are in love in Rochester.'

And we did it and, although it wasn't quite as successful as it was in West Sussex, it did very well indeed.

A Midsummer Night's Dream opened on a Thursday. On Sunday morning, I was in London.

Before reading the Sunday reviews for the *A Midsummer Night's Dream*, I thought I had better go for a swim, which I did. The reviews were quite good. Irving Wardle was still at *The Independent on Sunday*.

But, no sooner had I put the papers down then the phone rang. It was Annie Castledine who was directing the second production of the season, *Jane Eyre*. She said she was ill and had to drop out. Rehearsals began on Monday and I had to be in London rehearsing *Making It Better* for the West End.

I got on the phone and I tried to find a young man called Robert Delamere, who had assisted Stephen Daldry on *The Inspector Calls* and was a friend of Rufus Sewell. He had been at Hampstead a lot when we were previewing *Making It Better*. And, as my dad would say, I liked the cut of his jib. I thought he could probably direct.

Would he direct *Jane Eyre*, starting immediately? He couldn't because he had to spend every Monday with the tour of *The Inspector Calls*. Would he co-direct it with me, beginning on Tuesday? We could share the rehearsals. He said, 'Yes.' Did he want to read the script? Not necessary. This was all starting to look much better.

But, on the Tuesday rehearsals began, there was a snag. Annie had cast mainly what I think are called strong women. By that I mean women who wouldn't tolerate any macho crap. Unfortunately, Willis

Hall, the irrefragably Yorkshire playwright who had done the adaptation, made a comment to someone along the lines of 'Why aren't there more pretty girls in the cast?' Some of the women got angry. They refused to rehearse. Could I come up to Sheffield and sort it out? No, I couldn't. *Making It Better* opened that week at the Criterion.

Robert did sort it out. He is diplomatic. Willis apologized, although he didn't think he had done anything wrong. The rehearsals began. I went up on the Friday and saw a run-through of the first act. It was damn good and the show was on it's way.

Willis Hall

The most important and productive relationship I formed at Sheffield was with Willis. When we were setting up *Jane Eyre*, his agent had suggested him to do the adaptation. I knew his writing and readily agreed. In a few weeks, he had turned out an excellent piece of work. The show played to virtually full houses for it's entire run and, as it was the second show, after the successful *A Midsummer Night's Dream*, it meant that that we began well and established a relationship with the audience and, perhaps more important, the Board.

Mansfield Park

I had always thought that *Mansfield Park* should be adapted for the stage, partly because the crucial scenes involved the young people putting on a play. Also, I was enamored of Jane Austen both as a writer and as a person. I always thought we could have fun together.

My favourite moment in rehearsal involved Willis and his wit.

There was a big dance scene which included some addresses to the audience. As always, with a dance or a fight, you rehearse it into the ground. Probably more than necessary. It's a lot of fun. All that music and young people moving around is appealing to directors.

At one point, we asked Willis to rewrite a speech a little and he agreed. He went out into the hallway to work on it. After what seemed like quite a while, I asked the Assistant Stage Manager to go and ask Willis how it was coming along. The ASM returned. I stopped the rehearsal.

ME: Did you tell him?

ASM: Yes.

ME: What did he say?

ASM: He said 'Do you want it now or do you want it good?'

In the end, the whole show was good.

Two Bad Things

Not long after I started at Sheffield, two bad things happened.

Just when we were getting on our feet, the Arts Council sent a delegation to assess our work. This had happened to me once before when Peter James, John McGrath and Tim West assessed Hampstead and decided that it was being run inadequately, had no clear artistic direction and needed to change. It was a body blow.

About a year later, Hampstead without changing direction won the *Evening Standard* Award for Outstanding Achievement.

David Hare calls these people 'The Arts Police'. To Sheffield they sent an unlikely policewoman, Thelma Holt.

I had known Thelma for years. When she was running the Open Space with Charles Marovitz they invited my production of *Curtains* from the Traverse and Thelma was at the National when I was there. She was an eccentric woman who had started as an actress. Quite often, in Charles Marovitz' productions of Shakespeare, she would be required to take off most, if not all, of her clothes.

Years later, I saw her waiting for a taxi at the stage door of the National. I asked her where she was going. She said to the West End theatre where a play she had produced by Brian Clark was running. I said I would give her a lift. In the car, the dialogue went something like this:

ME: Don't you drive, Thelma?

THELMA: No, darling, I never got a license.

ME: Did you ever try?

THELMA: Oh, yes. I had a test. The little man failed me and I went home and told my mother. She said, 'Didn't they know who you were?'

ME: Who were you, Thelma?

THELMA: Nobody.

But, when she came to Sheffield with her committee, Thelma was somebody. She was assessing the work of a major regional theatre, which needed increased funding to pay the actors properly and, hopefully, allow them to rehearse for four weeks instead of three. The committee saw one of our productions, a revival of *Donkey's Years* by Michael Frayn, and decided that we couldn't have any more money. Admittedly, the Frayn play was a mistake. I loved the play and thought Sheffield would take to it, but I was wrong. I think it was too southern for Sheffield and in 1993 camp vicars and drunk politicians weren't as funny they were in 1976.

But the Arts Council assessment was wrong. We had done a successful *A Midsummer Night's Dream, Jane Eyre* and a cracking *Peter Pan* for Christmas. But one dud show was enough to convince a delegation from the Arts Council that we weren't doing well.

We managed without the increase but, about a year later, a really terrible thing happened.

Like everyone else, our budget was tight. It was big, but it was tight. A few thousand pounds either way could make a huge difference, which is why we were thrown into disarray by the discovery that the junior accountant had stolen nearly five hundred thousand pounds. The money simply wasn't there. All the budgets had to be rewritten and the situation was dire.

Here's how he did it. Any cheque issued by Sheffield Theatres had to have two signatures: the Chief Accountant or Artistic Director and either the Chief Executive or someone similar. This chap would get some cheques signed by one of these people before they went on holiday saying that he might need them and then he would simply forge the other signature, make it out to a fictional entity and pocket the money. All of this was greatly helped by the considerable amount of building and restoration work going on at the Lyceum Theatre which Sheffield ran along with the Crucible.

Thanks to the acumen of Stephen Barry, the Chief Executive, and a lot of help from the board, we overcame the blow but it did send us reeling for a while.

Grapes of Wrath

The Head of Publicity at Sheffield was a lovely man called, improbably, Roy Rodgers. He did his job quietly and diligently and gave me some excellent advice.

He said we should do the stage version of *Grapes of Wrath* which, as you know, is a great novel about the very poor and the dispossessed in California during the depression.

He said it would suit the Sheffield audience, many of whom were left wing. I was dubious but I read the version that had been done on Broadway by the Steppenwolf Company of Chicago in an adaptation of the Steinbeck novel by Frank Galati.

I am against stage adaptations of novels, which is weird because I have done quite a few. What can I tell you? Directors are perverse.

But this version fairly leapt off the page. I read it twice in one sitting and was determined to do it even though it had a huge cast. I thought we could get local amateur actors, if we could find any thin ones, to be the people in the camp. Thanks to Wendy Spon, we found quite a few, many of whom could actually act and, at times, the huge stage of the Crucible was full of people and energy. It was exciting. Patrick O'Kane, Ian Batholomew, Charlotte Cornwall were more than excellent. And when the company of forty sang *'The Battle Hymn of the Republic'* at the end, it was stirring. In fact, the whole damn thing was superb. We were very proud if it. Even Charles Spencer in the *Daily Telegraph*, who is thought to be right of centre, liked it and said that the show had *'Glimpses of greatness.'*

The trouble was nobody came.

A snowstorm hit Sheffield on the opening night and lasted for a couple of days. I went for a long walk the day of the second performance and dropped in to see some of the show in the evening. There were about a hundred people there and most of them were in the cast. I thought that if so few people would come to something as successful as that, it might be time to consider leaving Sheffield.

Sheffield was my comeback and, as it turned out, my swansong as an Artistic Director. I was more or less commuting from London to Sheffield. If you are running a theatre away from London, you have to spend a lot of time in the capital because that's where most of the actors, designers and directors live.

Hang on a minute, I hear you asking. Why didn't you concentrate on northern actors, designers and writers? Good question. And I should have done more of that. The truth is that I was living in two places: Sheffield, which was my work and London, where I was trying to repair a marriage.

In the end, it didn't work and I had to leave. Neither Paul Allen nor the Board wanted me to go and tried, in a low-keyed south Yorkshire way, to get me to stay longer but I was determined to 'Spend more time with my family.' I had never believed those words before when somebody left something, but in this instance it was true. I'm glad to say that I did spend more time with my family. Indeed, eventually, Felicity asked me to move in with her and Jacob in Chelsea and I did.

One of the refreshing things about working in Sheffield is that the people there are straightforward. They are positive, but they don't pull any punches.

At my going away party, given by the Board, they were extremely complimentary. Many nice things were said. Finally the Chairman rose and paid tribute to the work I had done, praising many of the productions.

But he couldn't resist pointing out that *Donkey's Years* was a disaster. What was the play about, he wondered, at some length, and what relevance did it have?

'Well, I said. 'It was interesting and funny to see a bunch of middle-aged men drink too much and give long, boring speeches.'

That got a good laugh.

In Sheffield I joked, but not too much.

And they presented me with a pewter plate and four mugs. The plate was engraved with this message.

You really have to imagine this read in a soft, South Yorkshire accent. The subtext is that I hadn't stayed there long enough:

PRESENTED TO
MICHAEL RUDMAN
FROM MEMBERS OF THE THREE BOARDS OF

**SHEFFIELD THEATRES
CONGRATULATIONS ON YOUR 2½ YEARS AS
THE ARTISTIC DIRECTOR OF SHEFFIELD THEATRES
1992–1994**

Freelance

There is a world of difference between directing a play at a theatre where you are Artistic Director and doing one for a commercial producer or another subsidized theatre.

When you are freelancing you are dependent on the good will of the producer and his whims, his assessment of your work and, more important, his budget.

Someone once said, I think it was me, that the budget is the only true fiction in our business. Producers, especially assistant producers or executive producers or whatever they are calling the yes man that year, are very fond of saying 'No, the budget won't allow that.' But what is the budget? It is the amount of money the producer has allocated and, of course, it can be increased or decreased depending on various factors, the main one being how well he thinks this show is to do at the box office.

Back to the budget. Here is an example: The director wants a particular actor to play a very important role. The producer agrees. The actor accepts. But, in the negotiations, the actor is asking far more than the producer wants to pay and thinks the actor is worth in terms of box office appeal. Or, perhaps the producer doesn't much like the actor and/or his work. What is the answer?

The budget won't allow it.

Another example. The director and the designer want certain features on the set and they want the scene changes to be quick and fluent. This costs money. Mainly man power. The producer doesn't think it's important. What's the answer?

The budget won't allow it.

So, it is better to be running your own theatre no matter how modest it may be. Very early on in my career, I was faced with a choice between becoming Artistic Director of the Traverse theatre and directing *Hair* in Israel for a big fee. The Traverse job paid £20 a week. The fee for *Hair* was £800, which was a hell of a lot of money in those days.

I talked for a long time about it with Peter Murphy. We discussed the pros and cons of each job. Finally, he said, 'If you take the Traverse job you'll have your own pitch. You can do your own thing.'

So, I did and he was right, as usual. When you are running the theatre you can, within limits, set the budget, choose the actors and designers and, of course, you usually decide the play and when it will be produced.

But freelancing can be fun and, occasionally, lucrative. Here are some examples of my freelance life.

Fallen Angels (2000)

One morning, I was shaving and the bathroom door was closed. Felicity, who has a strong voice, shouted to me.

'Bill wants us to do *Fallen Angels*.'

I answered without missing a stroke.

'Ok, if we can get Frankie.'

Frankie was Frances de la Tour who is, unquestionably, one of the best actors alive. I had worked with her twice before and both times it was wonderful and I knew that she would be the perfect partner for Felicity in this play. She is gifted, highly intelligent and, of course, very popular.

Unfortunately, it went downhill from there. Well, until we opened and it was a huge hit.

Bill Kenwright always has one of those, usually young, producers under him to deal with the nuts and bolts, the day to day making of the production, while he concentrates on the bigger picture. He is, of course, busy with many other productions and his beloved Everton Football Club.

For this production, the youthful producer was a chap called Harold who wanted to be a nightclub singer, which he now is. He was under-qualified, to say the least, to deal with this tricky situation. Felicity's agent and Bill had agreed a salary and billing. Frankie's agent was, quite rightly, demanding level pegging. Harold was trying to argue that Felicity was a bigger name and should have more. He was getting nowhere. He used to ring me every day to suggest other actresses for the role. Every time he rang I simply said, 'No. It must be Frankie. Give her what she wants.'

I had a lot of clout in those days. Finally, the deal was done. Equal everything.

The early rehearsals went well. Beautifully, in fact. We worked hard and laughed a lot.

I had always hoped that if we did the third act well enough, the play would emerge as what it was, a nicely crafted study of the upper middle classes with more than a hint of Chekhov. Well, minor Chekhov. I knew the play was better than its reputation, which was that of a neatly well-made comedy with a very funny second act in which two ladies get extremely drunk.

The third act is the key. I drew on my experience with Michael Frayn's *Donkey's Years* in which a lot of posh men have terrible hangovers and become even funnier than they were when drunk.

But, one day, towards the end of the third week of rehearsal when things were pretty well set, we were working on the first act when the relationship between the two women is established and enjoyed. We reached a point where they were both sitting on a sofa. It was lovely.

Suddenly, Frankie got up and started wandering around the room. After a bit I stopped it and asked her why she was doing that. I said I thought it was working very well before. She said that she had been studying the play the previous night in her kitchen and realized that to get up at that point was organic. I didn't know quite what she meant by that but I said by all means let's try it. We did it again. Again she got up and wandered. I didn't like it because precious moments of establishing the relationship between the two women were being wasted. I said it worried me a lot. She asked if we could do it again. She said that what she was doing was organic. This was getting tedious. We were opening in ten days. We tried it again. I said it didn't work. She argued. In exasperation I said 'Look Frankie, I'm beginning to think that what you mean by organic is Frankie being upstage center.'

You might think that was a very rude and direct thing to say to an actor, but I thought that Frankie and I enjoyed being direct with each other and shared a sense of humour.

When I was interviewing her for the part of the mother in *Brighton Beach Memoirs* at the National, we sat at a large conference table in the boardroom. Just Frankie, me and Annie Robinson, the casting director.

After about ten minutes of talking about the play, Frankie was becoming edgy and a little negative. I couldn't work out what was bothering her.

Finally, I said, 'Look Frankie, I'm offering you a leading role in a wonderful play at the National Theatre. Try to get over the insult.'

She thought that was very funny. We laughed together. She went home and rang her ex-husband and they both laughed over it. She accepted the part and did it brilliantly.

But Frankie didn't laugh at my remark about upstage center. She was furious. She got her stuff together very quickly and left the rehearsal room. I followed her to her car. She wouldn't lower the window or open the door. She drove off.

Bill Kenwright is a bit loud and assertive but he is a good producer and a good diplomat. A couple of hours later he got us all together in his office. He said it was going to be a big hit and we must all stick together. Frankie seemed reasonable. I apologized profusely for offending her. I said how much I admired her and loved her work. She knew this to be true. I pointed out that, as the director, I felt the need to get everything solid. We were opening in ten days in Windsor. I even quoted from Andrew Marvell, 'At my back I always hear. Time's winged chariot hurrying near.'

That seemed to work. We hugged and the next day we started rehearsal again. But nothing was ever quite the same again.

The play opened in Windsor and was considered by all concerned to be on its way to being a hit. It was particularly successful in Bath where, unlike Windsor, the audience had heard of Hollandaise Sauce. But then, unfortunately, we went to Woking.

Have you ever tried to find Woking? It's not easy. When I did finally get there for the Monday evening performance, I was five minutes late and had to sit in the balcony. Not a bad exercise for a director.

The performances were excellent. It is a large theatre, but the acoustics are good and both Frankie and Felicity have great diction. After the performance, I called notes for the next day. I really only wanted to tune things up a bit for London and I had one new idea which I knew would help.

It turned out to be a big mistake.

In the first act, the maid keeps entering and exiting while the plot is being laid and the relationships established. There was one exit and entrance that I found distracting and unnecessary. I asked her to cut that exit and remain on stage.

The actors were puzzled because they wondered if these women would discuss intimate things while a maid was present. I assured them that they would and that it would help to establish them as arrogant, wealthy upper middle class women with nothing to do who didn't much care about a what a maid would think.

That night we tried it and it worked. We even got two extra laughs.

I went to Frankie's dressing room for a chat. She was furious. She said she hated working with me. I was nowhere near as good as Trevor Nunn or Peter Brook or Howard Davies. I didn't know what I was doing.

And, more importantly, she was never going to attend another rehearsal.

That meant that from that moment up to and including the West End opening, throughout the run of the play, she would not go to a rehearsal or note session. That meant that any notes that I had for her would have to go through the company manager. And I did have some notes for her and they did go through the company manager, and she almost always took them.

The evening after the opening night and the amazing reviews, I saw Frankie backstage in the hallway. We hadn't spoken since Woking.

'Not bad?' I asked.

'Not bad,' she replied.

I think I have mentioned, probably too often, that the show was a hit. For example, the day the reviews came out, it took sixty thousand pounds in advance bookings. A very high figure for that time and place.

But I never think of it as a success. I am sad about Frankie. We had worked together very well indeed on two shows and we shared a sense of humour. I sent her flowers after her brilliant performance in *Boeing Boeing* and she wrote a polite reply and that's about it.

New York, New York

If you are looking for a truly challenging producer you have to go to New York.

Immediately after I finished at Sheffield, I did a play off off Broadway by Bruce Jay Friedman entitled *Have you Spoken to any Jews Lately?* (1995) Catchy title, isn't it? Off off Broadway meant, in this case, a basement with a very low ceiling on West 23rd Street, near 8th Avenue. The theatre was called the American Jewish Theatre.

It isn't there any more.

Our producer, the director of the theatre, was a strange small man called Stanley Brechner with a Russian girlfriend who spoke patchy English.

The play was a fantasy. A fever hot comedy dream. Two Jewish screenwriters are holed up in The Hamptons on Long Island. They feed each others paranoia that the Nazis are starting up again in America and are starting to take Jews away again.

Bruce is a very funny, insightful writer and a hell of a good storyteller. He has written hit plays and widely read novels such as *Mother's Kisses*. He also wrote some successful movies, *Splash*, *Stir Crazy*, *The Heartbreak Kid* and *The Lonely Guy*. In other words, he's not exactly chopped liver. But, as you will see, this didn't give Stanley Brechner much confidence.

The rehearsals were fraught. One of the leading actors decided he didn't want to do the play after all at the end of the first week. It took several days and many phone calls to change his mind.

But, on the whole, we started doing well until Stanley called a run-through. It's called a producer's run and it is quite common. The man who is putting up the money or responsible for the money watches the work and, sometimes, makes helpful suggestions.

After the producer run of *Donkey's Years*, Michael Codron asked Michael Frayn and me to meet him in a pub. He was charming for about three minutes and then he said, 'There is far too much good taste.' We knew what he meant and we improved it. It got a little broader and a lot better.

But back to Stanley Brechner and his producer's run. He invited his administrator, an ambitious young woman, and his Russian girlfriend. The play was supposed to be a comedy. The three of them sat there absolutely po-faced. There wasn't even a hint of laughter.

Stanley and I talked afterwards. He was worried. He doubted if he could open the show. He was afraid that it wasn't good enough and that, worse, it would offend his base audience. His biggest problem was a scene in which a Jewish man finds himself in a sadomasochistic fantasy including Nazis, a sexy blonde girl and whips.

I argued that the play was actually very funny and mainly because of that would hardly cause any offense. But, as is usual with these arguments, we just went on convincing ourselves that we were right. Finally, we agreed that we would hold a dress rehearsal and invite some heavy hitters whom we both knew and respected. Jack Gelber and Jack Temchin, for example. Stanley made it clear that if they didn't like it, he would cancel the production. I was alarmed but fairly confident.

It was a successful dress rehearsal. There were a lot of laughs and it was intriguing and, yes, sexy. Stanley agreed to open the show. But our troubles didn't end there.

In the early previews, there were a few complaints about the scene where the blonde lady in tights whips one of the Jewish men.

Afterwards the dialogue wasn't pleasant. It went something like this:

STANLEY: It's unacceptable. My audience hates it.

ME: A few people hate it, which is healthy.

STANLEY: My girlfriend doesn't think it's funny.

ME: Your girlfriend doesn't speak English.

STANLEY: She can speak English very well.

ME: Then why doesn't she ever do it?

STANLEY: We have a reputation to consider. We are a highly regarded theatre. Look at all these newspaper clippings on the walls.

The walls were, indeed, covered with positive articles about the theatre. I had read them during the intervals.

ME: I have a question.

STANLEY: What? What question?

ME: Why is there nothing on your walls from the *New York Times*?

Stanley got very angry and left. I went back to my cheap hotel room.

The next morning, he rang me. It was Christmas Day. We arranged to meet in a delicatessen on 72nd Street. I had matzo ball soup and he had a hot dog.

The conversation was more civil, but he was still saying that he didn't want to open the play. He gave me all kinds of reasons, again citing the sadomasochistic scene.

Then I had a brainstorm. I asked him a question:

ME: Stanley, why did you produce this play? You don't seem to like it all, so why did you do it?

STANLEY: For all kinds of reasons.

ME: You did it because Bruce is a big name and I am a bit of a name. Right?

STANLEY: I suppose that's true.

ME: Stanley, have you ever read this play?

(*pause*)

Stanley, have you ever read it?

STANLEY: To be honest, no, I haven't.

ME: I would like to suggest that you go home and read the play and call me and tell me what you think of it. I think you'll like it.

Stanley agreed to read the play and he said that he would call me later. I went back to my room and waited. Finally he called and he said that he had thought about it and that he would go ahead and open the play. I asked him if he liked the play at all.

He said that he had only read the first act.

Do I need to tell you that the play opened the following week and got a wonderful review from Vincent Canby in the *New York Times*, which Stanley immediately put up on three of his walls?

Making it Better (1992)

Not long after Chichester and Felicity both dropped me, I was in one of those black holes of the mind. I was jogging, swimming, trying to read and feeling sorry for myself.

Then Peter Murphy left a message for me to ring him immediately.

I was hopeful. Was it a new play at the Royal Court? Was it a West End revival of a Rattigan play? No, it was to appear on a BBC programme called *Did You See?* I was to be one of a panel of three to discuss and evaluate three television shows: BBC's comedy *Allo, Allo*, a Channel Four Cutting Edge documentary called *Volvo City* about Hassidic Jews in London and a BBC play called *Performance – The Trials Of Oz* by Tony Palmer with Alfred Molina. They would send us video recordings and we were to watch them before being interviewed by Jeremy Paxman.

I knew exactly what I was going to give them. Undiluted praise. I was not going to be the kind of pissy critic I had suffered from and I was not going to appear depressed and defeated. I was going to shower every programme with compliments. It wasn't hard. *Allo, Allo* was much better than people thought. It was possibly low brow but an excellent and successful example of broad comedy. The Cutting Edge documentary, *Volvo City*, was fascinating. The arrogance of the Jews involved was extraordinary, attractive and moving.

The other two panelists were Tony Robinson and Dame Shirley Porter. Robinson was intelligent and slightly left wing. Dame Shirley was extremely tough especially on the Jews. She was right wing and quite severe.

Paxman was amazed by what I was doing. He was surprised, especially by my praise for *Allo, Allo* but he seemed pleased with my contribution. He was a good interviewer. He brought out the best in me.

Minutes after the programme was transmitted, I got two phone calls. One was from my old friend Nicky Henson, who had been commiserating with me over my losses. He said it was great and that I looked dishy. Also, Felicity rang. She was complimentary and was very glad that I had worn the green desert boots that she had insisted on.

Early the next afternoon, when I returned from my run, there was a message from Michael Codron saying that he had enjoyed my appearance on the box (please don't ever underestimate the power of television) and that he was sending over a script for a new play by James Saunders that he was doing very soon with Hampstead Theatre. Peter Wood, who was going to direct it, had dropped out and would I read it? He said it was an 'SOS'.

I read the play that day. I liked it very much. I read it again and saw how it could be done and left a message for Michael saying 'Yes, oh yes.'

Jane Asher was playing the lead. I met her and liked her a lot. Two of the other parts were easy to cast, but that left the part of the young man. It is always a problem when you have to cast someone new to the business.

The role was that of a ridiculously attractive young Czech who had to speak in an Eastern European accent and to go to bed with both of the other leading characters, the male and the female. This made it more difficult. But Codron and Jenny Topper, the director of the theatre, already had somebody 'super' in mind. He was a young Russian actor who everyone was raving about.

I rang Joyce Nettles, the casting director, told her what we needed and asked if she could suggest someone. She came up with a further two names. I met all three of the young men in my office and felt torn, but favoured one of the English actors. So, we set up an afternoon of auditions.

The Russian chap was appealing. He hadn't completely mastered English but he spoke it well and was clearly intelligent. One of the English actors wasn't up to much, but the other was amazing. His Czech accent was authentic. He was tall and dark and charming. I was confident that he was our man, but both Jenny and Michael wanted the Russian. I'm not sure how much and in how many ways they wanted him, but they certainly wanted him to play the part.

This made it difficult. We discussed it at length. Finally, I asked if I could sleep on it and talk to them in the morning. They agreed. So, I went home, put on my tracksuit and went for a run. After a bath, I knew that we must cast the English chap, not only for his talent but also for his command of English, which was excellent.

The young Englishman's name was Rufus Sewell.

Making It Better was a hit at Hampstead and transferred to the West End.

And, Rufus, if you are reading this, please could I have the twenty dollars you borrowed from me fifteen years ago in New York.

Mrs Warren's Profession (2010)

English producers can also be tricky.

On tour the production manager. Mike Powell-Jones, had marshaled the set changes well enough to keep the show moving. There were three different locations and the sets were large, even cumbersome. Thanks to plenty of people working backstage behind the curtain, the transitions were quick enough and the play worked well.

When we got to the Comedy Theatre (now the Harold Pinter Theatre), we had a different production manager and there was hardly any space in the wings to store the set and furniture. That meant the changes were slow. What we really needed, according to the actors who were stood there watching the lengthy changes, was one more person to help. No one could remember doing a play that took so long to get from scene to scene. The evening was dragging.

The producer refused to hire one more person. It was too expensive. I beseeched him. I nearly used a phrase I had once heard from Michael Codron. He said, 'Michael, I beg you. I implore you from the bowels of Christ. Change those scene changes.' But, our producer was what many producers are sometimes. Adamant.

The budget wouldn't allow it.

When the play opened it got, on the whole, excellent reviews. Five bordered on raves but three of those five complained about the laborious scene changes. I believe their four stars could have been five which would have made a big difference to, guess what? The money.

The Old Masters at Long Wharf (2011)

Sam Waterston is a terrific actor.

When I did *Hamlet* with him in Central Park and later at the Lincoln Center in 1975, he played the part with what Keats called *'Rich anger'*. We became friends during this long period, but didn't work together again until 2011. He hadn't changed much except that he had become a vegan and an even better actor.

One of the things Sam likes about me is that I recognize and value his intelligence. Thanks to email, we were able to collaborate properly on Simon Gray's *The Old Masters* before we went into rehearsal. For *Hamlet*, which was in the land before cyberspace, I didn't get to consult him much before we began.

When we were looking for a regional theatre to start *The Old Masters,* the first really good one we were offered was the Long Wharf where I had done *The Changing Room* in 1972. I had happy memories of the place.

The Artistic Director of Long Wharf theatre is Gordon Edelstein. He is a sympathetic man who is a successful director himself, understands how difficult some things can be and knows what is important. He is a good producer.

From the beginning he was a big help with the casting and with the choice of designers. He had a clear idea of the direction the production was taking and the ways of getting there.

At first, I was against doing the play on a thrust stage because it is full of duologues and there isn't much movement. In fact, it worked well. Also, Brian Murray, who played the other leading role, had a lot of experience on the three-sided auditorium. As did Sam.

As demonstrated by my experience in *Mrs Warren's Profession,* one of the most important things in any production is the scene changes. I sometimes think that they are the main reason the good Lord invented directors. Many plays require more than a few locations and it is up to the director and the designer to devise something that will take the audience quickly and deftly from one to another.

The Old Masters opens on a big verandah. The second scene is a library with huge bookshelves. To go from one to the other was no easy thing. Both settings, designed by the excellent Alexander Dodge, were beautiful and highly detailed.

After the first few previews, it became clear that Alexander and I had not achieved what was necessary. It was taking much too long and the music and lighting were not helping enough.

After one preview, Gordon took Victoria Gray, the playwright's wife, and me to dinner and strongly suggested that I devise some dramatic action that could take place during the scene change. I was reluctant. Simon Gray, who was no longer with us, hadn't written anything. It didn't seem right. Gordon persisted. He had done a similar thing with Christopher Hampton's *The Philanthropist* and Christopher had been pleased. Wouldn't I at least try it? Alexander Dodge also thought it was worth pursuing. So, the next night we tried something. Sam and Heidi Schreck, who began the next scene, came on quite early in the scene change which was, as a matter of fact, interesting in itself because it was big and involved a lot of people. All Sam and Heidi did was read and work at their desks in the library in two shafts of white light that cut through the wash of red light which covered the rest of the stage.

It was clear to the audience that they should be watching two attractive actors whose stories they were already interested in and, although they were aware of the stagehands working around the actors, they focused on Sam and Heidi.

What can I tell you? When the next scene was ready, there was a round of applause. I was so pleased with it that I borrowed the device and used it *Chin Chin*, and it worked extremely well.

Chin Chin (2013)

Usually when you do a commercial play outside London, the West End theatre is already booked. Certainly that was the case with *Fallen Angels, Donkey's Years* and *Clouds*.

Not so with my latest job, *Chin Chin*, with Simon Callow and Felicity. After an eight-week tour, we are still in limbo and waiting to hear whether or not it goes into London.

Simon Callow is an extraordinary actor. He is a delight to direct. Of course, he is not just an actor. He also directs and writes successfully. He is extremely intelligent and erudite and by extremely I mean much more than me.

But, he listens.

I had always wanted to work with him since seeing him in Mike Ockrent's production of *Schippel* at the Open Space. He has great power and can work in broad strokes but also, when asked, he is capable of wonderful subtlety. Of course, polymath that he is, he is always working very hard on two or three things at the same time. When we were rehearsing *Chin Chin* he was performing his own play about Wagner in the evening and reading Michael Blakemore's book, *Stage Blood,* over lunch, which he was reviewing for *The Guardian*.

Rehearsals for *Chin Chin* were a joy. There is no other word for it. Everyone was constructive and funny. Ideas flowed back and forth. The stage managers were laughing a lot. Respect for Willis Hall's adaptation grew every day. The designers contributed, Bill Kenwright, the producer, made three constructive and positive visits to the rehearsal room and nobody got the flu.

The tour went well, even in Malvern where they haven't laughed since 1926 and that was at the General Strike. Cheltenham was particularly receptive and Bath was lovely. Everywhere except Nottingham and Cardiff the box office takings were high. The reviews were excellent. People were accosting Felicity in the street, literally grabbing her by the arm and telling her how wonderful she was. Vernon Dobcheff saw it three times. The production was/is fluid and fluent. The set and costumes are pleasing to the eye.

So, why are we waiting?

The answer, apparently, is money.

Nica Burns, who controls five West End theatres, saw it in Cardiff and said she liked the performances very much but didn't know how to sell the play. Bill Kenwright also wonders where to place it and he is trying hard, but it is difficult. And there is a long queue of attractive shows waiting for West End theatres. Also, by now, due to the delay, Simon has a big film and Felicity is doing *a* West End play in January. Howard Panter probably wants it for the Trafalgar in September, but the actors might not be free. The only possible time is March, and the only possible theatre is the Harold Pinter.

At least three times in the last two months, Bill Kenwright has said, at the end of phone conversations about *Chin Chin* that he would ring me 'tomorrow' or 'next week.' Once, at five past seven, he said 'I've got to go to a meeting outside the office at seven. I'm waiting to hear from

Howard Panter. I'll ring you in the morning.' I am still wondering which morning he means.

Meanwhile I am, as you know, on tenterhooks. First of all I want to know if my work is going to be seen in London and the work of my friend Willis Hall and the superb performances of Felicity and Simon.

But, most of all, I want to know what the hell I will be doing in March. And in two days, I will be seventy-five.

But, there are compensations. At the end of one of these conversations with Bill, he invited me to join him in the Director's Box of the Spurs v Everton match at White Hart Lane. If you don't know much about football, and why should you, you should know that for me, a fanatical Tottenham Hotspur supporter, that this is a lovely invitation to get.

Bill is, of course, generous. Many of his gifts are made by stealth and he doesn't seek credit so I won't divulge them here, but he has been known to fly the entire cast of a play to Las Vegas from New York and entertain them there and to fly the Everton football team to New York for the opening of one of his shows.

A day in the boardroom at White Hart Lane with Bill means an entertaining trip in a luxury car with him, a boyhood friend of his called Laurie, and Bill's charming partner Jenny Seagrove, whom he calls his 'Mrs.' There is Capital Gold on the radio playing hits from the sixties and early seventies, to which he and Laurie sing along. They know all the words and some of the songs are pretty obscure.

Then there is a delicious lunch with a wide assortment of hot and cold meats, vegetables salads, wine and, unfortunately, bread and butter pudding. Then there is the game itself seen from the perfect position. High enough up to see everything and close enough to feel involved. Then, at half time, there is tea and cakes. After the game there are drinks and more food followed by another enjoyable trip in the Jag back to Maida Vale listening to Capital Gold and the football news.

In all this time, five hours, this kind man didn't say one single word about *Chin Chin*.

Finally, as I was leaving, he said 'I'll ring you tomorrow.'

I said that I had read on *Whatsonstage.com* website that a show directed by Trevor Nunn was going into the Harold Pinter in our potential slot in March. Bill said that it wasn't going to the Pinter, it was going to the Haymarket. I thanked him for a lovely day, went home and had a few drinks.

The next morning, I read on *Whatsonstage.com* that *Relative Values*, directed by Trevor, was opening on March 19 at the Harold Pinter theatre.

I am telling you all this so you won't think directing commercial plays aimed for the West End is all beer and skittles.

And so, faithful reader, we come to the end of my career to date. Who knows? Rufus Norris at the National might decide that I need to be rediscovered. Vicky Featherstone at the Royal Court might want to employ a local director. *Chin Chin* might be a big hit in the West End. Michael Codron might come out of retirement. Some young playwright might hope that I could champion her or him like I did Michael Frayn or Pam Gems. Or, some clever lady or gentleman might read this book and say:

'Get me Michael Rudman.'

Highlight Reel

Young actors, and possibly some older actors, have what is called a highlight reel, which is a DVD of selections of their best work. Their agents give these out when the actor auditions or if a producer or director wants to know more about the actor.

I have a reel like this in my mind which I run on the back of my eyeballs when I feel like remembering something significant, to me, and successful episodes from my working life. Peter Hall once said to me 'count your blessings' and these memories are among my best blessings. What the French call *Les moments parfaits*.

These are in no particular order except, approximately, the order I think of them if I have trouble sleeping at night.

1980 – Alec McCowen and Geraldine McEwan in playbill, Terrence Rattigan's double bill of *The Browning Version* and *Harliquinade*.

If you've never directed a play or, even if you have, you can't possible imagine how much fun it is to direct Geraldine McEwan and Alec McCowen. It's certainly the most fun I've ever had with the lights on. And it's a special kind of fun. There aren't many big laughs. Nobody makes great jokes. There are very few anecdotes but, somehow, you find yourself smiling the whole time. And, at night, you sleep well.

Alec and Geraldine work hard. They learn their lines early. They ask pertinent questions. They help the other actors. They help the director work out what the rehearsal is hoping to accomplish. They are never late and they don't worry if the rehearsal goes over its allotted time.

Does that sound boring? It isn't.

One moment I love to remember is the moment Alec and Geraldine take their seats at the beginning of one scene. We had just agreed that the two leading actors in *Harlequinade* should have great affection, indeed love, sexual love for each other.

I had suggested that there might be a tiny bit of improvised dialogue before the scene to help establish this. The suggestion was greeted by the silence that often follows when a director suggests departing from the text to two seasoned professionals. But no one disagreed.

The scene began. Alec and Geraldine entered. They took their seats. There was a pause. Then Alec leaned towards Geraldine with a playful lustful look on his face and said quite loudly,

'Peach.'

I know it isn't funny, but it surely worked and Alec and I still call each other 'Peach' in every Christmas card and at the beginning of every phone conversation.

1961 – Sitting in the foyer of the *Oxford Mail* in 1963 with David Aukin waiting for the 12:30 edition, which would have a review of our production of *A Month in the Country* by Turgenev. This was the first full-length play that I ever directed.

The review was a rave. The best college production he had seen in fifteen years. We bought fifty copies.

1977 – The interval of the first run-through of the West End production of *Clouds* by Michael Frayn (with Tom Courtenay and Felicity Kendal).

DAVID AUKIN: What do you think?
ME: Do you smell something? I do.
DAVID AUKIN: What?
ME: Money!

1984 – The first night of *Death of a Salesman* on Broadway. After all the hotel rooms, the endless auditions (August to November), the arguments and the pages of notes from Arthur Miller, after rehearsing the big emotional scene at the end of the play over and over again, we finally got the first night at the Broadhurst. It went very well. No one was nervous not even the audience.

Now we cut to the last scene, you may remember that I kept trying to guide Dustin away from crying because I knew that he was controlling his tears the audience would be more moved.

On the first night, he was perfect and when it came to the penultimate scene, when Willy Loman's son tells him that he loves him, Dustin was on the point of tears when he said, *'He likes me, Linda.'* Then his wife says *'He loves you, Willy.'* and Dustin finally broke down. Tears poured from his eyes and down his smiling face. And, as if on cue, the audience, who had been sniffing a bit leading up to this moment, started sobbing audibly, especially people in the box above me to my right. I will never forget them. Rocking and sobbing and grieving for the smiling little man below them on the stage.

1977 – Seeing our touring production of *The Elephant Man* by Bernard Pomerantz in a cold, drafty hall in Manchester with about fifteen people in the audience including the five of us working on it and the slide projector failing to work and knowing, absolutely knowing, that it was going to be a big success. Of course, I didn't know that two years later I would be seeing the Broadway production from the standing room section of the Booth Theatre on Broadway. (Next year I can see a revival on Broadway with Bradley Cooper.)

1983 – Being called up on the stage by Ian McKellen after the last performance of my own play *Short List* at Hampstead to receive warm applause.

August 1972 – Edinburgh Festival, Traverse Theatre, Green Room. I was sitting in the Green Room, tired but happy, in the half hour break between two performances. One of the plays was *The Black and White Minstrel Show* by Cecil Taylor, which had been quite a struggle.

Casting it had been difficult. In the end, we were lucky because we got Tom Conti, very early in his career. He happened to be staying with his wife's parents in Edinburgh while we were looking for good Scottish actors. I drove round to their house with the script. He rang me the next day (sometimes he reads plays quicker than that) and he said he would do it, but only if the other leading male role was played by a Scot. This was tricky, as I had been thinking of Jack Shepherd, who I always thought of for almost every play, but I thought Tom was making sense.

I went to London to pursue Alan Howard, probably my favourite actor. He had read the play and was interested. I was so nervous about meeting him that I got no sleep at all the night before and I was pretty high on coffee when we met for lunch. Lunch went on until seven o'clock but eventually he agreed. After that, conversations with Alan became very brief. He simply did the part brilliantly and made excellent suggestions in rehearsals.

But Tom wanted to know if Alan was Scottish. He certainly didn't seem Scottish. I was delighted to tell him that Alan had been born in Bara so we got the ideal cast. But, when we opened, it was almost impossible to tell if the play was working. *The Scotsman* hadn't like it very much which meant that the audiences weren't very big and some nights there weren't many laughs, and laughs were vital to a play about socialists wife-swapping in Glasgow while being taken to a rent tribunal by their Nigerian boarder.

But something wonderful happened. A society of Scottish lawyers wanted a late night theatre outing and the actors agreed to do a performance for them. It started at 10.30 p.m. so the lawyers were well fed and bevvied. They absolutely loved it. They laughed from beginning to end.

So we put it in the Festival and I was sitting in the green room waiting for it to finish one night and, while it was being played to a full house, I saw Ian Holm come in to get ready for a performance of *Caravaggio Buddy* by Stanley Eveling with the same company of actors.

I felt that I was definitely doing something right.

1990 – Neil Simon and his wife laughing immoderately at a run-through of the first act of *Rumours* at Chichester.

Autumn 1992 – *A Midsummer Night's Dream* at Sheffield Crucible

Theatre. The rehearsals had been fraught. As I have noted, three weeks is not enough to rehearse a Shakespeare play with a large cast. But we did our best. There were some gifted and seriously sexy people in the cast and the audience found much of it very funny as, I suspect, they almost always do with that play.

There was a butch and manly young man playing Flute who, as you know, plays Thisbe in the play scene. I had suggested to him that it would be a good idea if he played Thisbe very well indeed, surprisingly well in the midst of all the am dram things that were going on around him. And he really did. He played it sweet and effeminate and very much in love. It was very moving.

But the highlight moment was when Alex Kingston, playing Hippolyta and Titania, started singing a song composed by Matthew Scott. First the acting company joined in and then, with only a slight encouragement from Alex, the audience joined in. It was, as it always should be with that play, a celebration and my time at Sheffield was off to a good start.

1986 – One moment in Pirandello's *Six Characters in Search of an Author* in the huge Olivier Theatre. The audience went absolutely silent when Barbara Jefford was speaking, as we had rehearsed it, barely above the level of audibility.

1976 – The first performance of Michael Frayn's under rehearsed *Donkey's Years* in Bath when a group of accomplished actors led by Penelope Keith made me look like a brilliant farceur, which I am not, by having a wonderful time entering and exiting at exactly the right moment for two hours.

2013 – My tall, super shy stepson, Charley Henley, is nominated for an Academy Award for his special effects in the film *Prometheus*.

1975 – The first night of *Hamlet*, Central Park, New York. After a short nap, I set out for the Delacorte Theatre in Central Park. The taxi dropped me off at the entrance to the park. I noticed that it was drizzling and I wondered if the show would go on. Then I saw a small African American boy zigzagging on a bicycle shouting, 'Not to be. It's not to be.'

I ended up drinking something called Harvey Wallbangers with a very entertaining man called Christopher Walken. I think they call it a Harvey Walbanger because after three or four of them you think, 'Hey, I think I'll bang my head on a wall.'

1967 – Robert Ryan talking to me after our production of O'Neill's *Long Day's Journey into Night* at the Nottingham Playhouse. 'Mike', he said. 'You're a damn good director. You play the music.'

1972 – *The Changing Room* at Long Wharf Theatre. The whole experience is a highlight for me. We played touch football for a week to get to know the actors and decide how to cast them. When I read out the cast on the second Monday, not one of them complained. We got through the nudity issue with ease, as I have described earlier. There was rough good humour throughout. Arvin Brown, the artistic director, was extremely helpful and even the Yorkshire accents proved possible for twenty-two American actors. I gave them a recording of a play done by the BBC by Wilfred Pickles, which helped a lot.

Then came the first night.

There was one big problem. The all-powerful *New York Times* critic, Clive Barnes, sitting in the second row, fell asleep during the first act. I can still see his head sinking to his chest. Fortunately, Arvin and Edgar Rosenblum, the administrator, noticed his condition and plied him with whisky and coffee in the first interval.

The applause at the end, the dancing and drinking at the all night party, the flirtations and soul to soul chats were all excellent, but my fondest memory is of the cast throwing me, wearing a suit and tie and smart shoes, into the large bath offstage that I had insisted on.

And a corollary to that memory is the note session I gave when I returned to New Haven to give notes after it had been decided to take the play to Broadway. I gave a few notes, quite a bit of praise, and one or two hopefully inspiring thoughts. As I folded my notebook, I heard a strange sound. The actors were applauding me. That has only ever happened twice since that time and one of those shows was a failure so complete that it is not mentioned in this book.

1993 – Seeing a queue all the way around a grassy Area in Central Park waiting for tickets for *Measure for Measure* (with Kevin Kline and Andre Braugher).

1984 – Watching the first night of a touring production of *Veronica's Room*, a modest thriller by Ira Levin, (with Barbara Jefford and George Sewell), and realizing that I was literally sitting on the edge of my seat.

2013 – My daughter Kate's wedding to James Risebero with their two children, Lucas and Rosa, in attendance.

1965 – Edward Woodward hitting a long high note to great applause at the end of his number in the somewhat musical, somewhat modern dress production of *Measure for Measure* at Nottingham (with Judi Dench and John Neville).

1980 – Peter Straker hitting the same note as Ed Woodward had in Nottingham in a strikingly similar production (with Norman Beaton and Oscar James) this time set in the Caribbean at the National.

1974 – Michael White, after a dress rehearsal of *The Ride Across Lake Constance* at Hampstead (with Alan Howard, Nigel Hawthorne and Nicky Henson), telling me immediately afterwards that without seeing the first preview, without reading any reviews, he was definitely going to take it into the West End. Where on earth is this man now when we need him?

1978 – At the Hampstead Theatre, the hysterical laughter throughout *Abigail's Party* (with Alison Steadman and Tim Stern) on the opening night. Bernard Levin, in *The Sunday Times*, wrote that it was difficult to enjoy the play because the audience was laughing so much.

1978 – Trevor Nunn hugging me after my speech accepting the *Evening Standard Award* for Special Achievement given to Hampstead Theatre.

1979 – Robin Bailey pausing at the perfect moment in the perfect way in a scene with Jean Anderson in *For Services Rendered* by Somerset Maugham at the National.

1980 – Alec McCowen breaking into sobs when he is given the Latin book by Graeme Henderson as Taplow in *The Browning Version* at the National.

1975 – Three minutes into the dress rehearsal for *Hamlet* in Central Park, Joe Papp gets up and crosses the entire width of the Delacorte Theatre to speak to me. All he says is, 'That's the first time I've ever seen this play begin correctly.' Two hours later, when John Lithgow (playing Laertes) breaks his ankle jumping into Ophelia's grave. Joe comes over again and said, 'You can't make a *Hamlet* without breaking legs.'

1999 – Getting a hole in one with a three-iron on the eighth hole at Richmond Golf Club on Robin Parkinson's Captains Day. I don't know who was more pleased, me or Stephen Greif, my gracious playing partner.

2000 – My son Jacob's *Bar mitzvah*.

1993 – The Delacorte theatre in Central Park. The first preview of my production *Measure for Measure* (with Kevin Kline and Andre Braugher). Rehearsals have been good. Kevin likes to take his time before committing himself to anything big. I've been wanting him to use a lovely Italian/Polish accent he came up with in rehearsal for when he is in disguise at the Friar. He has been uncertain. On his first line to Juliet, he uses the accent. Big laugh. Maybe two thousand people. The accent stays.

2010 – Carol Dudley, the amazing casting director, brings in Lucy Briggs-Owen to read for Vivie in *Mrs Warren's Profession*. Lucy is so interesting, so theatrical, so sexy and so truthful that we know after three lines that she is the one. Unfortunately, the producer wants a different young lady but, after two further auditions and what seems like two hundred phone calls, he agrees. Since then, Lucy has played leading roles at the RSC and is about to open in the West End with *Shakespeare in Love*.

1979 – Doreen Mantle's audition for *Death of a Salesman* in rehearsal room four at the National. When she did the 'Attention must be paid' speech, I cried.

1986 – Stephen Mackintosh's audition for *Brighton Beach* in the same room when, although he is a sixteen-year-old boy from Ipswich, he convinces me that he is a thirteen-year-old Jewish boy from Brooklyn.

2010 – San Sebastopol, California. Fred Washington, who for thirty years worked for my father, my mother, and my brother and who has been like a brother to me, makes everyone laugh for fifteen minutes at my brother's memorial service.

1973 – John Lithgow giving his acceptance speech for his Tony award for *The Changing Room*. It is good to know his hard work and talent can be rewarded even though he is very nice.

2011 – The first run-through of Simon Gray's wonderful play, *The Old Masters*, in New Haven when the performances of Brian Murray and Sam Waterston took off.

1978 – Oscar James's face lights up, as only his can, when I tell him *Gloo Joo* is transferring to the West end. *Gloo Joo* was a comedy about the attempt and hilarious failure to deport a West Indian. It goes to the Criterion and wins *Evening Standard Award for Best Comedy* of the year.

2002 – Electric Cinema, Notting Hill Gate. The first public showing of my daughter Amanda's film *Shadowman* with Liam Cunningham and Julia Ford. The film goes onto win many awards.

2013 – *Chin Chin* with Simon Callow and Felicity Kendal – It's a cold wet afternoon in Cardiff. There are only about one hundred and fifty people in the audience for the matinee, but Simon and Felicity are doing brilliantly. There are some good laughs. The scene changes go well.

Then, at the curtain call, which is enthusiastic, about twenty people, from all over the auditorium, rise to give what can only be called a standing ovation, whistling and shouting.

Not bad for a play that will probably never get to the West End.

1962 – *The Good Woman of Sezuan* by Bertolt Brecht at the Oxford Playhouse. When we chose to do Brecht's *The Good Woman of Sezuan* for the Experimental Theatre Club, David Aukin, who was playing the airline pilot, and I decided to the Berliner Ensemble and watch rehearsals. It was the kind of pilgrimage that others had made and it seemed like a good idea.

We went in my little Morris Minor so there were problems on the way. The Germans drive with fury on the autobahns and I was mainly trying to stay out of their way. It was an eight hundred mile trip. I hadn't realized how big Germany was.

The lady who received us was extremely nice. She ushered us into the auditorium and told us we could come and go as we pleased. We attended rehearsals for six days and were constantly amazed. For the last three months of rehearsal – yes, three months – they had a full set, costumes and lighting, but they went on rehearsing the acting. The physical production was, I suppose, epic, but the acting was beautifully naturalistic. There was none of the alienation that many English critics considered essential to presenting Brecht.

The attention to detail surpassed anything I have seen before or since. I resolved to rehearse our production as much as possible, afternoons and evenings for seven weeks, have a big, if not epic, physical production and keep the acting naturalistic.

At the same time, I was heavily influenced by an off-Broadway production of *The Threepenny Opera* I had seen – it was so successful that it ran for eight years – and I wanted to bring a fair amount of show biz to the evening.

Well, we did our best.

The moment I treasure was a Friday night at the Oxford Playhouse. Martin Esslin had been invited by the ETC Committee to see the show and address the audience afterwards. Esslin was an eminent theatre critic and academic and an expert on Brecht. He had written the most important book on the subject, *A Choice of Evils*.

After the show, which had gone extremely well, we all sat on the stage and waited for him to speak. I hadn't had time to be nervous about it because getting the play on had been difficult and complicated.

Esslin was extravagant with his praise. In the auditorium, there were all the bigwigs of Oxford Theatre, professional and amateur. He went on and on. I nearly got embarrassed. He answered questions from the audience. He heaped more praise on us.

I thought I could see a career in the theatre opening up for me.